HOW TO RAISE YOUR
CHILDREN FOR CHRIST

HOW TO RAISE YOUR CHILDREN FOR CHRIST

ANDREW MURRAY

 BETHANY FELLOWSHIP, INC.
Minneapolis, Minnesota

How to Raise Your Children for Christ by Andrew Murray

Copyright © 1975
Bethany Fellowship, Inc.
All rights reserved

Published by Bethany Fellowship, Inc.
6820 Auto Club Road, Minneapolis, Minnesota 55438

Printed in the United States of America

Library of Congress Cataloging in Publication Data:

Murray, Andrew, 1828-1917.
    How to raise your children for Christ.

    Published in 1952 under title: The children for Christ.
    Includes bibliographical references.
    1. Christian education—Sermons. 2. Christian education—
Home training. I. Title.
BV1477.M8 1975   649'.7   75-29344
ISBN 0-87123-224-3

the prayer of faith, manifesting itself in the godly training of the child, the blessing has been secured in covenant: "I will be a God to thee and to thy seed." As faith and prayer claim the promise and the power of God, the influence of the daily communion will make itself felt, and there will go forth from the consecrated lives of father and mother a secret but mighty power to mold the lives of the children, either preparing them as vessels of grace or establishing and perfecting them in it.

And so we come to the blessed but solemn truth: Let parents be what they want their children to be. If they would keep them from the sin of Cain, who loved not his brother, let them beware of the sin of Adam, who loved not his God. *Let father and mother lead a life marked by love to God and man*; this is the atmosphere in which loving children can be trained. Let all the dealings with the children be in holy love. Cross words, sharp reproof, impatient answers are infectious. Love demands and fears not self-sacrifice; time and thoughtful attention and patient perseverance are needed to train our children aright. When our children hear us speak of others, of friends or enemies, of the low, the vulgar, the wicked, let the impression be the love of Christ we seek to show. In all the communication of father and mother with each other, let mutual esteem and respect, tender considerateness and willing self-forgetfulness prove to the children that love is possible and blessed.

Above all, let us remember that it is the love of God that is the secret of a loving home on earth. It is where parents love the Lord their God with all their heart and strength that the human love will be strengthened and sanctified. It is only parents who are willing to live really consecrated lives, entirely given up to God, to whom the promise and the blessing can come fully true. To make our home the nursery and the type and the foretaste of heaven, ordinary halfhearted religion will not suffice. The love of God shed abroad in the heart and the home and the life by the Holy Ghost—this, this alone, will trans-

24

plant our home from the gates of Paradise Lost, where Adam dwelt with Cain, to within the Paradise Regained, where even amid the weakness of earth the image of the heavenly is seen, and the home on earth is in the likeness of the home above.

* * *

Blessed Lord God, we bow before Thee in deep humility. We desire to feel more deeply the terrible power of sin in ourselves and our children, and the danger to which it exposes our beloved home. We come to confess how far we as parents have come short in that pure and holy love which Thou didst mean to be the beauty and the blessedness of family life. In our fellowship with Thee, and each other, and our children, and fellow men—O God, forgive us the want of love! And oh, let not our children suffer through us as they grow up in our likeness! Deliver us, we pray Thee, from the power of selfishness, and shed abroad Thy love in our hearts by the Holy Ghost.

And, O God, bless our children with the spirit of love. May we so walk before them in love that Thy Spirit may use our example and our likeness to form them to Thy holy likeness. Give us a deep sense of our holy calling to train their immortal spirits for Thee and Thy glory. Inspire us with faith, with patience, with wisdom to train them aright. Oh, that our home on earth might be to them the pathway, the gate, to the Father's home in heaven!

Blessed Father, let us and our children be Thine wholly and forever. Amen.

THIRD DAY

The Family as Grace Restores It

"And the Lord said unto Noah, Come thou and all thy house into the ark; for thee have I seen righteous before me in this generation" (Gen. 7:1).

"By faith Noah prepared an ark for the saving of his house," and was made a witness to future ages that the faith of a believing, righteous parent obtains a blessing not for himself only but for his children too. The New Testament teaching that by faith Noah saved his house is in perfect accordance with what is recorded in Old Testament history: "Come *thou and all thy house* into the ark." Even Ham—who, as far as personal character was concerned, manifestly deserved to perish with the ungodly world—was saved from the flood for his father's sake and by his father's faith. This is proof that in God's sight the family is regarded as a unity, with the father as head and representative; that parents and children are one, and that in the dispensation of grace, even as in the ministration of condemnation, it is on this principle that God will deal with the families of His people.

We know it was this fact of parents and children being one that gave sin its terrible power in the world. When Adam sinned, his whole posterity was made subject at one blow, as it were, to sin and death. And was not the flood as well as the fall a proof of it? We see the children of Seth sunk as deep as the children of Cain, because Seth too was a son whom Adam had begotten in his likeness, with a sinful nature to be handed to his children too. Was it not this nature that gave sin such universal empire to a thousand generations? The family was sin's greatest stronghold; children inherited the evil from their parents. The unity of parents and children was the strength of sin.

Noah's deliverance from the flood was to be the introduction of a new dispensation—the first great act of God's redeeming grace on behalf of a sinful world. In this act God manifested the great principles of the economy of grace: mercy in the midst of judgment; life through death; faith as the means of deliverance, the one channel through which the blessing comes. And further, it was at this time revealed that the family was to be one means of grace.

The family had been sin's mightiest ally, the chief instrument through which it had acquired such universal dominion. This unit was now to be rescued from the domination of sin, to be adopted into the covenant of grace, to be consecrated and made subservient to the establishment of God's kingdom. How otherwise could the declaration be verified, "Where sin abounded, there did grace much more abound," if sin *alone* had the power through the parents to secure dominion over the children? No, in this very thing we are to have one of the brightest displays of redeeming grace—that the relation of parents and children, which had become the great means for transmitting and establishing the power of sin, was much more to become the vehicle for extending the kingdom of God's grace. And though many ages would have to pass before the promised Seed of the woman should be born, yet in anticipation of that holy birth the seed of God's people were to share in the blessing of their parents. It was on the strength of this hope that the children of righteous Noah were blessed with their father.

Let believing parents understand and remember this:

the father who is righteous in God's sight is dealt with not only as an individual, but also in his relation as parent. When God blesses He loves to bless abundantly; the blessing must overflow the house of His servant. For this temporal life and the supply of its many needs, the father must regard himself as the appointed channel through whom the blessings of nature and providence must reach the child. And he may count upon God's help. But the parental relation has a nobler destiny: for the eternal life, too, with its blessings, the believing father is to regard himself as the appointed channel and steward of the grace of God.

When once we understand this blessed truth and by faith accept God's word, "thee have I seen righteous before me in this generation," we shall be able to value the word that follows: "Come thou and all thy house into the ark." The seed of the righteous shall be blessed; the house of His servant God will bless. God gives the assurance that the ark in which the parent is to be saved is meant for his children too; for his sake, it is for them as much as for him. The ark is to be the house of the family.

As the blessing is to come *for his sake*, so *through his instrumentality* too. It is not only a promise but a command: "Come thou and thy house into the ark." God will not deal with the house separate and apart from him; the parent has to bring the children into the ark.

And if the question comes up as to the power of a parent thus to lead his children into the ark as certainly as he himself goes in, the answer is simple and clear: "*By faith* Noah prepared an ark for the saving of his house." God always gives grace proportionate to the duty He requires. Let the believing parent live, and act, and pray with and for his children as one to whom the ark and its salvation is indeed the one aim and joy of life and who is assured that his children are meant of God to be there with him. *Let him confidently trust God for the salvation of every child.* Let him in that spirit instruct and inspire his children. The children will grow up with the consciousness that to be with the father is to be with one who is in the ark—the blessing cannot be missed.

Beloved parents, listen to the wonderful truth of which Noah is God's messenger to you: there is room for your child in the ark. The God who saves you expects you to bring your child with you. Oh, it is no longer enough to pray and hope that your child may be saved! Accept in faith the assurance that he can be, and act out in obedience the command that you are to bring him in!

To each question as to how, let the answer be taken deeper to heart, "Come thou and all thy house." Go in and live in the ark; bring up and train your little children there, wholly separated from the world. God's blessing will use this training for their salvation. Abide in Christ, and let the child feel that to be near you is to be near Christ. Live in the power of the love and the redemption and the life of Christ; your house will be to the child the ark where Christ is known and found. Oh, if you have indeed heard that most blessed word, "*thee have I seen righteous*," let it teach you in the obedience of a joyous faith to fulfill the precept, "Come thou and all thy house into the ark"—may this word live in the heart of each believing parent!

* * *

O Lord my God, I have heard Thy message telling me that since Thou hast accepted me as righteous in Thy Son, Thou wouldst have my children saved too. I have heard Thy voice of grace, "Come thou and all thy house into the ark." Blessed be Thy name for the assurance of the salvation of his children that this message offers a parent's heart!

Lord, do Thou thyself open my eyes to see what Thy Word sets before me. Let me see in Noah the picture of a believing parent—walking with Thee, believing Thy word, obedient to Thy command. Let me see in the ark the type of my blessed Lord Jesus, a sure and a safe hiding place for me and my child. Let me see in the saving of Noah's house the sure pledge of what will be given to every parent who trusts Thee for his children, and obeys Thy voice to bring them in.

O my God, give me grace, like Thy servant Noah, so to walk with Thee that Thou mayest see me righteous before Thy face—so to believe the promise of Thy grace, so to obey Thy command and perform the work entrusted to me, that Thy blessing may abide on me and my children. And may it all be to the glory of Thy holy name. Amen.

The Child of the Covenant

"And, behold, the word of the Lord came unto [Abraham], saying, . . . he that shall come forth out of thine own bowels shall be thine heir. . . . And he believed in the Lord; and he counted it to him for righteousness" (Gen. 15:4, 6).

"Ye are the children . . . of the covenant" (Acts 3: 25).

Three times God gave to Abraham the promise that He would make of him a great nation, as the sand of the seashore in multitude. When God appeared to him the fourth time, Abraham poured out his complaint before God: "I go childless. . . . Behold, to me thou hast given no seed: and, lo, one born in mine house is mine heir." In answer the word of the Lord came to him, saying, "This shall not be thine heir; but he that shall come forth out of thine own bowels shall be thine heir." And then follow the memorable words, "[Abraham] believed in the Lord; he counted it to him for righteousness."

The great truth which this narrative sets before us is this: the promise and the gift on God's part, and on our part the reception and the birth of our children, is a matter of faith, a matter in which God takes the deepest interest. It is especially *as a parent*, in reference to the promise of a child, that Abraham's faith is exercised and found well pleasing to God. In the power of faith the natural longing for a child becomes the channel of most wonderful fellowship with God, and the natural seed becomes the heir of God's promise and the spiritual blessing.

The reason and meaning of all this is easily found. In Noah God had begun to acknowledge the validity of the oneness of parents and children in the dealings of grace. But it had been of little avail.

Immediately after the flood Ham's wickedness burst out, and it was not many years before the whole world had sunk into idolatry. The children of Noah had been born after the flesh. Before their birth God had not entered into covenant on their behalf. In character they had become independent men before God made them partakers of Noah's blessing. With Abraham He will deal otherwise; His way of dealing in covenant with His servants is to be advanced a distinct stage forward.

Everything connected with Isaac's birth is to be a matter of God's revelation and man's faith.

The covenant child before his birth is to be the object of God's care and the parent's faith. The very birth of the child God takes charge of, watching over and sanctifying by His word and by faith. Against nature and against hope God himself by His promise awakens the faith and expectation of a child. For twenty-five years this faith is tried and purified, till Abraham's whole soul is filled with believing expectancy, that so the child may in truth be the child of faith and prayer—a gift of God received by faith. Before the birth Abraham once again is sealed for God in the covenant of circumcision, so that full and clear proof may be given that the birth of the seed of His people is holy in His sight, a matter to Him of special interest, the object of His promises and His blessing.

In all this God would teach us that it is especially as parents, and even from before the first hope of having children, that His saints are taken into covenant with Him—are called to exercise Abraham's faith, and to receive their children from His hands. The children, not only when grown up but even from the birth, are to be partakers of the covenant. Yes, from *before* the birth, in the very first rising of hope, would God begin the great work of redeeming love by His Spirit. He would thus reveal to us how that wondrous power with which He had endowed man—bringing forth and giving life to a child after his own image—this power which sin had caused to become the great strength of Satan's kingdom, was again to be consecrated, and under God's own eye to be used to the extension of His kingdom and glory.

Hence it is that the Bible is so full of what cannot otherwise be understood—of divine promise and interposition, of human activity and expectation, connected with the birth of children. Everything concentrates on that one great lesson: the fatherhood and the childhood of this earth has a divine promise, and everything connected with it must be a matter of faith, a religious service holy to the Lord and well pleasing in His sight. I must believe not only for myself; if I would fully honor God, my faith must reach forth and embrace my children, grasping the promises of God for them too. If I would magnify the riches of God's grace, if I would with my whole nature and all my powers be consecrated to God's service, and if I would accomplish the utmost possible within my reach for the advancement of His kingdom, it is especially as parent that I must believe and labor.

God thought a long time was necessary for the strengthening and ripening of faith before Abraham received the promised child. This grace is a gift of high value, and cannot be attained but by a close walk with God and wholehearted surrender to His teachings and leadings. The faith which was sufficient to justify Abraham was not sufficient to receive the blessing for his seed; his faith had to be further strengthened and purified. Faith must ever be in proportion to the promise.

Believing parents will experience that there is nothing that so mightily quickens the growth of their faith as the reaching out after this blessing for their children. They will feel in it the mightiest stimulus to a life of entire devotion and unmixed faith, that they may have not only enough for themselves but to impart to their children, in harmony with that law of the kingdom: "According to your faith be it unto you."

But with this solemn lesson Abraham's story gives us the comforting assurance that God will give the grace to attain what we need. With what patience and longsuffering did He lead Abraham and Sarah until they were fitted to accomplish His purposes. Then it could be said of them, "Abraham *believed*" and became the father of many nations; and, "*Through faith* also Sarah herself received strength to conceive seed, and was delivered of a child. . . ." Even now will God, who has undertaken to sanctify His people soul and body and to fill them with His Spirit, himself train them for the holy calling of believing parents. He will teach us how the birth of our children can become the highest exercise of a faith that gives glory to God, and the truest means of advancing our spiritual life and the interests of His kingdom.

With us, too, the promise of God and the power of faith are the wondrous links by which the natural seed becomes the heir of the spiritual blessing, and the parental relationship one of the best schools for the life of faith. It is especially in a believing fatherhood that we can become conformed to the image not only of faithful Abraham, but of the Father in heaven himself.

* * *

O our blessed God and Father! What thanks shall we render to Thee for the wondrous revelation of Thy will in Thy servants Abraham and Sarah? The fatherhood and motherhood of earth Thou didst take into Thy covenant charge and keeping, didst sanctify and bless, that the seed of Thy people might indeed be holy to the Lord. Where sin had abounded and manifested its terrible power, Thou dost make grace much more to abound; and Abraham's child, the heir of sin and misery, Thou didst make the heir of the promise and its blessing. Blessed be Thy name!

Gracious God, open the eyes of Thy servants to see how, through the birth of Thine own Isaac, Thy dear Son Jesus Christ, the birth of our children hath indeed been redeemed from the power of sin, and Thy promise comes to us larger and fuller than ever Abraham could understand. Teach us, teach all Christian parents, to realize that if there is one thing in which Thou hast an interest, in which Thou givest abundant grace, in which Thou askest and aidest faith, it is for a believing fatherhood, for our receiving our children from Thee and for Thee. O God, enlighten and sanctify our hearts to realize that the fruit of our body is to be the heir of Thy promise. And let our parentage, like Abraham, be what binds us to Thee in worship and in faith. Amen.

FIFTH DAY

The Promise of the Covenant

"And I will establish my covenant between me and
thee and thy seed after thee in their generations for an
everlasting covenant, to be a God unto thee, and to thy
seed after thee" (Gen. 17:7).

". . .the children of the flesh, these are not the children of God: but the children of the promise are counted
for the seed" (Rom. 19:8).

We have here the first full revelation of the terms
of God's covenant, of God's dealing in grace with Abraham, the father of all who believe. Here is the great foundation promise of what God calls "an everlasting covenant." God had already revealed himself to Abraham
as his God and as the God who would give him a child.
The thing that is new and remarkable here is the assurance
that the covenant now to be established was to be with
his seed as much as with himself: "a God unto thee,
and to thy seed after thee." It is this promise that has
invested these words, through all the generations of God's
Church, with an imperishable interest. Let us see how
entirely the same promise is for the child as for the parent.

The *matter* of the promise is the same in each case:
"*I will establish my covenant*"; I will "*be a God* unto
thee, and to thy seed after thee." It is God's purpose

to stand in the same relation to the child as the father; the believing parent and the unconscious child are to have the same place before Him. God longs to take possession of the children before sin gets its mastery; from the birth, yes, from before the birth, He would secure them as His own and have the parent's heart and the parent's love sanctified and guided and strengthened by the thought that the child is His—"a God unto thee, and to thy seed."

The *certainty* of the promise is the same. It rests on God's free mercy, on His almighty power, His covenant faithfulness. God's faithfulness to His purpose is the ground on which the promise rests and its fulfillment may be expected.

The *condition* of the promise is in each case the same. In its twofold blessing it is offered to *the faith* of the parent, and has to be accepted by faith alone. If the promise *"I will be thy God"* be not believed, that unbelief makes the promise of none effect. God is true, His promise faithful, His offer of mercy real. But if it finds no entrance through unbelief, the blessing is lost. And so with the other half, *"a God to thy seed";* if the parent's faith accepts this for his child, God will see to it that his faith is not disappointed.

The *recipient* of the promise is the same. It is not as if the first half of the promise is given to the father, the second half to the child. No, it is the same person to whom the two parts of the promise come. In the one half the individual accepts it for himself, in the other half as a father for his child; but it is one act. The promise is not held in abeyance to wait for the child's faith, but is given to the father's faith in the assurance that the child's faith will follow. With Abraham, as with each believing parent, the same faith accepts the personal and the parental blessing. The blessing is in either case equally sure, if faith equally holds it fast.

But here a difficulty arises with many persons. They see that God's promises of mercy to sinners are free and sure, and have found, in believing them, that they have come true; they know that they have been accepted. But it is as if the promise with regard to the children is not equally simple and certain. They cannot understand how one can so confidently believe for another. They know that the only sure ground for faith is God's word; but they have not yet been able to realize that the word of God really means that He is the God of their seed. Their impressions are in accordance with this ordinarily held view: "God has established a general connection between seedtime and harvest, between faithful parental training and the salvation of the children. In neither case—the seedtime nor the training—is absolute certainty of success secured, or God's sovereignty excluded. It is enough that the promise expresses the tendency and ordinary result of proper training." It is evident that such a general principle, with its possible exceptions, cannot give the rest of faith the parent longs for. Faith needs the assurance that God's purpose and promise are clear and unmistakable; then alone can it venture all upon His faithfulness.

Such was the promise given to Abraham; such is the promise to every believing parent. It is not in the general law of seedtime and harvest that I am to find the parallel for my ground of hope on behalf of my child, but in that other very distinct and definite promise. The first half, "I will be a God unto thee," is the divine pattern and pledge of the second, "a God to thy seed."

When as a struggling sinner I first sought for mercy, it was not to some general principle (that seeking is generally followed by finding) that I trusted, but to the very definite divine assurance, "Every one that asketh receiveth, and he that seeketh findeth." I believed the promise; I came and was accepted; I found the promise true: "I will be thy God." So the promise is now brought that He is willing to be the God of my seed too. Wherever God comes with a promise, He expects faith to accept it at once. The promise was not conditional on Isaac's believing, it was intended to be its source and security. And so, as I stand in covenant with God as my God, and see how He offers to be the God of His people's seed, I have the right in faith to claim this promise, and to be assured of my child's salvation as firmly as my own, through faith in the God of truth.

The analogy between the two halves of the promise is complete. In the first it was the question, Could I trust the love and power and faithfulness of God to accept and renew and keep such a sinner as I am? Faith gave the answer, and secured the blessing. And now the other question, Can I trust the love and the power and faithfulness of God to accept and renew and keep my child? Faith can again give the answer, and this blessing too is secured.

And if the thought still come up, as it has come and troubled many, How about election? How can I be sure that my child is one of the elect? The first half of the promise again gives the solution. When I believed to the saving of my soul, I was sure the election and the promise of God never could be at variance with each other. Even so with my child. No believer in God's promise ever had to complain that God's sovereignty had hindered its fulfillment. "They which are the children of the flesh, these are not the children of God, but the children of the promise."

The promise is definite, "a God unto thee and to thy seed." Oh, let us like Abraham stagger not at the promise through unbelief, but be strong in faith, giving glory to God, and be confident that what He hath spoken He is able and faithful to perform. Let us look upon our children, let us love them and train them, as children of the covenant and children of the promise—these are the children of God.

* * *

O my God, how shall I sufficiently adore Thee for the grace Thou hast revealed in the promise of the covenant? As if it was not enough to take such unworthy sinners and make them Thy children, Thou dost offer to provide for their children too, and make the house of Thy servants the home of Thy favor and blessing. Thou meetest them with the sure promise once given to Thy servant Abraham: "I will be a God unto thee and to thy seed after thee." Blessed be Thy holy name!

And now, Lord, I beseech Thee, give me grace to take this promise and trust it with my whole heart. As sure as is the confidence I have that Thou hast accepted me and art my God, so confident may I be that Thou art the God of my seed. As I yielded myself all sinful to Thee, and Thou didst take me as Thine own, I give them, all sinful too, to Thee, and believe Thou dost take them as Thine own. As I accepted Thy promise for myself, I accept it for them. Give me grace now to look upon them as Thou dost, as children of the promise. May this be what gives me courage and hope for their training on earth and their portion in heaven. They are the children of the covenant, children of the promise. Faithful is He who hath promised who also will do it. Amen.

SIXTH DAY
The Seal of the Covenant

"Ye shall circumcise the flesh of your foreskin; and
it shall be a token of the covenant betwixt me and you.
And he that is eight days old shall be circumcised among
you, every man child in your generations" (Gen. 17:11,
12).

"He received the sign of circumcision, a seal of the
righteousness of faith." Such was the meaning, according
to the teaching of the Holy Spirit, of the ordinance of
circumcision given to Abraham. And yet there are many
who speak of it as if it were only the initiatory rite into
the temporal privileges of the Jewish people—as if it
meant one thing to him, something deeply spiritual and
sacred, and something else to his descendants! The whole
argument of the Epistle to the Romans reproved the Jews
for looking at it in so carnal a light and degrading it
from what it originally was: the holy sacrament of friendship and fellowship with God, the seal of the righteousness
of faith, the emblem of the covenant of the spirit in which
God would circumcise the heart, the sure sign of God's
faithfulness to Abraham and to his seed. There was no
need in the New Testament for repeating in express words
the truth, deeply inwrought into the life of God's people,
that their children were as truly in the covenant and had
as sure a right to its sign as they themselves. May the

Holy Spirit lead us to know the mind of our God.

We are taught that circumcision was a seal of the righteousness of faith. A seal is the confirmation of something that has been settled and transacted, the securing of privileges that have already been secured. Abraham had believed, God had counted his faith to him for righteousness and had taken him into a covenant of friendship. Circumcision was to him a divine seal and assurance of this. But it was also a sign, and that no arbitrary one, but with a spiritual meaning. It was a sign of that purity and holiness which was to be the mark of God's people. The most remarkable feature of the covenant was the passing on of the blessing from generation to generation, taking possession for the service of God's kingdom the very power of generation. Of this power sin had taken possession; the very first sign of sin with Adam and Eve was that they knew that they were naked and were ashamed. The very fountain of life was defiled and had to be cleansed. And so, when the little child of eight days old had to suffer the taking away of the foreskin of his flesh, it was in token of the defilement there is in our natural birth; a foreshadowing of that Holy One who should be begotten of the Holy Ghost, and of that second birth in Him, not of the will of the flesh, but of God, which was to be the blessing of the new covenant. It was a type of the circumcision not made with hands, the putting off of the body of the flesh in the circumcision of Christ, being buried with Him in baptism. The *seal* of the righteousness of faith under the Old Testament was the *sign* of the need of regeneration, a sign for the quickening and instruction of Abraham's faith and the setting him apart as a father for the service of God.

Circumcision could not be to the infant Isaac essentially different from what it was to Abraham. It was to him too a seal of his participation in that spiritual covenant of which God's promise and man's faith were the two marks. All unknowing, he had been taken, with his father and for his father's faith, into the favor and covenant of God. It was to him, as to Abraham, a seal of faith, faith already existing and accepted—not his own, but his father's. For Abraham's sake the blessing came on him. We find this distinctly stated later on (Gen. 26:3, 5): "I will bless thee . . . because that Abraham obeyed my voice, and kept my charge, my commandments, my statutes, and my laws." (And again (vs. 24): "I am the God of Abraham thy father: fear not, for I am with thee, and will bless thee: for my servant Abraham's sake."

Abraham had not believed for himself alone, but for his child; as a father he had believed and received the child in faith from God; the sign of circumcision in the child was the seal to the child of the father's faith. God dealt with father and child as one; the father believed for himself and his child as one; the child had the same place in the covenant, and the same claim on the seal of the covenant, as the father. And as he grew up it would be to him a seal not only of the faith his father had, but of God's promise waiting for his faith too, the reminder of the one thing required by God, the one thing well pleasing to Him and by which he in turn could pass the blessing on to his own seed.

What circumcision was to Abraham and Isaac, baptism is still to believers and their children. It, too, is a sign, only far clearer and brighter. If circumcision spoke of the shedding of blood and the purifying of the very fountain of life, the water in baptism witnesses to the blood that has been shed and the Spirit that has been given, cleansing and renewing. "There are three who bear witness: the Spirit, and the water, and the blood." Of all these blessings it is a sign and also a seal—a seal from God of the righteousness of faith—faith in His promise that is well pleasing to Him and is counted as righteousness.

The parent must meet God as Abraham did, as a believer. It is faith and faith alone that can enter into the covenant, that pleases God, that obtains the reward. He must believe for himself in that Christ who is the surety of the covenant, who is himself the covenant. He must believe for his child. "Thy God and the God of thy seed"; these are the unchangeable terms of an everlasting covenant. The faith that claims the first may claim the second too. It has the same warrant—God's word. It has the same hope—God's faithfulness. It obtains the same blessing of free grace—the salvation of my child as surely as my own.

* * *

O my God, we do thank Thee for the condescension to our weakness, manifested in giving us in visible sign a divine seal of spiritual and unseen blessings. Thou knowest our frame and rememberest that we are dust. Thou art the Creator of our bodies, not less the Father of our spirits; Thou hast redeemed them to be the temple of Thy Holy Spirit. In the body Thou dost set the seal of Thy acceptance of us and Thy right over us. Lord, teach us to understand this; and let holy baptism, the seal of the New Testament faith and life, be indeed to Thy people the sign that they are baptized into the death of Christ.

And grant, most gracious God, that where Thy people cannot yet see eye to eye in the dispensation of this ordinance, it may still be, not the symbol of division, but the bond of unity in the Spirit of love.

And teach us to recognize the deep spiritual meaning in the seal of the covenant, and to live ourselves as baptized into the death of Christ, circumcised with a circumcision not made with hands. Teach us in faith to claim the full spiritual blessing for our children too, and to train them for it. And so fulfill to us, O our God, in full measure the promise of the covenant: "a God unto thee, and to thy seed." Amen.

SEVENTH DAY
Keeping the Covenant

"For I know him, that he will command his children
and his household after him, and that they shall keep
the way of the Lord, to do justice and judgment; that the
Lord may bring upon Abraham that which he hath spoken of him" (Gen. 18:19).

Faith without works is dead. Saving faith is an energy,
the power of a new life, manifesting itself in conduct and
action. In true faith the soul becomes united to God and
seeks to enter into the divine will—the surest way of becoming one with himself. As faith grows clearer and
stronger, it always sympathizes more fully with God's
plans; it understands Him better, and becomes more conformed to His likeness. This is true not only of individual
but also of parental faith. The higher the faith of the
parent rises, the more the family will come under its
power and be permeated by the spirit of godliness. Parental faith in God's promise will always be known by
parental faithfulness to God's will.

Abraham is a remarkable illustration of this. As distinctly as God's Word speaks of his faith, it tells too of
his faithfulness as a father. In giving the reason why
God's purpose in regard to Sodom should not be kept secret
from him, He grounds it upon this part of his character.
Not as an eminent believer, not even as the father of

the promised seed, but as one called to be the faithful leader of his children and household in the ways of the Lord, God confers on him the high distinction of having His secret counsel revealed to him. Faithfulness in his household gave him access to God's secrets and to God's presence as intercessor for Sodom. Let us try to understand what this means, and why God puts such honor upon parental faithfulness. Let us look to its need, its character, its blessing, its power.

Think what *need* there is of this faithfulness. Without it the blessing offered to parental faith is lost and the purpose of God made void. Were God by direct interposition, or by special agents, to seek the salvation of the little ones, there would be no reason for the part the parent is allowed to take in the covenant. God's object in thus honoring him is distinctly that he, to whose influence the helpless babe is committed, should train it for God. God seeks a people on earth. The family is the great institution for this object; a believing and God-devoted fatherhood is one of the mightiest means of grace. God's covenant and the parent's faith are but preliminary steps; it is through godly upbringing by the parents that the children are led to enter upon and really possess the blessings secured in the covenant. They must learn to know, and choose, and love the God who has given himself to them. The most precious promises on God's part will not avail unless the child is brought up, in the course of patient and loving training, to desire and accept the proffered friendship of the Holy One, to obey Him and keep His commandments. God establishes His covenant with parents not only for their comfort, to assure them of what He will do, but also to strengthen them for what they must do, whom He makes His fellow workers in securing the children for Him.

What God says of Abraham further gives us an insight into the true *character* of this grace: "I know [Abraham] that he will *command* his children and his household after him." The spirit of modern so-called liberty has pene-

trated even into our family life; and there are parents
who, some from a mistaken view of duty, some from
want of thought as to their sacred calling, some from
love of ease, have no place for such a word as "command."
They have not seen of the heavenly harmony between
authority and love, between obedience and liberty. Parents
are more than friends and advisers: they have been
clothed by God with a holy authority to be exercised
in leading their children in the way of the Lord. There
is an age when the will of the child is to a great extent
in their hands, and when the quiet, loving exercise of
that authority will have mighty influence. We speak here
not so much of commanding in the sense of specific injunctions; we speak of what we see in the heavenly Father—the
tenderness of affection combined with an authority not
to be despised. It is the silent influence of example and
life which also exercises its commanding power, which
makes the child often unconsciously bow to the stronger
will and makes it happy in doing so.

The *blessing* of such parental faithfulness is sure and
large. God says: "That the Lord may bring upon Abraham
that which he hath spoken him." It was in the way of
a godly education that the blessing of the covenant were
to come true. God's faithfulness and man's faithfulness
in the covenant are linked by indissoluble ties. If Abraham
was to be blessed, and his seed with him, and all nations
again in his seed, it was only thus: he must, as a faithful
parent, pass on to others what he knew himself of God.
It is only as the children become partakers of the parent's
spirit that they can share his blessing. As it is written:
"Thou seest that faith wrought with his works, and by
works was faith made perfect, and he was called the
friend of God." In a way that passes all comprehension,
the faithfulness of God and man, each in his performance
of the covenant obligation, are inseparably and eternally
interwoven.

The solemn responsibility may well make us tremble.
But God's word meets us with divine comfort. The *power*

is provided in the purpose of God. The words of the text are most remarkable: "I know [Abraham], *that* he will command his children and his home." It was with this very purpose that God had chosen him and revealed himself; God himself was the security that His own purposes should be carried out. And so every believing parent has, in the very fact of his being taken into this relation with God, the guarantee that God will give the grace of faithfulness to prepare for the blessing as well as the reward upon it.

It is part of God's covenant that He will first teach man to keep it, and then reward that keeping (Jer. 32:40). A covenant-keeping God and a covenant-keeping parent— in these the children must be blessed. "The mercy of the Lord is from everlasting to everlasting upon them that fear, and his righteousness to children's children, to such as keep his covenant, and to those that remember his precepts to do them."

Believing parent, see here the two sides of a parent's calling. Be very full of faith, be very faithful. Let faith in the living God, in His covenant with you and your seed, in His promises for your children, in His faithfulness, fill your soul. Take God's word as the only measure of faith. And then be very faithful: take God's word as the only measure of your life, especially in the family. Be a parent such as God would have you to be. Study Abraham in his fatherhood as chosen of God, faithful to God, blessed of God, and find in him the type, the law, the promise of what your fatherhood may be.

* * *

O my God, hast Thou indeed taken me too into this wonderful covenant, in which Thou art the God of the seed of Thy saints, and makest them the ministers of Thy grace to their children? Open my eyes, I pray Thee, to see the full glory of this Thy covenant, that my faith may know all that Thou hast prepared for me to bestow, and may do all Thou hast prepared for me to perform.

O my God, may Thy covenant-keeping faithfulness be the life and the strength of my faith. May this faith make me faithful in keeping the covenant.

And teach me to realize fully what this parental faithfulness is which Thou dost ask of me. I would make this the one object of my home life, to train my child to serve Thee. By my life, by my words, by my prayers, by gentleness and love, by authority and command, I would lead them in the way of the Lord. O God, be Thou my helper.

Teach me, above all, that as Thou hast appointed this parental training for the fulfillment of Thy purpose, I may be assured that Thou hast made provision for the grace to enable me to perform. Let my faith see Thee undertake for me and all I have to do, and an ever-growing faith so be the root of an ever-growing faithfulness. I ask it in the name of Thy Son. Amen.

EIGHTH DAY
The Child's Surety

"And Judah said unto Israel his father, Send the lad with me . . . I will be surety for him; of my hand shalt thou require him" (Gen. 43:8, 9).

These are the words of Judah, when he sought to persuade his father to send Benjamin with him to Egypt. That he realized what his suretyship for the child meant and was ready at any sacrifice to fulfill its duties is evident from his pleadings before Joseph: "Thy servant is become surety for the child with his father," and offered himself as a slave in his brother's place. In this he was the type not only of his own descendant, the great Surety of His people who gave himself in their stead, but also of every parent to whom God commits the care of a child amid the dangers of the journey through life. The language and conduct of Judah will teach us some most helpful lessons.

Consider the *duties* of such a suretyship, as illustrated in Judah. He was thoroughly in earnest with the engagement he had undertaken. When the governor of Egypt had commanded that Benjamin should be kept as a slave, he at once came forward as a substitute. Not for a moment does he think of his own home and children, of Egyptian slavery and its hardships; everything gives way to the thought, "My father entrusted him to me, and I am surety for the lad." With the most touching earnestness he pleads to be accepted in the youth's stead: "Thy servant is become surety for the lad with his father. How shall I go up to my father, and the lad be not with me? Now, therefore, let thy servant abide instead of the lad as bondman to my lord, and let the lad go up with his brethren."

Oh that Christian parents realized, as Judah did, what it means to be surety for their child! How often, when our children are in danger from the prince of this world, when the temptations of the flesh or the world threaten to make them prisoners and slaves, holding them back from ever reaching the Father's home—how often are we found careless or unwilling to sacrifice our ease and comfort in seeking to rescue them from their danger! How often the spiritual interests of the child are considered subordinate to worldly prospects or position or profit, and the solemn covenant forgotten. How feebly we realize that it is only in a life of pure and wholehearted devotion, in which the selfishness and worldly-mindedness are crucified, and our life is lived for God, that we can really train children for heaven! When danger threatens, and our children appear to be growing up unconverted, we must bow at the foot of the throne until we see that our plea, "I am surety for the child," has touched the heart of the King, and we have His word to set him free. Oh that the ruling principle of parental life and love might be: without the child I will not see my Father's face.

Consider now, too, the *encouragement* Judah's example gives. It sets before us the abundant reward the faithful surety will reap. In pleading with the ruler of Egypt, Judah thought he was dealing with a stranger, a despot, an enemy. Little did he know that his pleadings were entering the ears of one who was his own and Benjamin's brother. He never dared to hope that it would exercise such a mighty influence, calling forth that wondrous revelation of the ruler weeping on Benjamin's neck, "I am Joseph." Wonderful picture of the power and the reward of a surety's supplication!

And yet it is not more wonderful than the parent-surety may expect. If we understood the sinfulness of our children's nature, and the dangers surrounding them, with what fervency we would plead with the great King and Saviour of the world for their salvation. It is there, not less than to Judah, that the blessing would come to us. It might be that at the first, as it was with him, we have little conception of the tender relation in which He stands to us and our children as a Brother; as we plead for the child, and show ourselves ready to make any sacrifice so he may be saved, we should have our reward in the blessed revelation of what Jesus is to us, as well as in the blessing on the child. The blessing to the pleading surety would be no less rich than to his charge.

In Jairus in the father of the lunatic, in the Syrophenician woman, and in the experience of thousands of parents, we have proof that while they thought only of obtaining what their children needed, their prayer led to experiences of the power and love of the Saviour, closer and more intimate fellowship with Him—personal blessing as they never had found in praying only for themselves. They saw Him with whom they were pleading on the throne descend and say, "I am Jesus"; they saw Him embrace their beloved one. Jesus was never so gloriously revealed as when they were pleading as parents and sureties for their children.

And just as Judah then learned to understand how Joseph was the true surety, who in the path of suffering had won the throne and their deliverance from famine and death, so parents will learn, the more they seek to fulfill their duties as sureties, to know and rejoice in Jesus as their Surety. He has not only undertaken their own personal salvation; He has secured the grace they need to fulfill their duties. Their surety is grounded in His.

The vicarious principle on which redemption rests, "One for all," runs through the whole of its economy; most especially does it appear in the family, that image of humanity as a whole. There the father is head, priest, king—even as Christ—over his own house; the father is, in a limited sense but most really, surety for the child. As he, the surety on earth, draws nigh to the King and discovers in Him the great Surety, the revelation will give him new confidence and strength and joy in the work he has undertaken. In the light of the redemption and love and friendship of Jesus, the thought "I am surety for the child" will gain new brightness; devotion to the training of the children will become more earnest; the readiness to make any sacrifice to save them from the world will be more spontaneous; and the pleading of faith will have more confidence and triumph.

* * *

Blessed Father, most earnestly do we beseech Thee to open the eyes of parents to see and know their holy calling. May they understand and realize that Thou dost say to them at the birth of each little one entrusted to their care. "At your hands will I require it." May they understand and realize, too, that with each little one they brought and gave to Thee, they accepted the solemn charge and gave the answer, "Of my hand Thou shalt require him; I am surety for the child."

O God, show us what the dangers are that surround our children. Give us the true surety spirit, the willingness to sacrifice all rather than be unfaithful to our charge. As we see the power of sin and the world threatening them, may we plead as for our own life, yea, with the offer of our life, that the children be now saved from sin and Satan. As Thine eye sees us day by day with our children, may this be the one desire of our parental love: that they may be wholly Thine. Be this our one aim in prayer and education..

O Lord Jesus, teach us as parents that, as Thou art our Surety, we are the surety of our family. O Thou who art the faithful Surety, make us faithful too. Amen.

NINTH DAY
Protecting Faith

"And when she saw him that he was a goodly child, she hid him three months" (Ex. 2:2).

"By faith Moses, when he was born, was hid three months of his parents, because they saw he was a proper child; and they were not afraid of the king's commandment" (Heb. 11:23).

The story of Moses leads us a step further in our study of the relationship between children and their parents' faith. It was faith that saw the goodliness of the child; it was faith that feared not the king's wrath; it was faith that hid the child and saved his life. In each child born of believing parents, faith sees the same goodliness, meets the same danger, and finds the same path of safety.

It was by faith Moses' parents *saw he was a goodly child.* The natural love of a parent's heart doubtless made the child a beautiful one in the mother's eye; but faith saw more than nature could. God opened the eyes, and there was the consciousness of something special, of a spiritual beauty, that made their babe doubly precious. And so the eye of faith sees in each little one a divine goodliness. Is this not a being created in God's image, with the faint light of a divine glory, of an immortal life, shining from it? Here is an object of the great redemption, destined to be a partaker of the precious blood and the

Holy Spirit of Jesus, to be the object of the joy of angels and God's everlasting love and pleasure—a child whose worth exceeds that of the whole world; a child that even in this life can be a brother of Jesus, a servant of God, a blessing for the immortal spirits of fellowmen. Surely, faith may call the little one unspeakably fair, seeing him shining as a jewel in the crown of the Lamb—His joy and His glory. We have indeed a surer hope than ever Moses' parents had, and a brighter light in which the heavenly beauty of our little ones is reflected. O Father, open the eyes of all Thy people that with each little babe Thou givest them, their faith may see a goodly child.

It is faith that sees but *fears not the danger*. Pharaoh had commanded that the children of God's people should all be destroyed. He knew that if the children were cut off, the people would soon die out. There would be no need of the trouble and danger of war; by a slow, silent but sure process the nation would be cut off. The Prince of this world still pursues the same policy. When parents take a decided stand for God, the world may despise or hate them; it soon learns that it is of little use to attempt to conquer them. But it knows a surer way. The spirit of the world claims possession of the children; if these are won, all are won. And too often Christian parents allow the world to prey upon their children. Children grow up in comparative ignorance about the blessed Saviour, are entrusted to the care of irreligious or worldly teachers, are allowed to associate with those whose spirit and influence is altogether worldly.

In many a Christian home, where at one time when the children were still young all was earnest and decided, the tone changed, and as they grew the power of religion was far less to be seen. And the Church is often too faithless or feeble to warn against it. How little it has realized that in the parental relation it has a mighty hold on the Church of the future. To what a large extent the education of the young has been left to the State, to the secular school, and to the spirit of the age, until the youthful heart has lost the simplicity and tenderness of which the Master spoke when He said, "Of such is the kingdom of heaven." Oh, what thousands on thousands of children are thus drowned in the mighty Nile of this world. Would God that the eyes of His people might be opened to the danger which threatens His Church! It is not infidelity or superstition; *it is the spirit of worldliness in the homes of our Christian people*, sacrificing the children to the ambition or society, to the riches or the friendship of the world, that is the greatest danger of Christ's Church. If every home once won for Christ were a training school for His service, we would find in this a secret of spiritual strength not less than all that ordinary preaching can accomplish.

It is faith that still finds *the same path of safety.* "By faith Moses was hid by his parents." They trusted God on behalf of this goodly child, one of the children of His covenant. These simple words tell us our duty, what our faith must do. Christian parent, hide your child. And where? Oh, hide him in that safest refuge, "the shadow of the Almighty," "the secret of God's countenance." Lay your child from its birth daily there in faith, and let your soul be filled with the consciousness that He has indeed taken charge of it. Let the mighty rock of God's strength and the tender covering of His feathers be your child's ark, while still he is all unconscious of temptation or danger. With the first dawn of reason, may the clefts of the rock and the love of Jesus be the place of safety to which you guide the youthful feet. In the quiet of home life, hide him from the excitements of the world without, from the influence of a civilization and culture which is of the earth. In that hiding, where the enemy cannot find, we have one of faith's highest duties. And when the time comes that your child must come into contact with the world, let it be a settled thing with your heart that He has accepted your trust, has taken charge, and cannot disappoint your faith.

The *reward* of faith of Moses' parents will be ours.

Not only was Moses saved, he became the saviour of his people. Your child, too, will not only be blessed but also be made a blessing. Each child has not the calling of a Moses. But in God's kingdom He needs not only a Moses but a Moses' mother and a Moses' sister for the fulfillment of His purposes. Let your faith, like that of Moses' mother, do its work; God himself will see to it that our labor is not in vain.

The education Moses' mother gave her son during the years of his childhood was such that all the years of training in Pharaoh's court could not obliterate it. His parent's faith bore fruit in his faith when he, at every cost, chose suffering with the people of God and was not afraid of the wrath of the king. Moses saw Him who is invisible. Train the child for God and His people, and when the time comes that he must go into the world, even into Pharaoh's court, he will be safe in the power of faith and of God's keeping. A child of faith will not only receive a blessing for himself but will be a blessing to those around.

God grant that the Church may indeed become a "Moses' mother," the faithful nurse of the children He entrusts to her care, hiding them and keeping them separate from the world and its influence. He will give a wonderful fulfillment of the promise, wherever He finds the fulfillment of the duty: "Take this child away, and nurse it for me, and I will give thee thy wages."

* * *

Gracious God, with my whole heart I thank Thee for the teaching of Thy Word, by which Thou preparest me to fulfill aright my holy calling as parent. I thank Thee for the example of Moses' parents and pray that the grace that taught them in faith to save their child may be given to me too.

I acknowledge, Lord, that I do not sufficiently realize the value of my children nor the danger to which they are exposed from the Prince and the Spirit of the world.

Lord, teach me fully to recognize the danger and yet never to fear the commandment of the king. Open my eyes to see in the light of heaven that each little one is a goodly child, entrusted to my keeping and training for Thy work and kingdom. Help me in the humility and watchfulness and boldness of faith to keep them sheltered, to hide them from the power of the world and of sin. May my own life be the life of faith, hid with Christ in God, that my child may know no other dwelling place.

And grant all this also to all Thy people, O my God. Let Thy Church awaken to know her place in this world and her calling to go out to the land to which God has called her. Let, in the training of the children, the mighty power of faith be seen—the difference between them that fear Thee and them that fear Thee not. Oh, give us grace to rear our children for Thee. Amen.

TENTH DAY

A Lamb for a House

"Take to them every man a lamb, according to the house of their father, a lamb for an house: . . . When he seeth the blood, . . . the Lord will pass over the door, and will not suffer the destroyer to come in unto your houses" (Ex. 12:3, 23).

Of all the Old Testament sacrifices, there is none that gives a clearer or richer revelation of the person and work of our Lord than the Passover. Often, however, the fact has escaped observation that the whole institution of the Paschal Lamb aimed at deliverance not of the individuals but of families; it dealt not with the persons but with the families, the houses of God's people. What else is the meaning of the expression. "a lamb for an *house*"? or (as in vs. 21), "Take you a lamb according to your families"? and "of the blood sprinkled upon the *house*? As so it is expressly declared, "When your children shall say unto you, What mean ye by this service? That ye shall say, It is the sacrifice of the Lord's passover, who passed over the *houses* of the children of Israel in Egypt when he smote the Egyptians, and delivered our *houses*."

Among the Egyptians it was the *firstborn* in every house who died, as representing the family. In Israel it was the *firstborn* who through the blood was saved from the

impending danger and consecrated for God. All this teaches that God lays down as a fundamental law in the Passover and the blood-sprinkling: "I deal with you not as
individuals but as families. As I chose and blessed you,
the seed of your father Abraham, so I still bless every
household through the believing father, who sprinkles the
blood in obedience to my command. The lamb and its
blood are the consecration of the dwellings and the family
relations of my people." In the hands of the father, God
thus places the destiny and the safety of the whole house.

Christ, our Passover, is slain for us. Even to the most
minute particular, the foreshadowings of the Paschal
Feast were fulfilled in Him. Have we any warrant in
God's Word for excepting this so important feature and
allowing the type to hold good in every respect but this?
In this one respect, is the Old Testament feast to stand
higher than the New and the blood which then was for
the saving of the house here to be only for the individual
and not be sprinkled on the houses too? The Christian
parent might then have every reason to envy the Jew;
he enjoyed the privilege, as he looked at the sprinkled
blood, of knowing that he had done it to the saving not
only of himself but his household too. Does not the Christian parent have the right, in definite and assured faith,
to claim the blood for his children? Christ, the Lamb
of God, is still "a lamb for an house"! His blood may
still be sprinkled upon the door that the destroyer enter
not. In the new covenant, and with the precious blood of
Christ, the principle still holds good: it is the believing
father's right and duty in faith to appropriate the blood
for his whole house. His faith has the divine warrant and
will be rewarded with the divine blessing.

Let me endeavor henceforth to live in this faith, fully
realizing this privilege. As I think of the precious blood
and seek to walk in the nearness to God which it gives,
let me claim its cleansing power for my house as well
as myself. Let me be assured that my faith as parent
has power and does secure a divine influence. Thank God,

as a father I may transmit the grace and blessing of redemption.

Not only my soul, but my house, can daily be kept under the sprinkling and cleansing of the blood. And each time I enter my door, in the light of heaven I may see it sprinkled with the blood of the Lamb. Parents and children stand under the cover and protection of the blood: the Lord is our keeper.

Every year in Israel parents had to renew the sprinkling. But the blood of the Lamb has been shed once for all. I can now each day again renew the consecration of my house to the Lord in the assurance of faith; the blood saves me and my children. In this faith I may confidently expect that the wondrous redemption of the blood will exercise its full and mighty influence until all our domestic life and its relations be sanctified, our house be wholly the Lord's, and each child be consciously and confessedly one of His redeemed.

To this end I must notice carefully how God commanded the parents to teach these things to their children (Ex. 12:26; 13:14). "The grace of God that bringeth salvation *teacheth* us." What is secured to the child in redemption must be made his own in free and personal appropriation. And this cannot be without his knowing it. The children were to be *taught* that they belonged to the redeemed people, that they belonged to the redeeming God. The parent was to act not only as priest and thus, in a sense, as mediator, but also as prophet and teacher. As he had dealt for the child with God in the blood-sprinkling, so he was to deal for God with the child in the instructions he gave them.[1] Let me seek grace and wisdom to teach my children what the blood has done for them, to make them know and love the God who accepted them before ever they knew Him!

One thing more is deserving of very special note. Every year the believing Israelite was to sprinkle the

---

1. See the next meditation for the further illustration of this thought.

doorposts with blood, so testifying that it was only in the blood that he and his house could stand before God; he was also to write upon these same blood-sprinkled doorposts the words of God's law (Deut. 6:7-9). In all the going-out and coming-in of his children, these words were ever to meet their eye. The freedom from Egypt's bondage and Egypt's curse was a freedom to serve God. God wills to be not only trusted but obeyed. It is "unto obedience *and* the sprinkling of the blood of Christ" that we have been chosen. The doorposts sprinkled with the blood and inscribed with the words of the law remind me of the blessed oneness of faith and obedience, liberty and service. I would in the joy of the great redemption train and educate my children to know, love, and keep the commands of their God. Day by day, in faith and prayer, in teaching and living, I would seek to set before them the blessedness of a faith that freely accepts all that God gives, with a surrender that gives all He claims.

"A lamb for an house"—I pray that God's Holy Spirit will reveal in its full power all the truths that cluster round this blessed word. A father redeemed by the blood; his children through him and with him partaking of the sprinkling; the father, God's minister every year anew to sprinkle the house; the father, God's witness and messenger to the children to teach them of this precious blood and of the God it reveals; the blood-sprinkled doorposts inscribed with the words of God's law—such is God's wondrous provision for getting full possession of His people.

* * *

Blessed Lord Jesus, the Lamb of God, which taketh away the sin of the world, the Son of God, whose blood cleanseth from all sin, in humble faith I claim that blood for myself and my children. May my own experience of its ever-cleansing power grow fuller and clearer. And may I by Thy Holy Spirit realize my right to claim it for my house.

O most blessed Saviour, may the power of Thy blood work in me so mightily that my faith may in full assurance accept it for each of my children as a present blessing. May we, under the covering of the blood, know ourselves protected from the destroyer.

O most gracious God, who hast given this wondrous ordinance of a lamb for an house, I yield myself to Thee afresh as the minister of Thy covenant. Use me, my God, to save my children, to train them for Thee and Thee alone. I would have the doorposts not only sprinkled with the blood but inscribed with the law. I would have Thy service the aim of my children. As Thou hast chosen us unto obedience *and* blood-sprinkling, may faith in the blood and surrender to Thy will be as the two doorposts between which we daily go in and out. The Lord make it so. Amen.

ELEVENTH DAY

The Father—Priest and Prophet

"And it shall come to pass, when your children shall say unto you, What mean ye by this service? That ye shall say, It is the sacrifice of the Lord's passover, who passed over the houses of the children of Israel in Egypt, when he smote the Egyptians, and delivered our houses" (Ex. 12:26, 27).

The Passover sets the believing parent before us in a twofold aspect: first, as dealing with God on behalf of the children and bringing down the blessing on them; then as dealing with the children for God and seeking to lead them up to Him. In the former capacity, he sprinkled the blood of the lamb upon his house, securing God's protection for the children. In the latter he had to instruct his children, telling them of what God had done and seeking to lead them to the personal knowledge and acceptance of this God as their God. Those two parts of parental duty are closely and inseparably linked to each other, the first being necessary as the root and origin of the latter. The parent's work as priest fits him for his work as prophet and teacher. The second is indispensable to the full appropriation of the blessing that the former has secured. It was after having sprinkled the blood for himself, and his child too, that the parent had to instruct him in the meaning of the holy mystery. His interposition with God and his experience of God's blessing on himself and child were his own training to fit him for the training of his child. As we keep this in view, we shall recognize the beauty of that institution by which God has chosen and appointed the believing parent the instructor of his children and realize its extreme fitness as the best means of securing a godly seed for the Lord.

It is the parent, *who has himself already experienced the salvation of God*, who is appointed to lead the child to know God. The knowledge of God is no mere matter of the understanding; it is to love Him, to live in Him, to experience the power of His presence and His blessing. It is evident that the man who would teach others to know God must be able to speak from personal experience of Him, must prove by the warmth of love and devotion that he loves this God and has his life from Him.

When God instituted the family as the great instrument of transmitting His fear, He so arranged it as to give it the highest possible efficacy. This consisted in his revealing himself to each head of a family as the God of his salvation. In the other sacrifices in Israel, the priest sprinkled the blood in the holy places; but in the Passover there was this peculiarity: *each father* sprinkled it *on his own house.* He thereby performed the act of faith by which the destroyer was kept from his house; and when he went forth from Egypt and undertook the journey to Canaan, he could bear personal witness to God's faithfulness and to the efficacy of the atoning blood of the lamb. He could speak as a living witness from personal experience. As a redeemed one he could tell of redemption; he could tell of the Redeemer-God.

It is even so now still: personal experience of the power of the blood can alone fit a parent for speaking to his children of God. Looking back upon the time when personal deliverance from sin was experienced and looking up to a God with whom in the spirit of adoring gratitude a personal fellowship is maintained, and looking forward to a home where the longing spirit knows it will inherit a place prepared by the Father—this and this alone fits a parent to speak truth in power. It is the parent who has himself experienced redemption who can tell his child of the God of Redemption, who can act in accordance with the injunction: "And thou shalt show thy son in that day, saying, This is done because of that which the Lord did *unto me* when I came forth out of Egypt" (Ex. 13:8).

And as parents in Israel every year had to renew the remembrance of that deliverance, so now it is the parent who lives in the fresh experience of the powers of redemption who can with ever-deepening earnestness teach his children the truth of God.

But please observe further: *this parent also has been constituted and accepted as God's appointed minister in the redemption of the child.* This gives an increased fitness for his work as instructor of the child. He not only can speak of a salvation he has experienced, urging and inviting the child to come and taste that to which he is as yet a stranger, but in sprinkling the blood upon the door of his house, he *saved his child too* from the destroying angel. He was honored to act with God on behalf of the child. What the child could not do, he did for him; and the deed was accepted. The child has initially been made partaker of the blessing of that sprinkling of blood, and in growing up, must come personally to accept what has been secured and sealed to him. And what a mighty vantage ground it gives the believing parent in his labor, when he can look upon his child in the light of that great transaction between God and himself! With what confidence it inspires his faith, how his energies will be roused, and what a strong motive in pleading with the child himself! He speaks to him as no longer a stranger to the covenant of grace but as a child of the covenant. He points him to a God who began to deal with him in the feebleness of infancy; he can attest to the reality of an engagement entered into between God and himself and sealed in the sprinkling of blood. He shows him how God dealt with the houses, with the families of Israel; and in the tone of the language which his faith adopts, he lets him feel that he cannot consent to one of his house refusing to acknowledge the God of the house.

And it gives him no less power in pleading with God on behalf of the child. He reminds the great Jehovah of the blood and the oath of the covenant and claims for his child the blessings of redemption—that just as he is a child of the redeemed people, he may grow up personally to accept and ratify the covenant. Next to his own personal experience of the blessing of salvation, this consciousness of what as a believing parent he has been allowed to do—his seed having been received with him into covenant—constitutes the fitness of the believing parent for his being the minister of God's grace to his child.

But there is another thought that brings out still more strikingly the wondrous adaptation of the family constitution for the working out of God's purposes—namely, that *it is grounded on the natural relation*, sanctifying its affections, and adopting them into the service of redemption. It is not merely a redeemed man saying to his fellowman, "Come and see what God has wrought for me." Nor is it a redeemed man saying to some child to whom he sustains a certain official relation and on whose behalf he has performed an act of atonement, "Come and let me lead you to your God." But *it is a father, with his own child*. In nature they are one, united by the closest and most wondrous ties. The child has his life from the father. The father looks upon him as part of himself, of his flesh and of his bones; he loves and cherishes him. This love seeks, even in nature, the happiness of the child and can often make wondrous sacrifices to attain it. And it is this love God lays hold of in the parental covenant, and purifies to be the minister and vehicle of His grace.

And with a parent's love there is a parent's influence. The weakness of the child renders him dependent, to a wondrous degree, upon the parent's will. The character of childhood is formed and molded by impressions; unceasing communion with the parent can render these impressions deep and permanent. The child's love to the parent rises and meets the parent's love, and the spirit of the parent can thus, in addition to the natural influence of birth, be breathed into the child. Of all this God's grace seeks to avail itself. And while it is the sole prerogative of the Holy Spirit to renew the soul and make a child of God, there is nevertheless a need for the means and instruments through which His gracious workings are prepared and applied, confirmed and established. Of all these instruments, there is none more wondrously devised or more beautifully adapted to its object than this of godly parentage. A parent made partaker of God's love and grace himself, accepted and blessed with the promises of the covenant and the Spirit, and then sent forth, in the power of consecrated parental affection, to make all the influences and relationships of domestic life the auxiliary to the great work of gaining the child for God—this surely is one of the most wondrous exhibitions of God's grace upon earth.

*   *   *

O my God, I come to Thee again with the earnest prayer for Thy teaching. Thou hast said, "I will be the God of all the families of Israel." Open my eyes to see clearly and my heart to feel deeply what Thy purpose is in this.

Since sin entered and ruined our nature, Thou wouldst early take possession of the little ones for thyself. Thou seekest to secure parents with all their love and influence to be Thy ministers. Thou enterest into covenant with them, giving them the right to claim the blood of the covenant for their children and in that blood the promise, "a God to thee and to thy seed." And then Thou sendest them, redeemed and having claimed and accepted redemption for their children, to use their influence for Thee and win and train their children for Thy love and service.

Lord God, open the eyes of the parents of Thy Church to their calling that they may honor Thee as the God of their families. And, O Lord my God, bless my own house! Give me grace, as one of Thy redeemed ones, to train my children for their God. May the joy of a personal experience of redemption and the love of the blessed Redeemer warm my heart, inspire my words, and light up my life to testify of Thee and to train my children for Thee alone. Amen.

TWELFTH DAY
Sanctify the Firstborn

"And the Lord spoke unto Moses, saying, Sanctify unto
me all the firstborn. . . . All the firstborn of man among
thy children shalt thou redeem. And it shall be when thy
son asketh thee in time to come, Saying, What is this?
that thou shalt say unto him, By strength of hand the
Lord brought us out of Egypt, from the house of bondage: And it came to pass, when Pharaoh would hardly
let us go, that the Lord slew all the firstborn in the land
of Egypt, . . . therefore I sacrifice to the Lord all that
openeth the matrix, being males; but all the firstborn of
my children I redeem" (Ex. 13:1, 2, 13-15).

"Let my people go that they may serve me"—in these
words so often repeated by the Lord in sending Moses
to Pharaoh, we see how service is the aim of redemption.
God makes His people free from the bondage of Egypt
in order to translate them into the liberty of His service—
the willing, loving, free service of a redeemed people.
The deeper God's people enter into the spirit of redemption, the deeper will be the insight into the blessed unity
of liberty and service, of liberty and necessity. There
is no true service of God without liberty, no true liberty
without service.

We have seen in the Passover the permanent place the
family and the children take in redemption. No less than
their parents were they redeemed to serve; all their train-

ing was to be a training for the service of God. When
Pharaoh said to Moses after the plague, "Go, serve the
Lord your God; but who are they that shall go?" the
answer was very distinct, "We will go *with our young* and
our old, our sons and our daughters." It was on this point
that the negotiations were broken off. The going of the
children the king would not consent to: "Let the Lord
so be with you, as I will let you go, and your little ones:
look to it; for evil is before you" (Ex. 10:8-10). And when
later on Pharaoh still wanted to keep the property, he
felt that this at least must be conceded: "Go ye, serve
the Lord; only let your flocks and herds be stayed: *let
your little ones also go with you"* (vs. 24). It is the
future of the nation that is to be secured for God; a people
that is really to serve God must, in the first place, see
to the little ones.

After the people had left Egypt, the very first command
God gave to Moses was in regard to the firstborn, who
were to be separated and sanctified for Him. In each
family the firstborn son was counted the chief and the
best. The father's attitude toward him is expressed in
these words of Jacob concerning Reuben: "Thou art my
firstborn, my might, and the beginning of my strength."

His was the birthright and the place of honor in the
family. He was the representative and head of all the
children. God looked upon Israel as His firstborn among
the nations. Because Egypt oppressed him and would not
let him go, God slew his firstborn. And now in commem-
oration of this and as a pledge of God's claim on all
the children and the whole people, every firstborn belonged to God and was set apart as His peculiar property.

And with what object? For none other but His service.
This comes out with great distinctness in the exchange
that was made when the tribe of Levi was taken instead
of the firstborn. "After that shall the Levites go in to do
the service of the tabernacle of the congregation, for
they are wholly given unto me from among the children
of Israel; . . . instead of the firstborn of all the children

of Israel, have I taken them to me; for all the firstborn . . . are mine" (Num. 8:15-17). And in the redemption money, which had to be paid at the birth of each firstborn for his release, the parents had the unceasing reminder that he belonged to God and His service and was represented in the Levites.

The principle involved in this is one of the deepest importance. *God claims our best children for His own direct and immediate service.* The whole people, old and young, were to serve Him; but the firstborn, the very best, were to be entirely set apart for the special maintenance of that service, not only by the part they took in the worship but by instructing the people in the law of their God. Let us try to take in fully the lessons the Christian Church has to learn from this.

In Israel all the firstborn and, as their representatives, all the children of Levi—a twelfth part of the whole nation —were exclusively claimed by God to be continually at His disposal in the service of His house. And in Israel that service consisted solely in the maintenance of what existed—nothing had to be done for the extension of the kingdom or the propagation of the knowledge of God among the heathen. The Christian Church has now not only to see to it that she maintains her hold on what she once has occupied; her calling in her redemption from sin is distinctly and essentially aggressive, to teach all the nations and seek the extension of the kingdom throughout the whole world. The question is naturally suggested: If Israel had to set apart one-twelfth of its children for the work of God, what portion should the Christian Church devote to the work committed to her? And what portion has she devoted?

Alas, that the answer to the latter question should be so sad! There is hardly a missionary society engaged in teaching and rescuing the ignorant and the lost that has not complained of the want of laborers. The call is being sounded forth louder every year that the doors to the hundreds of millions of heathen are opened wide, and yet how few, how sadly few, is the number of laborers. And why? Simply because Christian parents do not, as a rule, educate their children under the conviction that they are the Lord's. They do not place them at His disposal, do not train them to look upon this as their highest privilege, to be found worthy to bear the name of Christ among the heathen.

Let us just think a moment what would be thought of the loyalty of Englishmen to their Queen if it were found difficult to find men to form her bodyguard or accept appointments in her service. Or what of the enthusiasm of an army where the general could never obtain volunteers for a post of danger and of honor? And Jesus Christ, our King, who came to seek and save the lost, has said that these are His guard of honor, having His richest rewards, who forsake all for His and the gospel's sake. And yet, while in every profession there are complaints of more applicants than openings, the Master has to wait and His work has to suffer because His people do not understand that they and their children have been redeemed to serve Him who gave himself for them.

And what is the cure of this evil? And what can we do, each in our sphere, to wipe out this terrible reproach? What we can do is this: Let us devote every child to God and His service. Let us not pray that our children may be saved without thinking of giving them to serve. Let us cease choosing honorable and lucrative professions for our children, turning the truth that they can serve God in any calling an excuse for declining special service. Let us lay each child upon the altar, especially our firstborn and our best, and seek this one thing: that they may become worthy and fit to be set apart for the service of the King.

And let the Church learn as part of her preaching of redemption to lift aloud her voice and cry, "You are redeemed for service, you and your children." The reason so many a parent has prayed for the salvation of his child and been disappointed is that the prayer was utterly selfish; it was simply the desire to see the child happy, giving no thought to the glory of God or of consecration to His service. When God established His covenant with Abraham and gave him Isaac, He wanted to have Isaac at His disposal as a channel of blessing to the world. When God rewarded the faith of Moses' parents, He wanted a servant through whom He could save Israel. When God redeemed Israel's firstborn the night of the Passover, it was to have them for himself. Oh, Christian parent, when God offers the covenant to Isaac and Moses and Israel's firstborn, to your children, *He wants them for His service, His blessed service of love and liberty.* Has He not a right to claim it? Shall He not have it? He gave His Firstborn, His only-begotten, for you and your children; can anything be too precious for Him? Listen not to the thought that the demand is hard or the sacrifice great. Know that for yourself, as for your children, it is the path of honor and blessing. And let your example teach the Church that there are those who, because they love their children most intensely, know nothing better for them than to yield them utterly to the will and the work of their God.

*   *   *

O Lord, Thou art a great and a glorious God, and Thy kingdom ruleth over all. Thou alone art worthy to be praised; Thou alone hast a right to the love and the worship and the service of all Thy creatures. And this too is their blessedness: in heaven above and on earth below, blessed are Thy servants who stand around Thy throne and do Thy will.

O Lord, we do bless Thee that Thou dost ask and dost accept our children for Thy service. We acknowledge Thy claim; let them all be used for Thy service and glory. But especially would we offer Thee the first and the best.

O God, teach us to feel deeply that Thou hast need of them. For the building up of Thy temple, in the struggle of Thy kingdom with the power of darkness, in the gather-

74

ing of Thy people from the hundreds of millions of heathen, Thou hast need of our children. We give them to Thee. We will train them for Thee. We will wait in prayer and faith, and we beseech Thee to inspire them with a holy enthusiasm for the kingdom and its conquests. We beseech Thee to fill them and us with love to Jesus and love to souls that they may serve Thee as Thy Son did, giving their lives to save men.

O Lord God, who hast redeemed us and our children by the blood of the Lamb, let our firstborn—let all our children—be holy unto the Lord. Amen.

THIRTEENTH DAY
The Sabbath and the Children

"The seventh day is the Sabbath of the Lord thy God:
in it thou shalt not do any work, *thou, nor thy son,* nor
thy daughter. . ." (Ex. 20:8).

Among the most precious blessings which a child from
a godly home can take with him into the world is the
habit of reverent observance of the Sabbath. The separation from evil company, leading him to God's house, the
calm and thoughtful quiet it sometimes brings over his
spirit will, even if he is still a stranger to grace, be a
safeguard and a help, a schoolmaster to bring to Christ.
If he is a Christian, it will be one of his surest aids in
the growth and strengthening of the life of faith. The training is a part of a parent's duty that needs to be studied
in earnest prayer and for the performance of which much
wisdom and grace are needed. The Lord, who has enjoined the duty, will not withhold the grace.

Note in the words of the fourth commandment how
particularly the children are remembered. It is to parents
the command is given; it is in the keeping holy of the
day by their children, as well as by themselves, that their
obedience is to be manifested. "*Thou, nor thy son, nor
thy daughter,* nor thy man-servant, nor thy maid-
servant": it is not so much as a private nor as a national
but as a family ordinance that the Sabbath was first of

all appointed. Just as the terms of the covenant, "a God to thee and to thy seed," the words suggest the two thoughts that it is first the parent, and then the child through the parent, with whom God is dealing. The parent must first learn to keep the Sabbath day holy himself, then to train his child to keep it holy too.

The parent's obedience of this command precedes the training of the child to do so. Here is the principle which lies at the root of all true education: what I am to develop in my child I must first be myself. Example is more than precept; being more than teaching; what I am and do, more that what I tell him to be or do. The question is often asked how we can teach our children to revere and love the Sabbath, and in answer many lessons of great value have been given. But we cannot too earnestly insist on the truth that the first requirement is that the day should be a holy day to the parents themselves. It is as they serve God in the beauty of holiness, as the spirit of holiness breathes on and from them in the services of the Sabbath, as that day is to them a day not only of strict observance, but of joyful worship, of quickened devotion, of real loving fellowship with God, as the Sabbath is *a delight*, that the first condition will be fulfilled for teaching their children to love it.

Let Christian parents note this: God means the Sabbath to be to your child what it is to your own experience, a day you really love and rejoice in. Let us study its wonderful significance and rich blessing.

Look upon the Sabbath as the day of *rest*, of entering into God's own wonderful rest. The rest of God is in a finished work; by faith in that work we enter into that rest, and the great calm, the peace that passes understanding, keeps the heart and mind (Gen. 2:3; Heb. 4:3-10).

Look upon it as a *holy* day, the day God has given as a token and pledge that He who is holy makes us holy too (Ex. 31:13; Ezek. 20:12). It is in fellowship with God that we are made holy; let His presence, His love, His joy, be the mark as well as the fruit of keeping it holy.

Look upon it as a day of *blessing* (Gen. 2:3). Sin robbed mankind of this blessing. In the resurrection of Christ the finished work of creation was restored, perfected in a higher sense. Under the leading of the Holy Spirit, the first day of the week, the day of the Lord Jesus, the Sabbath of the new life, took the place of the Sabbath of death, when the Lord of the Sabbath was in the tomb. The Sabbath of creation, rendered void by the fall and the law, is now glorified in the Sabbath of redemption. And all the blessings of the living Christ—His finished work and resurrection power and eternal rest and the Holy Spirit, who descended from heaven on this new Sabbath—are to be made ours by this day. Let it be to us a day of blessing, in the fellowship of the Father's love, and the Son's grace through the Holy Spirit. In so doing we will have taken the first and the surest step for its being a blessing and a joy to our sons and daughters.

And now comes the second lesson. It is not enough that the parent keep holy the Sabbath day; the Lord lays it on him to secure the child's doing so too. As parent he is responsible for it, and must make it a matter of distinct effort and prayer. The training of their children to do so is a sacred obligation and requires, on account of its difficulty, the sacrifice of personal enjoyment, the exercise of thought and wisdom, and patient faith and love.

In seeking to do so, there are two dangers to be avoided. In human nature we find that there are two principles implanted in our hearts to guide us in action—pleasure and duty. The former leads us to seek what is agreeable and for our own interest and is one of the most powerful motives in all our conduct. When our pleasure, however, is at variance with the interests of others or the will of God, the sense of duty comes in to restrain and regulate the desire for pleasure. The reward of obedience to duty is that in course of time it is no longer a check to pleasure but becomes itself the highest pleasure. The art of education consists in so bringing pleasure and duty into harmony that without the sacrifice of either both may be attained.

In training the child to keep holy the Sabbath day, there is a danger of putting either of these principles too exclusively in the foreground. With our Puritan and Covenanting ancestors the former principle was urged, and the only sanction sought for keeping the Sabbath was the law. In our days we are in danger of the opposite extreme. To make the Sabbath interesting to the children, to make them happy on it—if possible to make them love it as a day of enjoyment—is so exclusively the object of attention that the thought of obligation is almost lost sight of. The idea is unconscioulsy instilled that the day is to be hallowed and loved only as far as it is made interesting and pleasant. Let parents seek grace from Him who, as divine wisdom says, guides in the midst of the paths of right, to be kept from the right-hand as well as the left-hand error.

Do not hesitate to speak of God's command and of duty. God trained Israel as He would a child in the life of law for the life of love in Christ. Education consists, in its first stages, more in training to right habits than inculcating principles—these come later. In connection with the Lord's day, be not afraid of the element of self-denial and quiet self-control which the thought of obedience to God's will and to your will brings over the child's spirit. They are part of the foundation of noble character. Tranquillity of mind and serenity of spirit are invaluable blessings; the quiet of the Sabbath helps to foster them. Holiness is much more than separation; it is a positive fellowship and enjoyment of God. But it begins with separation: the putting away of week-day toys and books and companions, the marking off of the day from other days. Even the little issues are, under wise guidance, a preparation for the truer hallowing of it later on.

This on the one side. On the other, exercise a wise and loving thoughtfulness as to the ways in which the day can be made a happy one. In the picture lessons to the younger ones, in the careful selection of suitable and interesting reading for the elder ones, in the merry singing of psalms and hymns and spiritual songs, making melody to the Lord, in the forethought with which possible transgression is guarded, in the tone of gladsome and loving reverence with which the day is spoken of and spent, in the personal Bible study and prayer, the believing parent will find the means of leading the child on to call the Sabbath a delight, the holy of the Lord (Isa. 63:13), and to inherit the blessing promised to those who do so.

Dear Christian parents, the thought of how we ought to train our children to love the Sabbath reminds us of our shortcomings. But let not this discourage us. We have God, the God of the Sabbath, who gave the day as a token of the covenant He has with us and our children, to sanctify us. We have Him to teach us and our children to sanctify His day. Let us look to Him to give grace to feel and show that the Lord's day is the happiest of the week. In the divided life of the ordinary worldly Christian it cannot be so. God's commandments cannot be obeyed without a wholehearted surrender to live for Him alone, without a life under the full power of His Holy Spirit. But if God be our chiefest joy, the desire after His service and love our highest aim, He himself will sanctify our Sabbaths, our hearts, our homes, our children, by His holy presence. And the Sabbaths will be but a part of a life holy to the Lord.

* * *

Most Holy God, I do thank Thee for the precious gift of the holy Sabbath day and the wonderful blessings of which it is the pledge. I thank Thee above all for the redemption of the Sabbath, in the death of Jesus from the power of sin and its restoration to us in the power and the joy of His risen life. Oh, grant that each succeeding Sabbath may lead me deeper into Thy rest, the rest of God in Christ, and so into the fellowship of Thy holiness and Thy blessedness. May a daily life that seeks its only joy in Christ, wholly yielded to the Spirit, prepare me for keeping the day holy.

Blessed Father, I especially ask for grace to train my children to love and hallow Thy day. I know that nothing but the joy of Thy presence in my own life can fit me for it. Give me this. And then give me the wisdom, as Thy servant, to bring to them the sense of Thy holy will and Thy lovingkindness, in claiming the day for thyself, and then giving it to them as Thy own day, that the fear of grieving Thee and the joy of pleasing Thee may each find due place in their hearts. So may the command and the promise, the duty and the pleasure, be one to them, and their delight in Thy day indeed meet the promised reward, "Then shalt thou delight thyself in the Lord." Amen.

FOURTEENTH DAY

The Children's Commandment

"Honour thy father and thy mother; that thy days may be long upon the land which the Lord thy God giveth thee" (Ex. 20:12).

"Children, obey your parents in the Lord: for this is right" (Eph. 6:1).

"Children, obey our parents in all things: for this is well pleasing unto the Lord" (Col. 3:20).

The first four commandments have reference to God, the last five to our neighbor. In between stands the fifth. It is linked to the first four, because to the young child the parent represents God; from him the child must learn to trust and obey his God. And this command is the transition to the last five because in the family is the foundation of society, and there the first experience comes of all the greater duties and difficulties with men at large. As the training school for all our relationships with God and man, this commandment lies at the foundation of all divine and human law, of all our worship of God, and all our dealings with man.

Of the ten, this one is especially the children's commandment. And on that account it is very specially the parents' commandment also. A wise ruler makes good subjects, a firm commander makes faithful soldiers; it is on the parents' character that the children's fulfillment of this precept will depend. And so we will consider what parents must be if they are to succeed in training their children to honor them.

The sentiment of honor, reverence, is one of the noblest and purest of which our nature is capable. The power of perceiving what is worthy of honor, the willingness to acknowledge it, the unselfishness that feels it no degradation, but a pleasure, to render it—all this is itself honorable and ennobling; nothing brings more true honor than giving honor to others. This dispostion ought to be cultivated most carefully in the child as an important part of his education. It is one of the chief elements of a noble character and a preparation for rendering to God the honor due to Him.

If the teaching of Scripture to honor God, to honor all men, to honor the widows, to give honor to whom honor is due is to be obeyed by our children, they must be prepared for it by learning first to honor their parents. If they are in later life to do what is so difficult—to honor all men, by recognizing even in the degraded and the lost the worth that belongs to them who are created in the image of God—they must be carefully prepared for it in the home school of family life. This is not only to secure a happy home and place the relationship of parent and child on a right footing, but to fit the child for all his future relations to God and his fellowmen and to lay in him one of the foundation-stones of a noble character and a holy life. God has placed this commandment the first of those on the second table. Parents may well study how they can train their children to fulfill it.

The child must honor the parent by obedience. "*Obey your parents*" is the New Testament version of "honor thy father and thy mother." The importance of this word "obedience" is more than the mind can grasp. God created man with his wonderful liberty of will that he might obey Him. Obedience to God was to lead to the enjoyment of God. By disobedience sin entered; in obedience—the twofold obedience of Christ and to Christ (Heb. 5:8, 9)—salvation comes. And on the parent the sacred charge is laid of training the child to obey, teaching him to link all the memories of happiness and love in home life with obedience, working the principle into the very mind and heart—not so much by instruction or reasoning as by training and securing the habit of obedience. The child is to be taught to honor the parent. The will of the child, no less than his mind and affections, is given into the parent's hands to mold and guide. It is in yielding his will to the will of the parent that the child acquires that mastery over it and over himself which will afterwards be his strength and safety, making him a fit instrument for doing God's will. Man was created free that he might obey; obedience is the path to liberty.

On this point parents often err; they often say that to develop the will of the child the will must be left free,, and the child is left to decide for himself. They forget that the will of the child is not free: passion and prejudice, selfishness and ignorance, all seek to influence the child in the wrong direction. The superior judgment, the calmer deliberation, the fuller experience of the parent are to decide for the child whose will has been entrusted to his care.

But are we not in danger of repressing the healthy development of a child's moral powers by thus demanding implicit submission to our will? By no means. The true liberty of the will consists in our being master of it and so our own masters. Train a child to master his will in giving it up to his parents' command, and he acquires the mastery to use it when he is free. Yielding to a parent's control is the path to self-control; and self-control alone is liberty. The child who is taught by a wise parent to honor and accept his superior wisdom will acquire, as he gives up his own way, the power over his will in a measure never possible to one who is taught that he need do nothing unless the parent has first convinced him of the propriety of the act and obtained his consent. The New Testament says very distinctly, "Children, obey your parents in the Lord: for *this is right.*" Not because the child approves or agrees but because the command is given by a parent—this is the true reason for its being obeyed.

In his attitude and conduct, too, the child is to be trained to honor the parent. Familiarity breeds contempt; in language and carriage and conduct, parents often tolerate an easy-going familiarity which, however it may be mis-called by the name of love or kindness, destroys those sentiments of respect and reverence in which true love has its strength and its real happiness. Manners are of more importance than many think; the neglect of good manners not only reveals a want in the disposition of those sentiments of respect and courtesy, but it reacts on the heart and fosters the selfishness and indifference that cares little for others' feelings. Locke has said that next to religion and virtue, manners are the most important thing in education—more so, he thinks, than learning. Let parents remember that in taking trouble to train their children to show them due honor and respect, even in apparently insignificant things, they are forming habits and breathing principles into them which will afterwards repay all their labor. "Him that honoureth me, I will honour" is God's principle which has its reflection in the life of earth too.

And it is the parent who is to cultivate and develop this sentiment in the child. The young child is guided, not by reflection or argument, but by feeling and affection. He cannot yet realize and honor the unseen God. He cannot yet honor all men, the wretched and unworthy, for the ideal, the unseen worth of their creation in God's image. The child can only honor what he sees to be "worthy of honour." And this is the parent's high calling: always so to speak and act, so to live in the child's presence, that honor may be spontaneously and unconsciously rendered. This can be only where, in quiet self-recollection and self-control, the parent lives in God's fear and presence and walks worthy of this calling, as one who has been placed at the head of a family to be not only its prophet, priest, but king too. Yes, a king receives honor. Let the parent reign as a king ruling in love and the fear of God, and honor will be given him.

Above all, let parents remember that honor really comes from God. Let them honor Him in the eyes of their children, and He will honor them there too. From parents who in everything seek to honor God, children will learn to honor God and them together. The parent who teaches his child to obey the fifth commandment has guided his feet into the way of all God's commandments. A child's first virtue is honoring and obeying his parents.

*　*　*

O my God, I come again to Thee with the request that Thou wouldst open my eyes and give me fully to realize the parent's holy calling to train his child for all that Thou wouldst have him be. I ask of Thee especially to reveal to me in Thine own light the full import of the fifth commandment that I may teach my child to fulfill it according to Thy will.

Fill my own soul, I pray Thee, with such honor and reverence for Thy holy majesty that both I and my child may learn what honor is. Teach me to claim honor from my child with the holy aim of leading him to honor Thee above all. May honoring his parents and honoring his God work in him the spirit of humility, which gladly renders to all their due.

O Lord, I look to Thee for grace to secure the keeping of the children's commandment in my home. Oh, grant that I may always live worthy of all honor. And may the holy power to train young souls to keep Thy commandments, to honor and serve Thee, be the fruit of Thy own Spirit's work in me. I ask it, my God, in Jesus' name. Amen.

FIFTEENTH DAY
Parental Instruction

"Now these are the commandments, the statutes, and the judgments which the Lord your God commanded to teach you, that he might do them in the land whither ye go to possess it: That thou mightest fear the Lord thy God, to keep all his statutes and commandments, which I command thee, thou, and thy son, and thy son's son, all the days of thy life; . . . thou shalt love the Lord thy God with all thine heart. . . . And these words, which I command thee this day, shall be in thine heart: And thou shalt teach them diligently unto thy children, and shalt talk of them when thou sittest in thine house, and when thou walkest by the way, and when·thou liest down, and when thou risest up" (Deut. 6:1, 2, 5-7).

"Thou, and thy son, and thy son's son"—with these words in the second verse, Moses gave expression to the truth that God gave His commandments not merely to the individual or to a single generation, but to all people throughout history. Each one who received the commandments of God was to strive not only to keep them himself but to hold himself responsible for their maintenance among his children. "These are the commandments . . . which the Lord your God commanded to teach you, . . . That thou mightest fear the Lord thy God, to keep all his commandments, . . . thou, and thy son, and thy son's son." In the following verses (5, 7) this idea is enlarged upon even further. In verses 20 and 21 is brought out the duty of expounding to the children the basis for that wondrous relation in which God's people stood to Him. They had been favored with the divine law, even the mercy and faithfulness of God who had redeemed them from the land of Egypt. All this concentrated in the one important and blessed truth that the fear and faith of God must be seen in family religion. The grand means for maintaining and extending the fear of God among His people is the faithful performance of parental duty, that His service and blessing should descend from son to son.

Parental instruction must be *from the heart*. We all know how little is learned from a listless or uninterested teacher. It is only the heart that gains the heart, the loving warmth of interest and affection that can awaken corresponding emotions in the pupil. God would secure all the influence of parental love to gain access for His words and will to the youthful and susceptible hearts of the children of His people. He therefore says, "*Thou shalt love* the Lord thy God with all thine heart, . . . and these words . . . shall be *in thine heart: and* thou shalt teach them diligently to thy children."

How easy and blessed the work, so often sighed over, if not neglected, to those who listen to God's guidance. As is your duty, love the Lord your God with all your heart. If you love Him, love His words too; let them live in your heart, let them have a place in your affections. And if the heart is filled with God's love and God's words, how easy it is to have them in your mouth too and to teach them to your children. Let holy love to God and His words mingle with all your fond and tender love to your little ones; and it will be a sweet and happy work to win the beloved on earth to the Father beloved in heaven.

As often as the work of instructing the children upon earth threatens to become a burden or a weariness, you may be sure it is a token of something wrong within: the love to God in heaven or the delight in His word has been fading. As you seek for fresh vigor to perform your work hopefully and joyfully, you only have to turn to the words that reveal the secret of a godly education. There is an unspeakable blessing in the wisdom that has so inseparably connected the heart's secret love with the mouth's spoken words: "*Thou* shalt love the Lord thy God *with all thine heart,* . . . and these words . . . shall be *in thine heart: and* thou shalt teach them diligently to thy children." The divinely appointed ministry, and means for the salvation of our children is parental love elevated and strengthened by the love of God, *guided* and *inspired* by His own Holy Word.

The parental instruction must likewise be *diligent and earnest:* "Thou shalt teach them diligently unto thy children"—"Thou shalt sharpen them unto thy children" (margin). The same word is used of sharpening weapons, arrows and spears, to make them penetrate deep. No cold declaration of His will, no mere intellectual knowledge, will be adequate. The dart cast or the arrow shot from the bow must be sharpened to pierce the heart of the enemy. And so the godly parent must use diligence to consider how he can best find access to the heart for the words that he speaks. He does this by carefully considering how he can best gain both the child's understanding and affections, seeking to avail himself of the best opportunities for securing his interest and studying the art of speaking in the spirit of love, not without the preparation of prayer. He does it by striving to make his whole life an attractive example of what he has taught. There is nothing that does so drive home the word of instruction as the confirmation of a consistent and holy life. Above all, he seeks to do it by waiting for the Holy Spirit who alone can make the word sharp as a two-edged sword. With His aid he may experience the truth of Eccles. 12:11: "The words of the wise are as . . . nails fastened by the masters of assemblies, which are given from one shepherd." God's promise is sure: from earnest, painstaking and prayerful effort the blessing of the Spirit will not be withheld.

And to this end the parental instruction must be *persevering and continuous.* "Thou shalt teach them diligently unto thy children, and shalt *talk of them* when thou sittest in thine house, and when thou walkest by the way, and when thou liest down, and when thou risest up." The entrance of divine truth into the mind and heart, the formation of habit and the training of character—these are not attained by sudden and isolated efforts, but by regular and unceasing repetition. This is the law of all growth in nature, and of this law God seeks to make use in the kingdom of grace, in dependence upon and subservient to the power of the Holy Spirit. This is the principle that is so beautifully applied by Moses to parental duty. The instruction he had enjoined was not to be by means of set times and stated formal lectures; the whole life with all its duties has to be interwoven with the lessons of God's presence and God's service. With a heart full of God's love and God's word, the ordinary avocations of daily life were to be no hindrance but helps to lead the youthful hearts heavenwards. The children were to feel that it was no matter that could be *done* for the day, in the moments of morning or evening prayer; the continued and spontaneous outburstings of the heart from the lips was to prove that God's presence and love were a reality and a delight. Sitting in the home or walking by the way, now in quiet rest, or in the labors and duties of the way, with the Bible or with the books of God's glory in nature—all equally afforded opportunity and material for recognizing the goodness of the ever-present One. The whole day and the whole life was to be the occasion for uninterrupted fellowship with the Holy One and for pointing the little ones to the Father in heaven. And lest the objection should be made that all the speaking would weary and estrange—an objection often made with terrible truth against mere speaking while heart and life deny the reality—lest this objection should be made, we point once more to the source and secret of all: "Thou shalt love the Lord thy God with *all thine heart.* And these words . . . shall be *in thine heart.*" Such wholehearted

love and piety! May you receive wisdom from on high
and be guided by divine love to know when and how to
speak—how to influence children's hearts with the flame
of your own zeal, finding a willing and loving ear when
others could only weary!

* * *

O Lord my God, I thank Thee for each new reminder
of the value that my relation to my children has in Thy
sight, and of Thy call to me as parent to carry out Thy
purpose. May each thought of loving and serving Thee
ever be connected with Thy word, "Thou *and* thy son";
and may each act of faith claim for the child all I seek
for myself.

Blessed God, give me wisdom and grace to be a teacher
of my children as Thou wouldst have. Thou sufferest
not any other to usurp the parent's place; Thou hast appointed him the first and highest teacher. Lord, teach
me, with all parents, to take home the lessons which
Thou seest we need to fit us for our work.

Fill our hearts with Thy love and Thy word. Love knows
no sacrifice, it counts nothing a burden; love rests not
till it has triumphed. Oh, fill us with Thy love; shed it
abroad in our hearts by the Holy Spirit. And fill us with
Thy word, that teaching our children will be the spontaneous overflowing of the heart. Make us diligent and
wise to do our work well. Sharpen Thy words deep into
our children's hearts too. And make us persevering all
the day, walking in Thy love and presence. Make our
whole life an influence, educating our children for Thee.

Father, help us for Jesus' sake. Amen.

SIXTEENTH DAY

A Consecrated Home

"As for me and my house, we will serve the Lord" (Josh. 24:15).

In God's dealings with Noah and Abraham, with Israel in the Passover and at Mount Sinai, we have repeatedly noticed the deep meaning of united mention of father and children in His commands and promises. "Thou *and* thy house," "thou *and* thy seed," "ye *and* your children," "thou *and* thy son." Such is ever the language of the Covenant God. In the words of Joshua we have the response from earth, "as for me *and* my house." The principle of divine dealing is accepted: the parent boldly vouches for his family as well as himself; the covenant engagement of the Father in heaven is met by the covenant obligation of the father on earth. Joshua is to us here the very model of a godly parent, and in him we can see what parental religion ought to be.

Let it be a *personal* religion. "As *for me* and my house" —he began with himself. We cannot too strongly press the truth that for a godly education the first and the most essential requisite is personal consecration. It is good to reflect on our responsibility, to study our duties and the best way of fulfilling them, to speak with our children, and to pray much for them—but all these may be called accessories. The first thing on the part of the parent is a life devoted to God and His service. It is this that creates the spiritual atmosphere the children are to breathe. This gives our performance of duty and our dealings with our children spiritual influence. This gives our praying and our working its value with God.

There must be no hesitation or halfheartedness in the consciousness or the confession of devotion to God's service. As often as the prayer for God's blessing on the children comes up, it must be in the spirit of David: "Thou, Lord God, knowest *thy servant*. Therefore now let it please thee to bless the house of *thy servant*." With God and men, in the home and out of it, in the hearts of parents themselves, it must be a settled thing: "As for me, I will serve the Lord."

But let yours be as distinctly a *family* religion. Take a stand for all who belong to you: "As for me *and my house, we* will serve the Lord." There are pious parents who do not understand that this is their duty and their privilege. They know not what God has put in their power. They imagine they honor God by thinking that the religion of their children is dependent on God's will apart from their instrumentality. They are so occupied, either with the engagements of their calling in this life or even with religious work, that they cannot find the time for speaking out and acting out the grand decision: "As for me and my house, *we will* serve the Lord." Or, perhaps, the father leaves the religion of the children to the care of the mother, and the mother thinks that the father as head is more responsible. They hesitate or neglect to come to a clear and definite understanding, and the religious education of the children does not take the prominent place it ought to in the relationship of parents with each other. Let each believing parent take Joshua's words—first in the depth of his own soul, then in fellowship with partner and children. The more we speak it out in prayer and conversation—our house is and must be holy to the Lord, our children must be trained first of all for God and His service—the more mightily will the power of the principle assert itself and help us so to guide the house that it too serves the Lord.

The words of Joshua teach us more. Let yours, like his, be a *practical* religion: "We will *serve* the Lord." There are many parents with whom the whole of religion consists in salvation, not in service. They pray most earnestly that all their children may be saved; if they see them spend their lives in the service of the world, they hope that they will yet be brought in before they die. It is no wonder that their education for this life has been a failure: the parents never understood this truth, that training their children for God's service is the most certain way of bringing them to salvation. Did we not hear God say of Abraham, "I know him, that he will command his children and his household after him, they shall keep the way of the Lord, to do justice and judgment; that the Lord may bring upon Abraham that which he hath spoken of him" (Gen. 18:19)? Do we not remember in connection with Israel's deliverance from Egypt the words of God, "Let my people go, that they may *serve* me"; and Pharaoh's, "Go ye, *serve* the Lord; let your little ones also go with you"? And the Holy Ghost has spoken, "How much more shall the blood of Christ purge your conscience to *serve* the living God."

All redemption is for service. God wills not that He should be worshipped without being served. The glory of heaven will be that "his servants shall serve him." Let our lives and our homes be consecrated to serving God: let obedience to His will, the carrying out of His commands, the doing His work, devotion to the interests of His kingdom, give family life its focus.

And then let yours be a *confessed* religion. It was in presence of tens of thousands of the children of Israel, with the first symptoms of the falling away that came after his death already beginning to show themselves, that Joshua witnessed this good confession: "Choose you this day whom ye will serve; . . . as for me and my house, we will serve the Lord." His was not the religion of the nation or the religion of neighbors—all might reject God, leaving him alone, and yet still the Lord Jehovah would be his God. As with Abraham leaving his father's house and Israel leaving Egypt, his too was to be a religion of decision and confession—a coming out and being separate, a peculiar people unto the Lord.

This is the religion we want in our family life, where not the example or authority of pious people, not inclination or pleasure, but God's own holy and blessed will is sought after as the law of the house. How often parents, whose early married life was marked by decision and earnestness, have afterwards become conscious of declension and coldness because they gave in to the desire to gratify their children or their friends. Though at first sight it may appear hard to be peculiar, if we trust God for His guidance and yield ourselves to His personal friendship and love to walk with Him, the blessing of separation will be unspeakable to ourselves and our children too.

If this page be read by parents who are conscious that their own and their house's service to God has not been as marked and clear as it should be, let me venture a word of advice. Speak with each other of it. Say out what you have often felt but might have kept to yourself, that it is your united desire to live as entirely for God as grace can enable you to do. If your children are old enough, gather them too and ask if they will not join in the holy covenant, "We will serve the Lord." Let that covenant from time to time be renewed in a distinct act of consecration, that the conviction may be confirmed: We do want to be a holy family, a house where God dwells and is well pleased. Ours must be a home wholly consecrated to God. And be not afraid that strength will not be given to keep the vow. It is with the Father in heaven, calling and helping and tenderly working both to will and to do in us, that we are working. We may count upon Him to inspire, to accept and to confirm and himself carry out the purpose of our heart: "As for me and my house, we will serve the Lord."

* * *

O Lord my God, I thank Thee for what I have seen this day in Thy servant Joshua, the leader of Thy people Israel into Canaan, in his faithfulness to Thee as father in his own home. I humbly ask Thee to give me grace to say as distinctly and as publicly as he did, "As for me and my house, we will serve the Lord."

Lord, may mine be a personal faith. Let Thy love to me, and my love to Thee, be its inspiration and its joy. May my children see that it is with my whole heart I serve Thee, that it has become a delight and my very nature.

And may mine be a family faith, exercising its influence on my home, gaining and training all to walk with me. Lord, remove every inconsistency and all weakness that might hinder anyone from being wholly Thine. May mine be a truly consecrated home.

May mine, too, be a practical faith, serving Thee day and night. Let the knowing and the doing of God's will, the working for His kingdom, the seeking His glory, be the one desire of our hearts.

May thus our home be a blessing to others, encouraging them to take a stand for Thee. Lord God, let Thy Spirit work mightily in the homes of Thy people, that everywhere this confession may be heard ringing out: "As for me and my house, we will serve the Lord." Amen.

SEVENTEENTH DAY

Consecrated Parents

"And Manoah said, Now let thy words come to pass. How shall we order the child? and how shall we do unto him?" (Judg. 13:12).

An angel of the Lord had appeared to Manoah's wife to predict the birth of a child. He would be a Nazarite unto God from his birth and a deliverer of God's people. The first feeling of Manoah, on receiving the tidings from his wife, was that to train such a God-given child for God's service, God-given grace would be needed. He therefore entreated the Lord, "O my Lord, let the man of God which thou didst send come again unto us and teach us what we shall do unto the child that shall be born." And when in answer to his prayer the angel came again, his one petition was, "How shall we order the child? and how shall we do unto him?" Let us consider the prayer, the answer, and the attendant blessings.

1. Notice the deep sense of responsibility for the holy work of training a child as a Nazarite unto God. The angel had already given Manoah's wife the needful instruction; but Manoah is so deeply impressed with the holiness of their calling as parents of this child that he asks for the angel to come again and teach them. What a contrast to the thoughtless self-confidence with which many Christian parents undertake the training of their

children. How little effort is made to realize the importance and solemnity of the work! How little real prayer for the preparation of the Spirit to fit them for it! How little true surrender to a life for God as the only fitness for training a child for God!

What would be thought on earth of a man offering to manage a bank or to navigate an ocean steamer who had no training to fit him for either? And what must be said of the presumption that feels no fear in taking charge of an immortal spirit of such priceless value, undertaking to guide it through the temptations and dangers of life? May all Christian parents learn from Manoah to feel and confess their ignorance and, like him, to set themselves at once to seek and obtain the needed grace.

We note, further, how Manoah's sense of need at once found expression in prayer. He believed in God as the living God, as the hearer of prayer. He believed that where God gave a charge or a work, He would give the grace to do it right; that where God gave a child to be trained for His service, He would give the wisdom needed to do so aright. Instead of letting the sense of unfitness and feebleness depress him, or the sense of his obligation set him to work in his own strength, he simply prayed. To him, prayer was the solution to difficulties, the supply of need, the source of wisdom and strength.

Let Christian parents learn from him. Each child is a gift of God as truly as Manoah's and should be trained for God and His service. Like him, we may count most confidently on the Father, who has entrusted the child to us to give the grace to train. But let us pray believingly, pray without ceasing, at each step of our work; we may depend upon it, God hears prayer, and no prayer more surely than of a parent seeking wisdom to train his child.

There is one thing more we must observe in regard to Manoah's prayer: it was after his wife had told him of the injunctions the angel had given that he thus asked for guidance. He longed to hear them himself, to have full certainty and perfect clearness. As parents, we have in God's Word plain and full directions as to the training of our children. Our own experience or that of others may have supplied us with much of great value to aid us in our task; all this does not diminish but only increases the need of prayer. For each child, each with separate needs, we need renewed wisdom direct from above. Daily renewed prayer is the secret of training our children for God.

2. And now comes God's answer. Manoah's story teaches here that God loves to answer a parent's cry. The angel had nothing new to communicate above what he had previously said to the woman; and yet God sent him, because He would not leave in the dark the one who seeks to know His will fully. The angel having come once encouraged Manoah to hope he might come a second time. They who have already had communications with God and have had divine teaching about their children will be those who desire more, praying for it most earnestly.

The answer to Manoah's prayer contained no new revelation, simply pointing back to the instruction previously given: "Of all that I said unto the woman let her beware; . . . all that I commanded her let her observe." In answer to our prayer, it may be that no new truth will be revealed, perhaps even no new thought impressed. But the answer to the prayer may be something better. As the Holy Spirit leads us back to what the Lord has already spoken, to study more carefully and adopt more unreservedly the principles laid down in Holy Scripture for the training of our children, we shall realize as never before how our children are the Lord's and must be kept holy for Him. Parents are God's ministers, in whose holy life the children are to be blessed.

It is this last thought that comes out with special clearness. What were the commandments that had been given and were now renewed? The angel had spoken only of the life of the mother before the birth of the child: the

Nazarite child must have a Nazarite mother. The giving up of the fruit of the vine, the sacrifice of the stimulus and excitement and enjoyment of the world and the flesh, not eating any unclean thing, separation to special purity and holiness—this was God's secret of parental duty. Education consists not so much in what we do or say but most of all in *what we are*; and that not only when our children are of an age to see and judge but long before, even before their birth. In that holy time of mystery, when mother and child are still one and influences from a mother's spirit pass into the child, God says, "Of all that I said unto the woman let her beware; . . . all that I commanded her let her observe." It is a life of moderation and self-denial that willingly gives up whatever is not helpful to entire consecration and fellowship with God; it is a life of purity and obedience that is the preparation for a mother's and a father's work. God's answer to the prayer, "How shall we order the child?" is: As you live, you train; live as a Nazarite, holy to the Lord, and your child will be a Nazarite unto God, a deliverer of His people Israel.

3. The blessing that attended Manoah's prayer was something more than the answer. There was the blessed revelation of God himself and the wonderful knitting together of the hearts of the parents. Before he left them, the angel of the Lord so revealed himself that Manoah felt, "We have seen God."

When he asked the angel's name, his name was WONDERFUL. And the angel did wondrously. This is still the name of the parent's God, WONDERFUL—wonderful in His love, wonderful in His ways, wonderful in His work, wonderful in what He does for us as parents, and wonderful in what He does through us for our children. Oh, let us worship the Lord, the parent's God, whose name is WONDERFUL! And let our prayer, like Manoah's, end in praise and worship, in faith and truth.

How rich was the blessing this revelation brought to the praying couple. What a picture the chapter gives us

of the way in which father and mother are lovingly to
help each other in all that concerns their children. Manoah's wife gets the message from the angel; immediately she tells her husband. He prays at once for more light
and fuller teaching. The angel comes again to her; she
runs to tell Manoah, who follows her. He hears again
what his wife had been told. When the sacrifice was offered and the angel did wondrously, Manoah and his wife
looked on together, and together fell on their faces to
the ground. And when Manoah was afraid, saying, "We
shall surely die, because we have seen God," she comforted him and helped strengthen his faith.

Blessed fellowship of love and faith, of prayer and
worship between husband and wife, to which the coming
and the training of a child can lead! Oh, it is not only
parents who are to be a blessing to their children, but
children to their parents too. As they talk together of
God's promises and His commands, as each tells the
other what has been revealed to him, as they unite in
seeking to know and carry out God's will, as they now
pray in the presence of each other, and then fall down in
worship before Him whose name is WONDERFUL, as
they unburden their fears, and encourage each other to
trust and hope—they will experience that the home school
is as much for training parents themselves as their children. There is nothing that opens the fountains of divine
love and of each other's love more than the prayerful
desire to know how to order the children God has given
for His service and glory.

* * *

Blessed Lord, as those whom Thou hast joined together
to train children for Thy holy service, we bow in united
worship before Thee. Make us by Thy Holy Spirit to be
so of one heart and mind that all Thou revealest to the
one may at once be witnessed to the other. Grant that
in our conversations and our prayers, in our weakness
and fear, in our faith and our worship, we may feel

what a blessing and help there is in Thy having sent us two and two to each little flock of children to be tended.

Lord God, we come to Thee now for wisdom for each child Thou hast given us. Of each one we would say, What shall be the ordering of the child, and what shall we do unto him? Open our eyes to see the treasures of wisdom in Thy Holy Word, in promise and instruction for parents and children. Especially reveal thyself to us, we beseech Thee, as the God of the covenant and the promise, the parent's God, whose name is WONDER-FUL. Teach us in holy fear and reverence, in childlike trust and joy, in purity of life and separation from the world, to walk before Thee, and so to train children that are Nazarites, holy to the Lord, prepared to fight for the kingdom, to be the deliverers of the oppressed. Amen.

EIGHTEENTH DAY

A Consecrated Child

"For this child I prayed; and the Lord hath given me my petition which I asked of him: Therefore also I have lent him to the Lord; as long as he liveth he shall be lent to the Lord" (1 Sam. 1:27, 28).

The communion between the believing parent and the Lord in reference to his child has been set before us under different aspects. In Samuel's story we have a new and very beautiful expression of the relation. Hannah has received a child from the Lord in answer to her prayer. The love and joy of her heart can find no better way of expressing themselves than in giving her child to the Lord again, to be the Lord's as long as he lives. Whether we think of God, of our child, of ourselves, there is every reason to say, "As long as he liveth he is given to the Lord."

Or does not the child already belong to God? Was it not to bear His own image, as His servant, for His own glory, that He created man—that my child, too, has been born? God looks upon him as His; he has only been lent and entrusted to me to train. This child is indeed not mine but the Lord's. And because I am naturally inclined to forget this, to love and treat the child as if he were altogether mine, I count it such a precious privilege, in a distinct act of surrender, to give him to the Lord for all the days of his life.

And God has not only a right to the child, but He needs him. The work He has to do upon earth is so great and He has so arranged for each his work that He would not miss one single one of His people's children. I have often heard of a mother joyfully sacrificing an only son, or all her sons, for her king or country. Shall I not count it an honor to give to my King the child which is His, which He has lent me and given the privilege of loving and training and enjoying? Have I not often asked what I can render to Him for His love to me? And shall I not delight to give to Him that which is my most precious possession upon earth? To Him who gave His Son for me, all I am and have belongs; my child too I have given to the Lord as long as he shall live.

But it is not for God's sake only; for my child's sake too I give him to the Lord. The more I love him, the more heartily I give him to God. Nowhere can he be safe or happy but with Him. I do indeed love my precious little one, and yet how little I can do for him! If I give him to God I know that He accepts him, and takes him for His own, to make him His own. He will make him one with His beloved Son, cleansing him in the precious blood, and in a second birth by His Spirit, give him a new and holy nature. He, the great God, will adopt my child as His. He will use me as His minister, giving me all the wisdom I need to train my child worthily as His.

And for my own sake, too, I give my child to the Lord. The child I give to God becomes doubly my own. I feel that the child I give to God, I can love with a more intense and holy love. I then hold him without the fear of ever losing him. Even if death were to come and take my child from me, I would know that he was taken from me only for a time to serve in the King's own palace. God gave him to me; I gave him back to God. God gave him once again to me; and once again I gave him back to Him. Giving my child has become the link of a most blessed friendship and fellowship between God and me.

Knowing that my child is His gives me the confidence that all the grace and wisdom I need for training will be given. I need have no care; my child is now the Lord's. Will He not provide for all His child needs? If the parent would love and enjoy and train his child aright, let him give the child to God.

Let us now consider how this consecration of the child is to be maintained and carried out in education. The grace promised for training a child, though most certain, is not given at once; but just as the grace for our own personal life it is given day by day. In the education of our children difficulties will often arise, and sometimes it seems as if God's help does not come. This is the time for prayer and faith. The power of sin may manifest itself in the child; in his natural character there may at times be more to awaken fear than hope. Our own ignorance, or unfaithfulness, or feebleness may make us fear that though God be faithful we may be the cause of our child's being lost. At such times, at all times, God must be our refuge. Let us maintain our consecration of the child and plead it: we did give him to the Lord; we abide by this; we refuse to take him back. We plead for grace for the child who has been given by us and accepted by God. This declaration will become in our souls a settled thing, that what we gave, God took, that the child is His now, and we can leave him with Him. Such faith will give rest and bring a sure blessing.

Let us use this as a plea with our child too. Even if we do not often say so in words, he should feel implied in all our relationship with him that he has been given away to God. Let him know that this is the reason we cannot give way to his will or allow sin in him—we have a charge from God to keep him for Him. Let him mark, in our holy gentleness and firmness, that this is not a profession but a principle that really animates us. This will gradually become a motive with himself. He has been given to God and accepted by Him; how could he disobey or grieve Him? Let not our words only but the whole spirit of our life and prayer and education make the child feel, "I am the Lord's."

Let us use this knowledge as a plea with ourselves, a motive to the faithful discharge of our duties. The pressing avocations of life, the spirit of the world all around us, the little direction we receive in regard to the consecration of our children make even godly parents grow unwatchful or negligent. And a really consecrated education needs a high tone of devotion in daily life, and that without ceasing. Let us from time to time look at our children in the light of this great transaction with God—I have given my child to the Lord—and stir ourselves to diligence, to faith, and to prayer.

God needs servants for His temple; let us ask Him what is the place He has for each child in His kingdom. If such a spirit animated each parent who has given his child to God, surely a far larger number of young Christians would enter Christian service. If we had consecrated parents as Hannah, and a consecrated education as Samuel's, we should have no lack of men to stand up and take their place in the service of God's temple. May God by His Holy Spirit teach us the full meaning and power of the words we use: "I have given my child to be the Lord's as long as he lives."

* * *

O Lord my God, hear, I pray Thee, Hannah's prayer as I come to Thee with the child Thou hast given me. I have heard that Thou dost allow the mother to give her child back again to Thee and that, having accepted and sealed him for Thine own, Thou dost entrust him to her again. O my Father, he is now *Thine*—and *mine*! My soul bows in the dust at the thought of this inexpressible privilege, this joint ownership of my child between God and me. I look to Thee for the grace to enable me to keep this treasure, to be given to Thee with usury.

Teach me, I pray Thee, to love him with a holy love, and to train him for the service of Thy temple. Teach me to speak to him of Thee and Thy love so that his heart may early be won for Thee. May my whole life be to him an inspiration, inviting and guiding to what is pure and lovely, to what is holy and well pleasing to Thee. And do Thou, in Thy great goodness, cause my child early to hear the voice that called Samuel; and may he in childlike simplicity and reverence answer, "Speak, Lord, Thy servant heareth."

O Lord, Thou wilt not despise a mother's prayer. Thou acceptest my surrender. By Thy blessing we shall be consecrated parents and a consecrated child. Amen.

NINETEENTH DAY
Parental Weakness

"Wherefore . . . honourest thy sons above me? . . . them that honour me I will honour, and they that despise me shall be lightly esteemed." (1 Sam. 2:29, 30).
"I will judge his house for ever for the iniquity which he knoweth; because his sons made themselves vile, and he restrained them not" (1 Sam. 3:13).

Some men are born to rule. It costs them no trouble, it is their very nature; they often do it unconsciously. Others there are to whom it never comes natural. They either shrink from it, or, even if they attempt it, utterly fail. They appear to be wanting in the gifts that fit them for the work; it is always a struggle and an effort. In ordinary life men can choose or are chosen for, the situations they have to fill as rulers or commanders. In family life we see a strange and very solemn spectacle: every parent has to rule, whether he be fit for it or not. Nor does the fact of his unfitness take away his responsibility; the terrible consequences of his failure to rule are still visited upon himself and his children. The picture of feeble old Eli, faithful to God's cause and ready to die for the ark of God, but unfaithful to his duty as parent, unable to restrain his sons, suggests to us the causes, the consequences, and the cure of parental weakness.

1. We have spoken of natural incapacity for ruling as

one cause. But this is never so absolute that determined effort could not to some extent remedy it, much less that the grace of God could not change it. We must therefore look for other causes. And of these the chief is the want of self-discipline. A Christian may not follow the easy or natural way, what he likes or what appears possible. His one question must be, What is duty? What has God commanded?

There is wonderful strengthening, even for the weakest character, in giving one's self up to the divine *ought* and *must* of God's will. The fear of grieving the Father, the desire to please Him, the assurance of His strength to aid our weakness—such thoughts rouse and nerve the energies of the soul. The will awakens, and nothing is so invigorating as the hearty effort to obey. Because some Christian parents do not realize that ruling their homes well is a simple matter of duty, a command that must be obeyed, many children are ruined by parental weakness. Not to restrain the child is to dishonor God, giving way to the child's will.

Closely connected with this is the good-natured weakness, misnamed kindness, which cannot bear to reprove, thwart, or punish a child. This is nothing but a form of sloth: it cannot take the trouble to rule and guide the child by God's Word, refusing the pain which punishing causes the parent. Alas, it chooses the greater pain of seeing the child grow up unrestrained. No grace of the Christian life is obtained without sacrifice; this very high grace of influencing and forming other souls for God needs special self-sacrifice. Like every difficult work, it needs purpose, attention, perseverance.

But the chief cause of parental weakness will be found deeper still—the want of a life of true devotion to God himself. God is the great Ruler and Educator; the powers that be—the parents' powers, too—are ordained of God; he who does not live under the command to God in his own life has not the secret of authority and command over others. The fear of God is the beginning of wisdom, of wisdom for the work of ruling too; failure in personal godliness is the root of parental failure.

2. And now let's look at the consequences of such parental weakness. There is one element in the law of consequences under which we live that makes it especially solemn and terrible. It is this, that ordinarily they are not experienced until it is too late to correct them. Our actions are seeds; no one who looks at the little seed could ever imagine what a great tree, what noble or what bitter fruit could come from it. Consequences, as seen in those around us, somehow hardly affect us; self-interest flatters itself with the pleasing hope that, in our case at least, the results will not be so disastrous.

Let me plead with parents (when conscience or experience tells them that they too have been guilty of consulting the will of their children more than the honor of God) to look at the picture of Eli and his home under God's judgment. Let them ponder carefully what God says. Let them remember that throughout the universe there is no well-being but in harmony with the law of our being. In earth and heaven, in nature and grace, in the individual, the family, and the Church, obedience to the law under which God constituted a creature is the only possible path to happiness. To disobey that law is to court misery. And if parents, destined of God to bear in the home the likeness of His own fatherly rule, give way to weakness, they must expect the natural results.

It may not always become manifest in the same degree or with equal speed, but in the loss of their child's character, in the loss of peace and happiness, in many cases in the loss of the soul for ever, they must reap what they sow. God appointed parental rule in the family as the symbol of His own authority, in which parents and children alike are to honor Him; to dishonor Him is to lose His favor and blessing.

3. In speaking of the causes, we have already indicated some of the cures of parental weakness. To continue, the first one is this: the determined purpose, by God's grace,

110

to do God's will. My duty is never measured by what
I feel is within my power to do but by what God's grace
makes possible for me. And I never can know fully how
much grace will enable me to do until I begin. Let the
weak parent accept this as a God-imposed duty: he must
rule his children. Let him remember that not to rule and
restrain his children means both parent and child are
dishonoring God by not doing His will. Let him yield himself to the God of grace, with the purpose to do His
will, however impossible it appear; the surrender will
be accepted and the grace not withheld. Step by step,
amidst many a failure, the honest effort to do God's will
cannot remain without its reward.

Next to this, let the parent who has failed study some
of the simplest laws in the art of ruling. Ignorance and
neglect of these are often the cause of failure. Ruling,
like any other art, must be learned.

Some of these rules are as follows: Do not give too
many commands at once; begin, if need be, with only
one. If you secure obedience to one, your own and the
child's consciousness of your power to rule is established.
Do not command what you cannot enforce or what the
child has not the power to obey. Prove your authority
when it is easy for you to secure obedience and for the
child to render it. In all learning we proceed from the
easy to the less easy. Let the command be given in quiet,
deliberate tones, with full self-control; hasty, ill-regulated
injunctions lead to disobedience. Self-rule is the secret
of all rule; as you honor the law yourself in self-command,
others learn to honor it too.

Above all, let the Christian parent who would rule well
remember he is God's minister, doing God's work. God
loves the children, and wants them trained for himself.
He is your covenant-God; depend upon Him to be your
help and strength. It is God who, through you, will rule
your home. Yield yourself to Him. Not only pray for help
but believe most certainly it is given. Not only believe
but act in the assurance that it is given and is beginning,

little by little, to work in you. Say to your Father that you desire to do your duty at any risk, and to honor Him with your children. And in the spirit of a quiet, restful assurance, you may count on God's strength working in your weakness.

* * *

O my God, with fear and trembling would I bow before Thee, the righteous God, who wilt not give Thine honor to another nor suffer sin, even in Thy servants, to go unpunished. Impress deeply upon my heart, O Lord, the solemn lessons Thou dost teach Thy Church by the terrible sight of Thy judgment on the house of Eli, Thy servant.

Not to rule and restrain our children but to give them their own way is to honor them more than Thee. Before we think it, weakness becomes wickedness, in ourselves and our children too. Thou hast made every parent after Thine image, a king in his home, that he may rule his home well and command his children in the way in the Lord. On his exercise of authority, and their rendering of obedience, Thou hast made Thy blessing dependent.

O God, have mercy upon us! Let the thought of Thy command to rule our home, of Thy judgment on disobedience, of Thy promised grace to those who give themselves to obey, of Thy blessing on a home ordered in Thy fear, stir us with our whole heart to fulfill our holy calling. And let us, above all, believe that as we and our children fulfill Thy will, we are in the path of true blessing for this life and the life to come. Amen.

TWENTIETH DAY

The Father as Intercessor

"And it was so, when the days of their feasting were
gone about, that Job sent and sanctified them, and rose up
early in the morning, and offered burnt offerings according to the number of them all: for Job said, It may be
that my sons have sinned, and cursed God in their hearts.
Thus did Job continually" (Job 1:5).

What a beautiful picture of a man in whose heart the
fear of God lives! He fears lest his children sin against
God or forsake Him in their heart. He is so deeply conscious of the weakness of their nature that, even when
he does not know of positive transgression, the very
thought of their having been in circumstances of temptation makes him afraid. He so fully realizes his position
and privilege as father that he sends for them to be
sanctified, and takes upon himself the continual offering
of the needed sacrifice. Job is another example among
Bible saints of a servant of God in whom faith takes up
the whole home in its intercession and whose fear of God
extends to the sin of the children too. God could hardly
have said of him, "That man was perfect and upright,
one that fears God, and escheweth evil," if this element
of true piety had been wanting. The book might have been
complete without it, as far as the record of Job's patience
and faith is concerned, but we should have missed the

much-needed lesson that a man's entire consecration to God implies the consecration of the home life too. Let us study the lesson his example teaches.

1. A deep fear of finding sin in himself or his children is one of the marks of a godly parent. It is to conquer and free from sin that God entered into the parental covenant with Abraham. It was on account of sin, and to deliver from its cause, that the blood of the lamb was sprinkled in the Passover. It was to lead from sin to the service of God that parents were constituted the instructors of their children. In all God's dealings with us in redemption and grace, in His revelation in Christ and His cross, He has one object: to save us from sin and make us partakers of His holiness. And if the parent is to be God's fellow worker, if the authority God delegates to him is to be used aright, and if the blessing promised to him is to come true, God must find the parent in harmony with himself, hating sin with a perfect hatred and seeking, above everything, to keep it out of his home.

How superficial our views of sin are! And how easily we are satisfied! Under the appearance of what is good and loving, sin may be lurking. Our children may be growing up renouncing God in their hearts! Let parents ask God to give them a right sense of what sin is in their children—its curse, its dishonor to God, its power. And let us ask Him to work in us a very deep and very clear conviction that His great object in taking us into covenant as His ministers to the children is that sin may be cast out of them. This is the one thing at which He aims, that the power of Christ's victory over sin may be seen in them, that we and they and our home may be holy to the Lord.

2. Very special watchfulness, where there is special temptation, will be the natural result of such fear of sin. Job knew that at a time of feasting there would be special danger. As the days of feasting were past, he sent for his sons and sanctified them. These children must have received a strong impression of the fear of sin in their

God-fearing father, and thus would be awakened in them the need of watchfulness and the fear of forgetting God. Every thoughtful parent knows there are times and places when the temptations of sin come more speedily and more easily surprise even the well-disposed child. Such are the times, both before and after a child goes into the company and the circumstances where he may be tempted, that a praying father and mother should do what Job did when he sent for his sons and sanctified them.

A Christian man, only lately converted, has told of the indelible impression made by his mother taking him into her room, just as he was in full glee to start on his first long journey from home, and praying with him that he might be kept from sin.

Let us ask God to make us very watchful and very wise in availing ourselves of opportunities. There are times when the conscience of a child is especially sensitive and a word fitly spoken will sink deep into the heart. There are times when conscience has been slighted and when a word of prayer will help to awaken it and restore its authority. A parent in sympathy with God's purpose as to destroying sin, holding himself at God's disposal, will be guided from on high as to when and how to rouse and strengthen in the child the consciousness of sin and its danger.

3. A godly parent has power with God to intercede. Job not only spoke to his children, he sanctified them through the burnt offerings he offered. The parent who has accepted the sign of the sprinkling of the blood for his child, who has sprinkled the blood on the doorposts of his home, has a right to plead that blood with God. His faith obtains pardon for the child. And he has a right to intercede for the grace that can save and sanctify.

We have, through the whole course of God's dealings with parents, from Noah downwards, seen that God gives the parent the right and the power to appear and act in behalf of the child and that such representative action is accepted. To lay hold of this clearly is the very essence of parental faith; to act upon it is the secret of parental power and blessing. The whole family constitution is based upon this. All the other influence a parent is to exert depends much on his being clear on this point: I am the steward of God's grace to the child; I represent the child with God and am heard on his behalf. This makes him confident in saying, I represent God with my child; I have God's help to give me influence and power. I have overcome the power of my child's sin in pleading with God for him; I am sure of conquering it in pleading with my child.

Dear parents, let us plead very earnestly that God may by His Spirit enlighten our hearts to know this our calling—to intercede and prevail for our children. We want the Holy Spirit to shine upon God's purposes with us that in our family life the first thing shall be, not the happiness of parental love and fellowship, not the care of providing all the good gifts they daily need, not the thought of their education for a life of prosperity and usefulness, but the yielding ourselves to God's redeeming love to be every day the ministers of its grace and blessing. Let us live to secure God's purpose: the deliverance from sin. And our family life shall evermore be lighted up with God's own presence and with the joy of the heavenly home, of which it is the nursery and the image.

* * *

Gracious God, I humbly ask Thee to print deep in my heart the lessons Thy holy Word was given to teach. May Job, who has taught Thy saints so much of patience in the hour of trial and of Thy wondrous grace in delivering from it, be to all parents a lesson and a model of the God-fearing parent.

Teach us, we pray Thee, the fear of God in its full power and extent, trembling at the sins of our children and interceding for them as for our own soul. Oh, teach us, Lord, to fear sin, the one thing Thy soul hateth, and may we make it our one care that the children sin not.

Teach us to realize our God-given position as interces-
sors and to plead the blood for them as definitely and
as believingly as for ourselves. May we know in faith
that we are heard.

And teach us so in prayer to bring them with us, praying
at the right time and way, that from us they may learn
both the fear of God and the confidence of faith. O
God, if we are indeed Thy children, may this element
distinctly mark our piety and our faith,, stamping home
and family life as wholly the Lord's. Amen.

TWENTY-FIRST DAY
The True Good

"Come, ye children, hearken unto me;
I will teach you the fear of the Lord.
What man is he that desireth life,
And loveth many days, that he may *see good*?
Keep thy tongue from evil,
And thy lips from speaking guile.
Depart from evil, and *do good*;
Seek peace, and pursue it" (Ps. 34:11-14).

There is a science called ethics which seeks to discover the laws which regulate human conduct, so teaching the art of living aright. In the pursuit of its object, this science seeks to find out the moving principle which urges men to act as they do—in other words, their aim in life. In the discussions on this point, the word that comes up universally is *the good*. Men propose to themselves some good or other as the reward of their efforts.

The students of ethics are divided into two great schools, depending on the meaning they attach to the word *good*. With some, it expresses the good of *well-being*, the possession or enjoyment of what is desirable. They maintain that happiness, the fear of pain and the desire of pleasure, is and ought to be the motive of conduct.

Another school takes higher ground. It maintains that, though the desire of happiness is innate and legitimate, it may not be man's first or ultimate aim. Happiness will be the accompaniment and the reward of something higher. The good not of well-being but of *well-doing* is the only true good. The ideas of right and wrong are deeper and holier than those of pleasure and pain. To teach men to do good is their ideal.

In the words of our psalm, children are invited to come and learn the secret of a happy life. The call appeals to the desire for happiness: Who is he that would *see good*? The teacher promises to show the path to the enjoyment of true well-being. That path is, "Depart from evil, and *do good.*" God has so ordered our nature that well-being will follow well-doing: to do good is the sure way to see good.

But our inspired teacher goes further. He not only tells of our *seeing* good and *doing* good, but would teach us the secret of *being* good. This, human science cannot teach. The value of uprightness and purity in the inner motive, making conduct really good, can be taught; but it cannot show us what the true, the only pure and purifying motive is. The Psalmist tells us, "Come, ye children, hearken unto me; I will teach you the fear of the Lord"— the beginning of all wisdom and goodness. It is our personal relation to God that makes conduct really good. To fear God—this is being good; then follows doing good; then seeing good.

Christian parents have in this call, "Come, ye children, hearken unto me," words prepared for them by the Holy Spirit to use with their children. They are God's ministers to teach the children the fear of the Lord, the path to the true, the highest good.

To begin with, *seeing good*: "What man is he that desireth life, and loveth many days, that he may *see good*?" Parents need not be afraid of promising their children that all shall be well with them if they do indeed fear God. With a Creator of infinite goodness and wisdom it cannot be otherwise; doing right and pleasing Him must bring blessing and happiness. The desire for happiness may not be the first or the only motive for a man's

conduct. Experience has proved that those who make it
their first object fail, while those who give it a second
place, subordinate to duty, find it. God commands us to
be happy. He promises us joy, but always in connection
with our being in the right relation to himself and His
will. So the previous verse (vs. 19) says, "They that seek
the Lord shall not want any good thing."

The promises that God will do us good are many. "I
will surely do thee good," He said to Jacob. To Israel
He spoke: "Do right and good, that it may be well with
thee." His peace and presence, His guidance and help,
will come to those who do His will. Such obedience and
doing good will bring a blessing even for this life too.

Let our children learn early that if they would see
good it will be found with God. Let them learn it of us,
not as a doctrine, but as a personal testimony. Let us
show them that the service of God makes us happy and
that the good which God bestows is our one desire and
our highest joy.

The next step is *doing good*. Let us seek in the hearts
of our little ones to link inseparably well-doing and well-
being. "*Blessed is* the man that feareth the Lord." The
Christianity of our day has learned to seek only safety
in religion but pleasure and happiness in the world. We
will need a very clear testimony to fill our children with
the thought that to do God's will and serve is in itself
blessedness and enjoyment.

And now comes the teaching as to what doing good
is: "Keep thy tongue from evil, and thy lips from speaking
guile. Depart from evil, and do good; seek peace, and
pursue it." Sins of the tongue, sins of disobedience, sins
of temper—these are the three principal temptations for
children, against which parents have to guard them.

"Keep thy tongue from evil, and thy lips from speaking
guile." The tongue reveals what is in the heart. Parents! study above everything to make your children
true—first in words, and then true in heart and deed.
A child's truthfulness and integrity may be the beginning
of his walking in the truth of God. "I have no greater

joy than to hear that my children walk in the truth."
Let this be your aim even with the little children.

"Depart from evil, and do good." To a young child
that which is evil is that which his parent forbids. The
parent is to him a conscience, as God. Train your little
ones to flee from evil, to depart, to come away from
everything naughty and forbidden. And keep him occupied
with what is good, that which is allowed by you and
pleasing to you. Stir and strengthen his young will, train
him to *do* good—not to think and wish and feel good,
but to do it. It is the will, and what it does, that makes
the man.

"Seek peace, and pursue it." To quarrel is a sin that
comes too easily to children. Let us train ours to respect
the rights of others, to bear and to forgive when our own
are affected, seeking redress from the parent only.
"Blessed are the peacemakers, for they shall be called
the children of God."

But we have the highest good to speak of yet: we must
not only seek good and do good but *be good*. Only a good
tree can bring forth good fruit. And what is it to be
good? What is the disposition that makes the good man
or the good child? "I will teach you *the fear of the
Lord*." There is none good, and no good, but God; if we
seek and find Him we find all good. It is in the fear
of the Lord that good conduct has its spring, that virtue
has its worth. "In singleness of heart, fearing God: whatsoever ye do, do it heartily, as unto the Lord." The personal relation to God carried out into all our conduct
constitutes the fear of the Lord. It is not the fear of a
slave, but of a child, twin sister to hope and love: "The
Lord taketh pleasure in them that *fear* him, in those that
hope in His mercy."

How can the fear of the Lord be taught? Dear Christian parents, you know the answer: by walking in the
fear of the Lord all the day. Seek to train your children
to understand the connection between seeing good and
always being blessed and happy, and doing good where

we always choose what is right, and being good, having a heart filled with the fear and love of God. Let them see you walk in the fear of the Lord all the day, His holy presence resting on you and brought with you into daily life. Let them see in your conduct that religion is a holy sentiment and emotion, a power in the heart which moves the will in everything to do what is good. And let the light of your eyes and the brightness of your face be the exposition and the confirmation of God's truth, "*Blessed* is the man that feareth the Lord."

* * *

O my God, I ask for grace to take to heart and wisely apply in dealing with my children the lessons of Thy Word.

May my whole relationship with them be full of the joyful assurance that the fear of the Lord is the path to the enjoyment of all good and that Thy service is happiness. Let this be so real that all thought of pleasure in the world or sin may pass away.

Help me to teach them the fear of the Lord by instruction, and example, and the spirit of my life. May thoughtfulness, and truthfulness, and lovingness mark the conversation of my home. May the life of all be holy to the Lord. Day by day I would show them, through Thy grace, how departing from every evil, doing good, and following after peace and holiness is what Thy fear teaches.

Give me grace, above all, to teach them that the fear of the Lord itself is the true good, the principle of all good. May we walk as children in the full light of Thy countenance, fearful only of offending Thee or not rendering Thy holy majesty the reverence due to Thee. And let ours be the true Christian life of Thy disciples of old, who, walking in the fear of the Lord and in the comfort of the Holy Ghost, were multiplied.

O my God, I beseech Thee, make me a parent such as Thou wouldst have me and let on me and my home Thy blessing rest. Amen.

TWENTY-SECOND DAY

Training

"Train up a child in the way he should go; and when
he is old, he will not depart from it" (Prov. 22:6).

This promise is the scriptural expression of the principle on which all education rests, that a child's training
can decide what his later life will be. Without faith in
this principle there could be no thought of anything like
education; when this faith is elevated to a trust in God
and His promises, it grows into the assurance that a parent's labor will not be in vain in the Lord.

Education has been variously defined as fully developing a child's faculties, fitting him to fulfill his destiny,
developing in him all the perfection of which he is capable.
Such definitions have their value for every parent who
would thoroughly understand his work. Yet their application is dependent upon the further statement of what his
faculties and his destiny really are and wherein his highest
perfection would consist. It is only when the real aim
of education is clearly and firmly grasped that its work
can be successful. Just as in our text everything will
depend on a correct view of what is "the way he should
go," only then can the training do its work in the assurance of the divine fulfillment of the promise.

There have been so many failures in religious training
that a spirit of doubt has grown up as to whether a

principle like this can be regarded as holding universally good. With such doubt we undermine God's covenant. Let us rather believe that the failure was owing to man's fault—"Let God be true, and every man a liar." Either the parent did not make "the way he should go" his one aim in the child's training, or the training in that way was not what God's Word had ordered it to be. Let us see what the Word teaches us on each of these points.

As to "the way he should go," we need be in no doubt. The names Scripture gives to this way make clear what it is. "The way of the Lord," God calls it, when He speaks of Abraham training his children; and we often read of "walking in his ways," "the way of his footsteps," "the way of his commandments." It is called "the way of wisdom," "the way of righteousness," "the way of holiness," "the way of peace," "the way of life." This is "the new and living way" opened by Christ for all who will walk in His footsteps; it is Christ himself, the living Way, of whom Scripture says, "Walk in him."

There are many religious parents who are most anxious to see their children saved but who do not choose this way for them; they do not decide on it distinctly as the only way in which they are to walk. They think it too much to expect that their children should walk in it from their youth, and so they do not train them to go in it. They are not prepared to regard the walking in this way as always the first thing. It is not their first aim to train wholehearted, devoted Christians. There are worldly interests which must not be sacrificed. They are not always ready themselves to walk in that way only and wholly— "the narrow way"; they have chosen it, though not exclusively and finally. They have their own thoughts as to the way they and the child may go. No wonder that with a great deal of apparent religion their education fails; a mistake here is often fatal. There may be no doubt or hesitancy; "the way of the Lord" must be heartily accepted as the only way in which their children should go.

"*Train up a child* in the way he should go." *Train* is a word of deep importance for every teacher and parent to understand. Training is not telling, not teaching, not commanding, but something higher than all these (without which the teaching and commanding is often more harm than good). It is not only telling a child what to do, but showing him how to do it and seeing that it is done, taking care that the advice or the command given is put into practice and adopted as a habit.

Let's look at the way in which a young horse is trained. It is made to yield its will to the master's until at last it is in perfect sympathy with him and yields to his slightest wish. How carefully it is directed and accustomed to do the right thing until it becomes a habit, a second nature! Its own wild native tendencies are checked and restrained when necessary. It is encouraged and helped to the full exercise of its powers in subjection to this rule, and everything done to make it bold and spirited. I have seen a coachman with thoughtful care watch his young horses, sitting ready at any difficulty to help them with voice and hand lest they should lose their confidence or be overcome by some difficulty. And I have thought, Would that parents bestowed this care on training children in the way they should go!

Training may now thus be defined: accustoming the child to do easily and willingly what is commanded. Doing right, doing it habitually, doing it from choice—this is what we aim at.

Doing right. The parent who wishes to train not only tells or commands, but sees that the thing is done. To this end he seeks to engage the interest and affection of the child on the side of duty generally, as well as of the duty to be performed specially. Knowing how naturally thoughtless and fickle a child's nature is, he urges or encourages until the thing involving self-denial or difficulty is performed. He is careful not to give too many commands or to give them hastily; he begins with commands to which submission is most easily secured, so that the thought of obedience may not be linked too much with the thought of what is displeasing or impossible. But the great thing, whether he appeals to the motive of authority or of love, of duty or of pleasure, is that he watches the child through the struggle until the consent of the will has become deed and action.

Doing right habitually is, we said, an element of training. Success in education depends more on forming habits than inculcating rules. What the child has done once or twice he must learn to do over and over again until it becomes familiar and natural; it must feel strange to him not to do it. If the educator be content with the first acts of obedience, sloth, forgetfulness, reluctance to make effort, the evil of his nature and self-will may soon come in and break the power of the habit. The parent should silently watch and, if there is danger of a retrograde step, help and confirm the habit until its mastery is secure. Going on from a first and a second command in which obedience has been secured, the principle is extended until the child comes to feel it quite natural that in all things he should do the parent's will. And so the habit of obedience is formed; this becomes the root of other habits.

Doing right from choice. This is something higher, the true aim of education. You may have good, obedient children in whom there never has been much resistance to a parent's training, who render habitual and willing obedience, and yet, when left to themselves in later life, they depart from the way in which they were trained to go. The training was defective; parents were content with habits without principles. The training of the young horse is not complete until he delights, full of joy and spirit, to do his work. It is the training of the will that is the aim of education. Beginning with *obedience*, the parent has to lead the child on to *liberty*. These apparent opposites have to be reconciled in practice; to choose and will for himself what his parent wills, to find his happiness not only in obedience to the parent's command but in the approval of the thing commanded—this is what the child

must be formed to do. And here is indeed the highest
art and the real difficulty of training a child in the way
he should go.

But just here the promise of divine grace comes in.
No mind yet understands the wondrous interplay of God's
working and our working in the matter of our salvation—
and as little in the salvation of our children. But we
need not understand it to be sure of it, or to count on
God's faithfulness. Where the believing parent seeks not
only to form the habits of obedience but in prayer and
faith to mold and guide and strengthen the will of the
child in the way of the Lord, he may count upon the
workings of God's Holy Spirit to do what God alone can
do. In covenant with God as His fellow worker and
minister, he does not shrink back from this highest and
holiest of tasks, the training of a will made after the
image of God's will. He reckons on a divine wisdom to
guide him; he counts on a divine strength to work with
him and for him; he trusts in a divine faithfulness to
make the word true and sure in all its fullness, "Train
up a child in the way he should go, and when he is old,
he will not depart from it."

* * *

Holy Lord, with fear and trembling I bow before Thee
in view of the work to which Thou hast called me. O
my God, I feel deeply that I lack wisdom; I come to
Thee, who givest liberally and upbraidest not. Thy word
has said, "It shall be given."

Lord, give me the spirit of wisdom that I may understand
aright the wondrous nature of that immortal spirit which
has been put into my charge, with its power of mind
and emotion and will. Give me wisdom that I may know
the way in which the child should go, even the way of
Thy footsteps. May he learn from me that as there is
no other way well pleasing to Thee, so there is no other
way that can give us true pleasure. And give me wisdom
that I may know how to guide and influence the will that

---

1. See Principles of Training, p. 11.

it may give itself first to my will and then to Thine, to choose only and always Thy way. Lord, give me wisdom to train my child in the way he should go, even the way of the Lord.

And, O my God, strengthen my faith to hold fast the blessed assurance that a godly training in Thy fear and under the rule of Thy spirit cannot fail. Thy promise is sure, Thy power is infinite; Thou wilt bless the seed of Thy servants. Amen.

TWENTY-THIRD DAY

Choosing the Good

"Before the child shall know to refuse the evil, and choose the good. . ." (Isa. 7:16).

Of all the wondrous powers with which God has endowed man, his will—the power of determining what he does, and so what he is—is the most wonderful. This is indeed the deepest trait of the divine image. God gave man to a very large extent the power of deciding and making himself. The mind, with all its wondrous capacities; the soul, with all its wealth of feeling; the spirit, man's moral and religious nature—all these have been given that he might be able to exercise that royal prerogative he has from God: to will, so fashioning his own being and destiny for eternity.

And it is to the parent that the solemn task is entrusted of teaching the child how to use this will aright. This delicate instrument is put into the hands of the parents to guard, to direct, to strengthen, and to train the child for the glory of the God who gave it. Parents might easily shrink from the task with trembling. But if they learn how wisdom can be obtained to train a child's will, most would count no sacrifice too great to secure it. To those who seek the wisdom from God in faith and in His fear, success is possible, is even promised.

The problem is one of great delicacy: to combine the greatest degree and the fullest exercise of personal liberty with perfect obedience. God's Word has more than once taught that obedience is the child's first virtue—that in yielding it, his will is to be exercised. He is to obey, not because he understands or approves but because the parent commands. In this he will become the master of his own will as he voluntarily submits it to a higher authority. Obedience from this principle will thus secure a double good: while guiding the will into right habits, it strengthens the command the child has over it. When this has been attained, a safe foundation has been laid for the further exercise of the child's free will in the deliberate choice of what appears to him best. It is this that the parent must regard as his highest and most blessed work. *"Before the child knows* to refuse the evil, and choose the good"—in this first stage of childhood, simple obedience is the law. As he grows out of it, it is still a parent's influence that must train the young will to exercise the power on which in later life everything depends; he must now be trained himself to refuse the evil and choose the good.

And how is this to be done? The choice of the will depends upon the impulse and motives which prompt it to action. These impulses and motives again depend upon the objects presented to the mind and the degree of attention with which they are regarded. In our fallen nature, the soul, dwelling in the flesh and surrounded by the world, is far more alive to the visible and the temporal than the unseen and the real. It is deceived by what appears pleasing or beautiful; the influence of what is present and near outweighs that of the distant, though of infinitely greater worth. It is the work of the parent to present to the child the true motives of action, and thus aid it in refusing the evil and choosing the good. The beauty of virtue, the nobility and happiness of self-denial, the pleasure that duty brings, the fear and the favor of God—not in these words, but clothed in forms suited to a child's apprehension—the parent holds up to his view objects that awaken emotions by which the will is guided gladly to choose the good.

Amid the thoughtlessness of childhood, which lives in the seen and the present, the parent acts as a conscience to the child, calling him to be true to his higher instincts and convictions and leading him to the true pleasure with which duty rewards even the young. But the training of the child aims specifically at teaching him to refuse the evil and choose the good when there is no parent near to help.

In conscience every man possesses a guardian and helper of inestimable value in the path of right. A wise training can do much to establish the authority of this inner rule, leading the child to look upon the indwelling guest not as a spy or a reproachful enemy but as the truest friend and best companion. Let the authority of the parent and of conscience be linked together, that even in the parent's absence the weight of his influence may be felt. If the success of all true education consists in aiding the pupil to teach himself, the aim and success of moral training must especially consist in forming the habit of ruling himself and always listening to the inward monitor. Cultivate in the child the power of self-control, of recollection, of quiet thoughtfulness, that he may always wait to listen for the gentle inner whisper that tells him to refuse the evil and choose the good.

Conscience, however, can only tell to do the right; what the right is it cannot always teach. The mind may be wrong in its views of good and evil, and faithfulness to conscience may even lead to choose the evil and refuse the good. The inner light shines upon the path of what we think duty; it is only the light from above that shows what that duty really is. "Thy word is a lamp unto my feet, and a light unto my path." One of the most precious influences of a godly education is not so much the knowledge of what the Bible contains as the consent of the heart to take God's Word as the standard of good and evil, desiring to let it decide in every choice. The

authority of the parent, of conscience, of God's Word—
here is a threefold cord that cannot be broken, binding
the child to the throne and the will of God, there to know
to refuse the evil and choose the good.

We need hardly repeat again how such an education
is not to take the place of divine grace but to be its servant
—both in preparing the way for God's Spirit by forming
a strong and intelligent will to be afterwards used in God's
service, and in following up the work of grace by guiding
it in the path where all God's perfect will is to be accepted
as the rule of conduct. Such a training, that the child
may know to refuse the evil and choose the good, is of
unspeakable value. When once the eyes of the parent are
opened to the meaning of the words, he will see how in
every step of life, in every action, there are two motives
contending for mastery; and the choosing between the
evil and the good is the solemn lifework being carried
on all the day. He will recognize the responsibility entrusted to him of awakening, guiding, strengthening that
young will on which such infinite issues depend, and will
feel that if he can do this one thing well, he has done
his highest work. To know to refuse the evil and choose
the good will be to choose Christ and holiness and eternal
life.

Dear parents, God's highest gift to man in creation
was the will, that he might choose the will of his God.
Your highest work is to take charge of that will in your
child and be God's minister in leading it back to His
service. Pray earnestly for light on this holy trust committed to you. Study carefully the wondrous character
of this endowment of the divine image. See in it the power
to which the gospel comes; make it free to choose God
and His service, Christ and His love. Realize your own
incompetency to influence a will in which the powers of
light and darkness are wrestling for supremacy. And cast
yourself on the covenant for the leading of the Holy Spirit
in your work, for the renewal of the Holy Spirit in your
child, that it may be your and his joy to see his will

given up to choose the good, to choose God.

* * *

O Lord my God, how holy is the work Thou hast committed to a parent. Open my eyes, I do pray Thee, to see its responsibility. May the traces of the divine image to be seen in the child's power of willing stand out clearly to me. May the tremendous issues for time and eternity depending upon the right use of his will be ever before me. May I feel the danger from the corruption of sin within and the temptation from without. May I realize the wonderful power entrusted to me in Thy giving the child's will into my keeping. And may a due sense of my own weakness and Thy almighty power working in me combine to keep me humble and yet hopeful, conscious of my weakness but confident in Thee. O God, teach me to form and train the will of my child to refuse the evil and choose the good.

Lord, make me very gentle and patient, and very watchful, because of the sleepless vigilance of the enemy and the hourly danger of my child. May I be ever faithful to fulfill my commission well, and very full of trust, because Thou art my help and my Father.

O my God, do it for Jesus' sake. Amen.

TWENTY-FOURTH DAY

God's Spirit in Our Children

"... I will pour my spirit upon thy seed, and my blessing upon thine offspring: ... One shall say, I am the Lord's; ... and another shall subscribe with his hand unto the Lord... (Isa. 44:3, 5).

In the prophecy of the outpouring of the Holy Spirit quoted by Peter on the day of Pentecost express mention is made of the sons and daughters; here too the blessing of an outpoured Spirit is made to the seed and offspring of God's people. The root-principle of the covenant, promising grace to the fathers for the children, to the children for the fathers, is to be the mark of the dispensation of the Spirit too. The promise is accompanied by a very distinct statement of the fruit of the Spirit's coming on the offspring. Not resting content with a religion inherited from the fathers, the children would openly profess their personal faith with the words; "I am the Lord's." Through the power of the Holy Spirit the religion of parental training would become the faith of a personal profession. Let us seek to grasp the two thoughts: the personal acknowledgment of the Lord as the fruit of the Spirit's work, and the sure promise of the Spirit to do that work.

Among all earnest parents there is the desire that as their children grow up, they may come forward to make personal confession of the faith in which they have been raised. If we enter fully into the mind of God, it will be one of the great aims of parental training to rear our children for such a profession. And yet there are many Christian parents who hesitate to admit this. To some the dangers attending a distinctly religious education, of cultivating a formal and traditional faith, appear so great that they leave their children to themselves. They would never think of asking them whether they can say, "I am the Lord's," or encouraging them to do so. They do not believe in the conversion of children. They feel that children are so impressible and so much the creatures of their surroundings that such a profession is not to be counted on and ought rather to be avoided. Others are themselves so much in doubt about what they consider the intricate question of assurance of faith that, having themselves no liberty to say, "I am the Lord's," it is no wonder they never think of helping their children to say it. It is, they think, only the advanced believers who dare speak thus; in them it would be presumption and pride. With others still, though they admit in theory the duty of making such a confession and the possibility of a child making it too, yet the heart is so cold and worldly that the warm, loving confession of Jesus as their Lord is never heard from their lips. Family worship and religious profession testify to anything but the living, loving attachment to a personal Saviour. Their children would never learn from them to say, "I am the Lord's."

And yet we see here promised so distinctly that the Spirit's working in us a living, spiritual faith will manifest itself thus. The experience of these last years has proved to many who formerly were in doubt that a distinct profession of Jesus as Saviour is as sure a fruit of the Spirit's presence among the children as among older people—and that it can be quite as trustworthy too. A little reflection, too, will convince us that nothing can be more natural than this fruit of God's blessing on the labors of believing parents. Do we not tell them from their youth that God is love and that He gave Jesus to be a Saviour? Do we not tell them that they belong to God, not only in right of creation and redemption, but in virtue of our having given them to Him and His having accepted them? Why should it appear strange if the child believes what we say, and speaks it out: "I am the Lord's"? We tell them that Jesus receives sinners who confess their sins and give themselves to Him to be cleansed. What we ought to hope for as the fruit of our instruction is that when he feels his sins, the child will go and confess them to the blessed children's Friend, believing that He does not cast him out but accepts and pardons.

Oh, let us be very careful of casting suspicion on the childlike, "I am the Lord's"! We teach the children that it implies a giving of ourselves to be His property, to do His will, and to acknowledge Him as Lord and Master. And if their young hearts are touched and consent, oh! let us beware of refusing or doubting their profession or of reproaching them if they fail. Let us remember the promised fruit of the Spirit's working among the children: "I am the Lord's."

Are we then to think that there is no danger at all connected with it? And are we to rest content with the momentary impressions which speak the words without inquiring further? By no means. As with those who have come to years, so with children: impressions may be temporary and profession superficial. We have been warning against the disposition that doubts the reality of all children's conversion and profession; God's Word teaches us what will give them sincerity and reality. Let us consider well the second lesson our prophecy teaches: it is the Spirit's working that will make true "I am the Lord's."

And in what way is the outpouring of the Spirit to be given? Blessed be God! the promise was fulfilled on the day of Pentecost. The Spirit dwells in the Church of Christ, in the hearts and the homes of His believing disciples. There may now at times come special outpourings of the Spirit in revival movements of wider or smaller extent, when the young come forward in numbers to confess their Lord. But for this we have not to wait. In promising the Spirit to the offspring of His people, God would have us expect that parental instruction, a consecrated home life, and His ordinances of family religion are to be the means the Spirit is to use and bless for leading the children to Christ. The Spirit ever works in the Word; to the child the parent is the God-ordained minister of the Word. The blessing of the new dispensation is this, that the parent may count on the Holy Spirit for his children too, from their youth up, and that all his teaching and training, his word and work, though it be in weakness and in fear and in much trembling, may be in demonstration of the Spirit and of power.

But then everything depends upon the parent himself as a minister of the Spirit. He must live and walk in the Spirit, he must be led and sanctified by the Spirit, he must speak and pray in the Spirit, and he must in faith claim and accept the promise of the Spirit for his child. It is possible, we said, that a child's profession, "I am the Lord's," may be of no value. This depends greatly on the parents and those who surround the child. He takes the meaning of the words very much from them. If to them it is the language of a joyous faith and consecration, the child unconsciously catches the meaning from the spirit in which he sees them live. If they watch over his weakness and continually speak words of help and encouragement, even the little child can prove the reality of the change of which this profession was the token.

Dear parents, let God's thoughts for your children enter your hearts and rule there. These two thoughts especially: (1) God's Spirit and my children belong to each other; I may in faith claim the Spirit's dwelling and working in them. (2) My child may know and say that he is the Lord's; the fruit of the Spirit is the faith of the heart and the confession of the lips, "Jesus is mine." Let this promise be your strength as you deal with God, your strength as you deal with your child: They that wait on the Lord shall not be ashamed.

* * *

O Lord God, we draw nigh to Thee to claim the fulfillment of this promise on behalf of our beloved children. Lord, may they from their very youth have Thy Spirit poured out upon them that even in the simplicity of childhood they may say, "I am the Lord's."

O Lord, be pleased to this end to fill us, Thy servants, with Thy Holy Spirit. May all our home life and our parental influence be a channel through which the Spirit reaches each child. God, help us so to live that the life that breathes around him may be life in the Spirit.

Especially we ask Thee, gracious Lord, to give us great singleness of aim in training our children for Thee alone. Oh, that the indwelling of the blessed Spirit may not be thought of as something hardly to be expected but as the one gift the Father loves to bestow, and the first thing the child needs in order to grow up into a noble man and Christian! Lord, let our training of him, as Thy exclusive sacred property, knowing and saying he is Thine, be our one desire. And we can count on this, that each child we so consecrate to Thee Thou wilt, by Thy Spirit, consecrate for Thine own. May we experience how wonderfully the parents' work and the Spirit's work blend in securing the seed of Thy people for Thyself. Amen.

TWENTY-FIFTH DAY

From Generation to Generation

"My righteousness shall be for ever, and my salvation from generation to generation" (Isa. 51:8).

When we speak of a generation in the history of man, we think of the shortness of human life and the continual change among men. "One generation passeth away, and another generation cometh: but the earth abideth for ever." What a contrast between man and the heavens above, the mountains around him—always the same. Even more, what a contrast between man whose life is but a span and the unchangeable, the everlasting God.

We shall find in God's Word that it links together, rather than contrasts, these opposites; it lifts man out of the transitoriness of life to find his refuge in the unchangeableness of God. "As for man, his days are as grass; . . . but the mercy of the Lord is from everlasting to everlasting upon them that fear him, and his righteousunto children's children." "O my God, take me not away in the midst of my days: thy years are throughout all generations. Of old hast thou laid the foundation of the earth; and the heavens . . . shall perish, but thou *shalt endure.* . . . Thou art the same, and thy years shall have no end. The children of thy servants *shall continue,* and their seed shall be established before thee" (Ps. 102:25-28). Death may separate one generation from another, but

God's mercy connects them, passing on from one to another; His righteousness, which is everlasting, reveals itself as salvation from generation to generation.

At every point where God meets and acts with man, there are two sides to be regarded—the divine and the human. So it is here, too, in the transmission of God's salvation from generation to generation. God's faithfulness inspires that of man and therefore demands and rewards it. In some passages it might almost appear as if everything depended upon man and his keeping the covenant; and so it does indeed. But not as if this keeping of the covenant were to be the means by which he secures the blessing. No, it is in the mercy and truth of God, as these are known and trusted, that human faithfulness has its strength and security. To know God's purpose, to believe God's promise, to adore God's unchanging faithfulness communicates to the soul the very spirit of that faithfulness and binds us firmly to Him, so that He who is all in all can work out His purpose in us.

Let us first look at the divine side of this salvation from generation to generation. In Isaiah we have these words that express this truth with great frequency and distinctness: "As for me, this is *my covenant* with them, saith the Lord; my spirit that is upon thee, and my works which I have put in thy mouth, shall not depart out of thy mouth, nor out of the mouth of thy seed, nor out of the mouth of thy seed's seed, saith the Lord, from henceforth and for ever" (Isa. 59:21). This speaks of New Testament times. When God made His covenant with David, He anticipated generations in which there would be disobedience and therefore punishment (II Sam. 2:14; Ps. 89:30-33). But here the promise of the Spirit and the Word in the mouth of God's Anointed One and His people is not to pass from the mouth of the seed's seed. And, blessed be God, there are familes in which for generations, even for centuries, the Word and the Spirit have not departed from the mouth of the seed's seed.

Then we have that other beautiful promise: "*I will*

direct their work in truth, and *I will* make an everlasting covenant with them. And their seed shall be known among the Gentiles, and their offspring among the people: all that see them shall acknowledge them, that they are the seed which the Lord hath blessed" (Isa. 61:8, 9). Or, as it is otherwise expressed in Isaiah 65:23, ". . . They are the seed of the blessed of the Lord, and their offspring with them." The covenant with Abraham and David was also an everlasting covenant, but its fulfillment was reached over the heads of generations that proved faithless. But here, in the power of the promised Spirit, believing parents may claim and expect, from child to child, to see the blessing of the Lord. This is to be the fruit of the outpouring of the Holy Spirit; the promise, "Thou, and thy son, and thy son's son," is to have its literal fulfillment. And this not for our comfort and joy and the blessing on our children only, but that God may be known and glorified. "Their seed shall be known among the Gentiles." To be God's witnesses on earth—if need be, among the Gentiles to the end of the earth—it is for this that the Word and the Spirit are not to depart from the mouth of our seed from henceforth and for evermore.

Let us look now from the human side at the fulfillment of this promise: "My salvation from generation to generation." Most strikingly God's purpose is set forth in the words of Psalm 78:4-7: "We will not hide them from their *children*, shewing to *the generation to come* the praises of the Lord and his strength, and his wonderful works that he hath done. For he established a testimony in Jacob, and appointed a law in Israel, which he commanded our fathers, that they should make them known to *their children;* that the *generation to come* might know them, even *the children* which should be born; who should arise and declare them to *their children;* that they might set their hope in God, and not forget the works of God, but keep his commandments." We read in Psalm 145:4, "One generation shall praise thy works to another." The triumphant joy of that psalm of praise is the spirit in which the parents tell their child of God's glory and goodness.

Here we have the human side. Parents who know God show His praise, and His strength, and His wonderful works to their children. Parental instruction is in the ministry of the Spirit, not less but more than in the old covenant, a testifying for God in the spirit of praise, telling what He has done to us, His strength and His wonderful works. And so the children are taught not to forget the works of God, but to set their hope on Him and keep His commandments, to trust and to obey Him. And so His righteousness, which is from everlasting to everlasting, becomes salvation from generation to generation.

Parents, it is God's will that His salvation should be from generation to generation in your family too, that your children should hear from you and pass on to their children the praise of the Lord. Oh, let us seek to enter into God's plans, and with our whole heart labor earnestly to secure the blessing and to please our Father! We know what is needed—nothing but wholehearted devotion to God. But nothing less will do. God's salvation must not be a secondary thing, something to be enjoyed along with other things. It must be the first thing. We must set our whole heart upon it, even as God does. It must be the one thing we live for, to glorify this God. It is such a life, proving to the children the joy of God's salvation, a blessedness and a delight, that will influence them to come with us. It is this wholehearted devotion that will give strength to our faith and confidence to our hope. Under its inspiration our prayers will be persevering and believing. It will impart to our instruction the joyful tone of assurance, and make our whole life the model for our children. It is one generation living for God that will secure the next for Him; I may ask and expect that my wholehearted consecration to God will, in His infinite mercy, be blessed to guide them; His salvation is from generation to generation.

* * *

Gracious and most blessed Father, I bow before Thee once again with the prayer that Thou wouldst open my eyes and my heart that I may fully apprehend Thy holy purpose with an earthly parentage, transmitting through it Thy blessing. O my God, let Thy word, "my salvation from generation to generation, " so fill my heart that my calling and duty, with Thy promise and purpose, may be equally clear to me and the salvation of my children be as sure as my own.

And grant, Lord, that in Thy light I may realize and manifest fully what salvation is—salvation from sin and its power unto the holiness and the service of God. Let it be in me a salvation that fills the heart with gladness, and the lips with praise, and the whole life with purity and love. Let the salvation in which I walk and in which I train the children indeed be not what man calls so but the salvation of God.

O my God I do beseech Thee, give me grace that this be the one heirloom of their parents my children cherish, the one thing transmitted in our home from child to child, the salvation, the love, the joy, the service of God. Yes, Lord, Thou art the eternal and unchanging one; let it be from generation to generation. Amen.

TWENTY-SIXTH DAY

The Crowning Blessing

"I will pour out my spirit upon all flesh; and your sons and your daughters shall prophesy. . ." (Joel 2:28).

This is the promise of which the day of Pentecost was the fulfillment and the interpretation. The coming of the Comforter, the baptism with the Holy Ghost and with fire, the endowment with power from on high, the receiving the power of the Holy Ghost to be His witnesses to the end of the earth—all these precious promises of Christ were comprehended and fulfilled in the fulfillment of Joel's prophecy. It contains the title deed to the birthright of Christ's Church: the Holy Ghost from the throne of the exalted Saviour, her power for testimony and for suffering, for triumph and for blessing, and the heavenly sign with which she has been marked and sealed.

What a place is given to the children in this foundation promise! "Your sons and your daughters shall prophesy, your old men shall dream dreams, your young men shall see visions." The seed of God's people have such a place in His heart that even in the promise of Pentecost the first thing introduced is not the disciples now anointed to preach but the sons and the daughters prepared to prophesy. Let us attempt to take in what it teaches us of God's purpose, of a parent's hope, and of a child's education.

1. *God's purpose.* With the gift of the Holy Spirit to His Church, God had an object: the power from on high for her work of testifying to the ends of the earth. The very last words of the Master (Acts 1:8) speak of this. All the other blessings of the Spirit—assurance, joy, holiness, love—have as their aim fruit-bearing and the power to bless. It is because many Christians do not understand this that there is often a weary and fruitless seeking for the blessings of the Spirit, when they would come as unsought if there were but a wholehearted surrender to the Spirit. He is given to empower the Christian for God's service and work. No wise man wastes power; he economizes it and puts in just sufficient for the work. According to the work our will undertakes and our faith expects to perform is the power, the measure of the Spirit God gives.

This is true in our children too. In Joel's prophecy God reveals His purpose with our sons and daughters. Under the mighty breathings of His Spirit they are to prophesy. What this prophesying is Paul tells us: "If all *prophesy,* and there come in one that believeth not, or one unlearned, he is convinced of all, he is judged of all: thus are the secrets of his heart made manifest; and so falling down on his face he will worship God, and report that God is in you of a truth" (I Cor. 14:24-25). This is prophesying in the power of the Spirit, convicting even the unbelieving and unlearned. And for such prophesying God wants our sons and daughters. And for such prophesying we ought, in this dispensation of the Holy Spirit, to educate our sons and daughters.

The world is in sore need of them. The Church is suffering for want of them. Supply always creates demand. Because there is so small supply, the Church thinks it has done something great when there is annually some increase in the amount of its subscriptions and the number of its agents. But, oh, if there were a heart to enter into God's purpose, and the Church and parents understood what glory it is to train our sons and daughters to be prophets of the Most High, witnesses and messengers for Jesus our Lord, what a change it would bring in our modes of operation! As the children of this world do their utmost to obtain some high commission in the army or navy, some good appointment in the civil service or in business, why should not the children of God press around the throne of their Father, seeking no favor so earnestly as that He would fulfill this promise in their children, making them His prophets wherever He has need of them? God's purpose is that the Holy Spirit should take possession of our sons and daughters for His service; that our sons and daughters should be filled with the Holy Spirit, consecrated for power for service. They belong to Him and He to them.

2. *The parent's hope.* Just imagine believing parents entering fully and heartily into this purpose of God, acting upon it as a settled fact that they are training their children for the service of God's Spirit. Could any doubt still arise in their minds as to whether they might count on the conversion of their children? "Aim high" is a daily maxim; you will accomplish more than he who is content with a lower range. This is the blessing of full consecration: while it aims at the highest that God has promised, the secondary gifts, which others struggle lifelong for in vain, fall unsought to their share. Nothing will give such confidence for the salvation of our children, of the Spirit's working for conversion and renewal, as the consciousness of having surrendered them undividedly to the service of God and His Spirit.

And it will equally inspire us with confidence in regard to fitness for parental duty. We have no conception of the extent to which self-interest enfeebles faith and self-sacrifice emboldens it. If I know I am seeking the salvation of my children for their own and for my sake, the soul cannot rise to the confident assurance that all grace for training my child will be given. But let me lose all selfish thought of myself and them, placing them at God's disposal, and it will become impossible to doubt that my

Father will give me grace for the work I do for Him.

Though there is a diversity of gifts, and I may not see each child used in the direct service of the Master, I may be sure that the heart's purpose is accepted, and the effort to train all my children to be the vessels of God's Holy Spirit has had its elevating influence on my own soul, on my home, on each of my children, whatever their external calling in life may be. The more distinctly I acknowledge to the family that in this dispensation the Spirit claims all, the more may I depend upon His presence with me and mine. Such a purpose in God's heart and such a hope in the parent's heart will influence the children's training.

3. *The children training.* Cultivate every mental power, keeping in view the preparation of a sharp instrument for the Master's use. Cultivate natural virtues—diligence and decision, order and method, promptness and firmness—with the high aim of having the child more fit for the work to be done. Cultivate every moral power to be the form prepared for the Holy Spirit's filling. Let obedience to conscience and to law, let self-control and temperance, let strict integrity and justice, let humility and love, be the aim in education, that the Holy Spirit may have a noble Christian, an efficient servant of the Lord, a true prophet.

The prize that parents seek for their children is often counted worthy of any sacrifice; there have been those who have willingly suffered want to give their sons a liberal education or to secure for their daughters a position in the world. Oh, let us so set our hearts upon the promotion we seek for our children that all thought of sacrifice passes away as we study and labor, as we pray and believe, to have them counted worthy of a place among the separated ones whom the Spirit of the Lord anoints for His work.

And now we close our meditations on the Old Testament testimony of the place children occupy in the purpose and promise of God. We have seen what God would be to our children—a God in covenant, with the covenant blessing of the blood and the Spirit of Jesus. And we have seen what He wants our children to be to Him—a covenant seed, to receive and transmit and multiply the blessing through the earth. And we have seen what their children can in turn become—the ministers of the covenant, sprinkling and pleading the blood with Him and receiving the Spirit from Him; by example and training and life communicating the blessing as channels for the Spirit's training future generations for His service.

God help us to learn these three lessons. God help us to believe and receive all He is willing to be for our children through us. God help us to give and train the children for all He would have them be. God help us to be faithful sureties for our children, to seek for them nothing less than God seeks, and so to live that from our homes may go forth sons and daughters to prophesy in His name.

* * *

O Lord our God, we thank Thee again for the institution of the family, Thy divine appointment for transmitting Thy salvation to all generations. And we thank Thee for the revelation of thyself as the covenant God to the children of Thy servants, pledging thyself to fulfill all Thy promises of blessing. And we thank Thee most of all for the promise of the Spirit—Thy Holy Spirit, the Spirit of Thy Son—to dwell in our sons and daughters.

O Lord, fulfill Thy promise to our children. Give us grace to train them for Thee, believing for the Spirit's working, of the Spirit's coming with power. Give us grace to prepare them to be meet for the Master's use, every gift cultivated and consecrated for Thy service. Let our sons and daughters prophesy in the power of the Holy Ghost.

O Lord, bless all believing parents. Let Thy claim on their children, let Thy promise of the Spirit, let the inconceivably high privilege of offering their children to Thee for service, let the power promised to parents, let the crying need for laborers, let the Spirit's seeking for those whom He can use as the prophets of the Most High so fill their hearts that all their training may be in harmony with Thy purpose: "Your sons and your daughters shall prophesy." Amen.

TWENTY-SEVENTH DAY
The Heavenly and the Earthly Father

"If ye then,being evil, know how to give good gifts unto
your children, how much more shall your Father which
is in heaven give good things to them that ask him?"
(Matt. 7:11).

We began our meditations from the Old Testament
with the home on earth and picture of the home in heaven.
The glory of the New Testament is its fuller revelation of
the Father in heaven. We can have no better beginning
for our New Testament studies of what God intends family life to be than to see what light the fatherliness of God
casts upon our own fatherhood, upon what we are to be
to our children.

1. First we note how Jesus wants us to rise from and
through the experiences of fatherhood on earth to know
the Father in heaven aright. Not as if our fatherhood
were the original and the reality, to be used by way of
comparison and illustration to make God's relation clear
to us. By no means. God is the true Father: from eternity,
in His very nature, He is the God of love. Fatherhood
was the glory and the blessedness of the Divine Being.
And our fatherhood on earth has been given as a reflection
of His, to lead us to a participation in its honor and joy.
We, too, are to taste the blessedness of begetting a

son in our likeness, having in him the object of our love, the reflection of our image, a companion and helper in all our work.

But because this fatherhood in heaven is so high above us, we are to study the father-heart on earth, from it continually rising into a truer and fuller apprehension of what God is to us. Home life is a school as much for training parents as children; the deepest mysteries of God's love are best studied by a parent in his own bosom. As we think of our love to our children, the joy they give us, the tender sympathy their troubles wake, the patient kindness their dullness or waywardness requires, the ready response with which their needs and requests are met, Jesus wants us to look up and calculate *how much more* all this must be in God, the good and perfect one, the fountain of love. He wants us to banish every shadow of unbelief from the heart, and live our life in the sunshine of God's love.

As we see what influence a parent can exert on his child, breathing his disposition and even his will into him, securing his unbounded trust, He would have us be sure that the Father does love and is able to breathe His own mind, His own disposition, what Jesus calls His own Spirit, into us. And as we claim and strive to secure the love and obedience of our children, as we long that they should find their happiness in our will, our friendship, our company, He asks us to remember that the Father loves to meet us in secret, that the voice and the trust of His child are His joy and will meet a rich reward. What a study for every father and mother: each pulse of love and joy that swells their hearts marks the revelation of divine love and joy bending over them, longing to meet the response of their childlike love and joy. In the light of the fatherhood of earth, we rise to what fatherhood in heaven is.

2. But then, again, the fatherhood in heaven will cast its light also on the fatherhood of earth and teach us what it ought to be. In giving us the place and the name

and the power of father, God has in a very real and solemn sense made us His image-bearers. He asks and expects us, in doing our work, to copy Him, to act as like Him as possible. The parents who desire to bring a full blessing to their children must make God's fatherhood their model and their study.

They must enter into God's purpose and make it their own, giving themselves to pursue it with their whole heart. The heavenly Father seeks to educate children into His likeness. He has nothing higher to bestow on them; with nothing less can He be content if they are to have a place forever in His home. God has appointed parents on earth to be His ministers and fellow workers, to carry out His plan. How can they, unless they understand it and make its realization the first object of family life?

From the Father in heaven they must learn, too, the way in which that purpose is to be attained. In His dealings with His people, parents will see how He came first, as with Abraham, in love and kindness, securing trust and confidence; then with law and its authority, to lead on to self-knowledge and self-renunciation; then with the gospel of full liberty in the Spirit that we might no longer be children but men. From Him parents will learn to combine love with authority, and through them to aim at the free and hearty surrender to all God's will. In the tenderness and patience and self-sacrifice of the divine love, in the firmness and righteousness of divine rule, the parent will find the secret of successful training.

Above all, from the father must be learned how very personal such training is. How the Father has come down to us in Christ; how in His own example He shows us that He wants us to be as He is; how in giving us His Spirit He would have us understand that fatherhood longs to draw the child into perfect likeness and oneness with itself. As the earthly father gazes and studies, it will dawn upon him that the highest duty of our fatherhood *is to be what the child is to be*. A father must breathe his own spirit into the child; that he as a child of the heavenly

Father receives His Spirit day by day can breathe this into his child too. Is it not a solemn but most blessed thing to be a parent? First a child of the heavenly Father, and then His image, His substitute, His picture to the child on earth.

3. This brings us to a third lesson. The earthly father must not only take the Father in heaven as his model and guide, but he must so reflect Him that the child may naturally rise from him whom he sees to the unseen One whom he represents. A child loves his parents by natural instinct; as the child sees in the father all that is holy and worthy of honor, natural love becomes the homage of an affectionate and enthusiastic admiration. In a Christian father a child ought to have a better exposition than the best of sermons can give of the love and care of the heavenly Father and all the blessing and joy He wants to bestow.

But to attain to this the parent must consciously and distinctly aim at making himself and the name he bears the ladder by which the child can climb to the Father above. It is when the bright, living, happy piety of the parents, a mingling of holy reverence to God with childlike love, shines on the children from their early youth that the name of God as Father will become linked with all that is lovely and holy in the memory of a child. It is not so much a matter of reflection or thought but as the life-breath taken in all unconsciously that the fatherhood of earth will have been the gate of the Father's home above.

And is it possible so to live that all this shall be true? The one thing the Father loves to give, the sum and center of all His good gifts, is His own Holy Spirit—His Father-Spirit to be in us. And we have but to believe, and as we believe, to receive, and as we receive, to yield to and live in the Spirit; and He will make our fatherhood the image of God's, and from us too there, will flow streams of living water to bless our children.

What a world it would be if every Christian father

set himself in true earnest to realize and fulfill his calling
and in his little home circle as God's ambassador to bear
God's name—the holy name of father. In a holy partner-
ship with the Father in heaven, he yielded himself to
be taught and sanctified and used to train children for
the Father who is in heaven. Shall not we all who are
fathers join, and shall not all mothers, with whom the
fathers are so truly one and on whom they so depend
for what they are to be as fathers in the family, join
too in the fervent prayer that the Father would make
us all the worthy bearers of that name?

* * *

Our Father which art in heaven, we unite in an earnest
prayer for all Thy children who bear the holy name of
father. Give us, we beseech Thee, more insight into Thy
fatherhood and into the unspeakable riches of blessing
for us and our children included therein. From the wonderful traits of Thine own likeness in our feelings towards
our children let us rise up to believe and enjoy the divine
fullness of love which Thy heart and Thy name offer to
us. Let our fatherhood so teach us the blessedness of being
the children of Thy Father-love.

And then, our Father, give us to see how really Thou
dost command and expect that our fatherhood shall be
nothing less than the reflection and the outflow of Thine
own. Oh, may these two fatherhoods indeed be one—one
in purpose, one in method, one in principle, one in spirit.
O God, we want to be fathers to our children just as
Thou art to us; make us such, so that Thou canst fully
use us as the channels for thy Father-grace to our little
ones. May they see in us true pictures of Him of whom
we teach them to say, "Our Father which art in heaven."

Father we look to Thy Son and the "how much more"
He taught us for the answer to our prayer. We count
upon the tenderness and the faithfulness of Thy love and
upon Thy mighty power and Spirit to bless the parents
of Thy Church who cry to Thee. Amen.

TWENTY-EIGHTH DAY
Children of the Kingdom

"But the children of the kingdom shall be cast out into outer darkness" (Matt. 8:12).

In what close union we have here before us the wonderful privilege and the terrible danger that come with the place our children have in the Church of Christ. They are children of the kingdom—what more glorious! They can be cast out into outer darkness—what more awful! The only way certainly to avoid the latter is fully to grasp the former, to let it be not a name but a power ruling and renewing the whole life. To this end let us try to apprehend all it implies.

Children of the kingdom! What kingdom? The answer is simple: the kingdom of God! And where is this kingdom? In heaven. It is that divine rule or dominion which is in heaven and the whole heavenly world. Its center is the throne of God, on which He dwells. He is the Holy One from whom all life and all law and all love flow forth. Around that throne are powers and principalities and dominions, with their untold myriads of holy spirits who do His will and are the messengers of His power. The mark of that kingdom is that in God everything is love and blessing; in His subjects, everything obedience and joy.

And how can this heavenly kingdom be here on earth?

When God created the heavens and the earth, it was with the object of securing new territory in which His heavenly empire might be established. But the power of another kingdom, the kingdom of Satan, interfered; and in the fall of man the coming of the kingdom was delayed. For four thousand years it was promised and hoped for, but the kingdom of heaven was not yet on earth.

And how did this kingdom come? It was in the fullness of time, when the King himself came to earth, that the message was heard: The kingdom of heaven is at hand, the kingdom of heaven is come unto you. He came, first, as a subject and a servant to show us the spirit that animates all the subjects of the kingdom—implicit obedience, delight in doing the will of God. In that obedience unto death He broke the power of Satan and of sin, showed forth the wondrous love with which as our King he loved us and set us free for the blessed life of serving and obedience like His own. And then when as King He ascended to heaven and took His seat upon the throne, the kingdom could come. In the outpouring of the Holy Spirit the kingdom came in power and was set up in the hearts that had been prepared to receive Him and to enter the kingdom.

And who were the subjects of this kingdom? Jesus said, "Except a man be born again, he cannot see the kingdom of God." Nothing less than the Spirit of God, the Spirit of heaven, coming in and taking possession of a man could fit him to enter, or even see the kingdom, or to live as one of its subjects. But with this solemn message Jesus also spoke: "Blessed are the poor in spirit, for theirs is the kingdom of heaven." To become an heir of the kingdom, nothing was needed but the consciousness and confession of poverty, of having nothing that we might possess all.

And the marks of those who truly belong to this kingdom? Nothing less than the marks by which the King was known on earth: obedience and love towards God— obedience to the uttermost, an absolute surrender to His will. And towards man, love—giving itself to live and die to bring the blessings of the kingdom to all around. "The kingdom is not in word but in power"; the kingdom of heaven above everything is in the infinite power of the eternal life. As the kingdom comes down, the Holy Ghost, the power, comes also to give the strength to live as members of the kingdom. In each one of whom the kingdom truly takes possession, the prayer "Thy kingdom come" becomes the desire of the heart, and everything is subordinate to its extension and manifestation of its glory.

And who are the children of the kingdom? Jesus spoke this word even of the Jews who rejected the kingdom. God had in His great mercy committed the promise of the kingdom to Israel, and all its children were its heirs. And now our children—born under its influence, destined for its blessings, brought into the fellowship of the Church, which is the nursery and training school of the kingdom— our children are children of the kingdom: "of such is the kingdom of heaven."

And what is needed to secure for them the possession of the kingdom to which they have thus been made the heirs? That they may lose it is possible—children of the kingdom may be cast into outer darkness. What is needed above everything is this, that they be so educated and trained under the influence and power of the heavenly life, in the very spirit of the kingdom, that the blessing which their name, expressive of their destiny, brings may become their own personal and everlasting possession.

And who is to train them thus? Christian parents! This is our holy privilege. As children of the kingdom, they are entrusted to us to keep and nourish. The keynote of our education, the watchword in all our desires and efforts on their behalf, our plea with God for them and with them for God, must be this: They are children of the kingdom. To parents God has entrusted the high commission of leading their children on from the place where their title is yet only a name and a promise to the life of possession and full enjoyment.

And what is needed to enable the parent to do this? Nothing less than that with his whole heart *he himself live in and for the kingdom of heaven.* The atmosphere of the home must be the spirit of heaven; Christ's command "Seek ye first the kingdom of God" must be the ruling principle of all its conduct. Unconsciously the child must receive the impression that not only personal blessing but the interests and extension of God's kingdom are the hope and the joy of life. Parents whose citizenship is in heaven, who have in truth entered the kingdom and live in it, will alone be found worthy or fit to train the children as heirs of the kingdom.

And how are parents able thus to live? "My kingdom," Jesus said, "is not of this world. It is from above, from heaven, from God. From heaven, from God the Spirit the life and the power of the kingdom must come each day. Coming out of the world, daily rising upward and entering into the holiest within the veil through the blood, the believer must tarry in God's presence in worship and surrender until the anointing is fresh upon him; only so can he come into his home and consecrate it as the nursery for children of the kingdom.

As long as we are content with just enough religion to save ourselves and our children, we must not be surprised if they remain unsaved. Only in seeking to be filled with the Spirit, to have our whole life, like Christ's, sacrificed for the kingdom, may we count on the blessing of a successful education. "My kingdom is not of this world." The spirit of the world ruling in the parents, perhaps even unconsciously, destroys all that they hope to effect by their purposes, their precepts, or their prayers. In Christ's command "*first the kingdom*," we have the secret and the certainty of a successful education.

Parents, your children are children of the kingdom, the kingdom of God in heaven! Hold and love and train them as such, for God alone. From God alone be your hope. From above must be your help. Seek it in much prayer. Accept it in childlike faith that believes that you have what you ask. Yield yourself to it, denying self,

158

not allowing self any say in the guidance of your life or home. Yield yourself to it, keeping the ear open every hour to hear the voice of the Holy Spirit, through whom alone the laws and the powers of the kingdom can work in us.

Above all, remember Jesus! *He said,* "Suffer little children to come *unto me,* for of such is the kingdom of heaven." He is the King; in Him we have the kingdom. Live with Him, on Him, in Him. He loves our children and looks after them; His presence and love will fill us and them with a holy enthusiasm for the kingdom. So will they grow up in the kingdom and for the kingdom. And we shall taste the joy unspeakable of having our home, with its life and love and training, within the kingdom—yea, of having the kingdom of heaven within our home. * * *

Our Father which art in heaven, Thine is the kingdom, and the power, and the glory. Blessed be Thy name that by Thine almighty power Thy kingdom, the kingdom of heaven, hath come to this earth, and will come until the whole earth be filled with Thy glory. Blessed, too, be Thy name, that we and our little ones are the children of the kingdom. O Father, we look to thy Father-love to give us who are fathers and mothers grace to realize how sacred our calling and our home is, because we are training children of the kingdom for Thee. Teach us, we pray Thee, never to put asunder the words our Lord has joined together—the children and the kingdom. May all our love and fellowship and influence help to link them inseparably with the kingdom. May they ever know that they are living and growing up in it.

Blessed Lord Jesus, who didst say of the little ones, "of such is the kingdom," we do beseech Thee, reveal to us what Thy kingdom is in its spiritual reality and glory—which is here even on earth as the rule of God by the Holy Spirit in the hearts and lives of His people.

May the kingdom of God be within us in such power, and we within it in such truth, that our children may not only have the name, but that the very atmosphere they breathe in our home be such as will make them really children of the kingdom. Amen.

TWENTY-NINTH DAY

A Mother's Persevering Prayer

"A woman of Canaan came out of the same coasts, and cried unto him saying, Have mercy on me, O Lord, thou Son of David; my daughter is grievously vexed with a devil. . . . Then Jesus answered and said unto her, O woman, great is thy faith: be it unto thee even as thou wilt" (Matt. 15:22, 28).

In the Old Testament we found God's promises of blessing clear and sure on the godly training of children. Nor were His threatenings on the neglect of this duty less distinct. And in more than one terrible example we saw with what relentless power the threat came true. In the sons of Aaron and Eli, in the family of David and Solomon, proof was given that the personal righteousness of the father could not save the ungodly child. And we found no answer to one of the most solemn questions, one which has been as a burning fiery furnace to many a parent's heart: Is there still hope for a child grown up in sin and passing out from beyond the reach of a parent's influence?

It is in Christ Jesus that God has revealed how completely the power of sin and Satan has been broken. It is in Christ Jesus that God has shown us what it is possible for His grace to do. It is in Christ Jesus, too, we must seek for the answer to every question of a parent's heart.

His earthly life revealed all that the Father is willing to do for us, and in Christ is a parent's hope for a wandering child.

As we study this carefully, we will be surprised to find how many of the most precious and encouraging words of Christ have been spoken to parents in reference to their children. "Fear not, only believe"; "All things are possible to him that believeth"; "O woman, great is thy faith: be it unto thee even as thou wilt." Such words, which have countless times been the strength and comfort of the penitent seeking pardon or the believer pleading for some spiritual blessing, are in the first place the parent's property, the blessed assurance that there is no case in which a child now in Satan's power is beyond the reach of a Saviour's love and a parent's faith. Let us see how wonderfully this will come out in the well-known story of the Syrophenician mother, as we think of her daughter's misery, her prayer's refusal, her faith's perseverance, and her rich reward.

Her daughter's misery: "My daughter is grievously vexed with a devil." How many a mother is there who has a child possessed with an evil spirit far more terrible than that of which we read here? In this case it was more sickness than sin, it was the power of Satan in the body more than the soul. But, alas, how many of the grown-up children of Christian parents there are who are under the power of Satan, given up to pleasure or worldliness, to self-will or to sin.

Let our story encourage these parents to believe that, however hopeless their case appears, there is One who is mighty to save, the parent's Friend, the children's Redeemer. Let them come to Him with their need and cry out in prayer, "My child is grievously vexed with a devil." Let them make full confession of their child's lost estate. Beware of excusing their sin by the thought of what is good or lovable about them, or by laying the blame on circumstances or companions. Bring them to Christ and say that they are lost, under the power of Satan, that they have deserved and are on their way to eternal damnation. Hide not their wretchedness. Ask not that they may be saved and made happy and taken to heaven. Ask nothing less than that they may turn from the power of Satan unto God, that they may be translated from the power of darkness to the kingdom of God's dear Son. Ask that they may be born again, changed from being the children of the devil and enemies of God to being His friends and children. Honor God by confessing their sin fully and clearly, acknowledging His righteous judgment; ask distinctly and definitely for a full salvation.

Her prayer's refusal is the second lesson this woman has to teach us. Christ appeared to turn a deaf ear to her prayer. At first He did not answer her a word. When He did speak, His answer was worse than His silence. It cut off all hope; He was not sent to the heathen. A second answer, given as she had come nearer and had again worshipped Him, saying, "Lord, help me," appeared to heap contempt on her misfortune; she was not only a heathen but a dog.

Here is a true picture of what passes in the heart of many a pleading parent, They hear of Christ's love and power and begin to pray with great urgency. But He answers not a word; there is no sign of thought or change on the part of the lost one. Still they pray, and it is as if the power of sin grows stronger and the loved one only wanders farther off. Conscience begins to speak of parental sin and unworthiness. Others, who are holier and have more power with God, may be heard; how can we expect that God should work a miracle for us? And the parent settles down in a quiet despondency or a vague hope that tries to shut its eyes to its own wretchedness. Oh, the dark, heartrending uncertainty as to the salvation of that child!

Her faith and perseverance—it is for this especially that the mother's example is held up to us. She refused to be denied. She met silence and argument and seeming contempt alike with one weapon—more prayer, more trust. She had heard of the wondrous Man and His compassion; she saw it in His face; she heard it even in the voice that refused her. She would not believe He could send her away empty. She hoped against hope; she believed against appearances and, what is more, against His very words; she believed and she triumphed.

And now, mother! you who are pleading for your prodigal child, you have her example. And not only her example but a thousand words of promise, a revelation of the Father's will and the Saviour's power and love such as she never had. Let her faith and perseverance put your unbelief to shame. In the face of all appearances and all doubts, let your faith rise and claim the promise of an answer to prayer in the name of Jesus. Yield yourself to the Holy Spirit that He may search out and bring to the light everything not according to His will, that you might confess and cast it out. Trust not to the fervency of your desires or the wrestling urgency of your petition. Put your strength in God's promise and faithfulness, in His power and love. Let the soul, in restful deliberate confidence in Jesus, praise Him for His promise and His power to save. In this confidence let nothing shake you from the continuous and persevering prayer of faith. The prayer of faith is always heard.

The wondrous blessing she obtained is for us too. Not only was her daughter delivered from this grievous trouble but there was something almost better, a spiritual blessing: our Lord's delighted approval of her faith. "O woman, great is thy faith: be it unto thee even as thou wilt." Yes, it is in the earnest, believing supplication for a child that the parent's heart can be drawn out toward the Lord, can learn to know and trust Him aright, can rise to that insight into His love which is most pleasing to Him, bringing down into the soul the consciousness of His good pleasure. Mother, you who are pleading for loved ones far from the fold, come nearer, come nearer to Jesus. He is able, indeed, to save them. He waits for your faith to take hold of His strength, to accept their salvation.

Oh, let not your child perish because you refuse to come and take time with Him until His love has inspired you with faith. Mother, come nearer, tarry with Jesus in prayer, trust Him; your child can be saved.

* * *

Blessed Lord Jesus, I too, like the Syrophenician woman, have a child grievously vexed with a devil. Like her I come pleading, "Have mercy on me, O Lord, thou Son of David."

O Lord, I confess the sin of my child. Thou knowest it all: unconverted and an enemy to Thee by nature, he has rejected Thy love, choosing the world and sin. I confess my sin, too, Lord! Thou knowest how bitter the thought is that had my life been less in the world and the flesh, purer and holier, more full of faith and of love and of Thee, my child might have grown up differently. Lord, in deep sorrow I confess my sin; oh, let not my child perish! Son of David, have mercy on me.

Blessed Lord, I put my trust in Thee. I look in faith to Thine almighty power. The things that are impossible with man are possible with God. I look in faith to Thy promise to hear prayer. Lord, I believe Thou hearest me; help mine unbelief. I lay this perishing child at Thy feet and plead Thy love. Saviour, I do believe in Thy love and claim deliverance for my child. In this faith I will praise Thee for Thy grace. I will tarry at Thy feet day by day in the rest of faith, praising Thee and looking for Thy fulfillment. Make haste, O my Lord, for Thy name's sake. Amen.

THIRTIETH DAY
The Heavenliness of a Little Child

"Whosoever therefore shall humble himself as this little child, the same is greatest in the kingdom of heaven. And whoso shall receive one such little child in my name receiveth me" (Matt. 18:4, 5).

The disciples had come to Jesus with the question, Who is the greatest in the kingdom of heaven? He had spoken often of the kingdom. To them it suggested the idea of power and glory; they could not but wonder who would have the highest place. How utterly strange and incomprehensible must have been the answer Jesus gave to their question. He called a little child and set him in the midst of them. He told them that as long as they were thinking of who would be greatest, they could not even enter the kingdom; they must first become as little children. And then in the kingdom the humblest and the most childlike would be the highest. And whoever received one such little child in Jesus' name would be receiving himself. The deeper the sympathy with the child-nature, recognizing Jesus and His name in it, the closer and more complete the union with himself.

How wonderfully applicable this is to parents! In creating a family, God sets a little child in the midst of a mother and father. And in that little child He opens to them the mystery of the kingdom of heaven and the spiritual world. He tells them that if they want to know about heaven and what will prove their fitness for its highest place, they must study the child-nature. On earth they will find nothing so heaven-like as a little child, no surer way to the highest enjoyments of heavenly dignity than in receiving little children in His name; for in doing this they will receive himself in whom the kingdom is. These are the three lessons we parents must learn.

First, the heavenliness of the little child. Wherein does this consist? Our Saviour uses one word: "Whosoever shall *humble* himself as this little child, the same is greatest in the kingdom." The greatest will be he who thinks least of being greatest, because he loses sight of himself in seeking God and His kingdom. The great beauty of childlikeness is the absence of self-consciousness. The true child loses himself in that which is around him. The curse of sin is that it makes man, every man, his own center; even when he seeks the kingdom of heaven he is still thinking how he can be greatest in the kingdom. In the true child self does not yet manifest itself; it lives and is at rest outside of itself in the parent. It loves and rejoices in being loved; it is truthful and trustful to all around, showing itself as it is, counting upon others to be what they appear. This naturalness and simplicity of the child, Jesus tells us, is something heavenly, the thing in nature most allied to the kingdom. And the lesson we need to learn is that there is nothing a parent should seek to preserve and cherish more carefully than this heavenly childlikeness. It is the secret of that beautiful calmness and serenity which is the image of the peace and the rest of heaven.

The spirit of the world is the very opposite; with its rivalry and its ambition, its seeking excitement and possessions, it destroys all that is so beautiful and heavenly in the child, making way for the show and self-seeking that are its marks. Especially Christian parents who have the means for gratifying taste and pleasure at their disposal are in danger of destroying the simplicity and tenderness of the child-life by stimulating the desires which are of the earth. And so, in the midst of a great deal of Bible-teaching and hymn-singing, the very heart of true religion may be eaten out by the artificial and unchildlike spirit of the homes in which the children are reared.

Parents, make a study to find out what the thought of Jesus' heart was when He spoke so strongly of the need for being childlike, the only path to heaven and heavenly greatness. Value the childlikeness and simplicity of your little one as its heavenly beauty; realize that the little one, in its tender susceptibility to impressions, is all alive to what surrounds it—to the fostering influence of the heavenly life or the withering effect of a worldly life. Believe that between the Holy Spirit, who brings heaven down to us and reveals it within, and the heavenliness of childhood, there is a wonderful suitableness for each other. Train your children in that holy, happy stillness which keeps the heart open to His workings.

But how shall the parent succeed in doing this? Our Lord's words have a second lesson. If we are to watch over the heavenliness of our children, we must ourselves be childlike and heavenly-minded. Christ put a little child in the midst of strong men to teach them. Parents often owe more to the teaching of their children than their children owe to the teaching of their parents. Our children lose their childlikeness all too soon because parents have so little of it. The atmosphere of the home should be that of simple, happy, trustful living in the Father's presence. Amid many of the proprieties of religion the spirit of the world too often reigns. To be great in the kingdom of heaven is all too seldom the object of earnest desire. To be the greatest by being humble and childlike, as Jesus puts it, the least and the servant of all—this is hardly a popular goal in life.

Let parents study to be childlike. There are very few studies more difficult, very few that will bring a richer reward. The little children entrusted to us have a higher worth than we know; their very size, with which we often connect weakness, is what to Him, who looks at things in the light of God, constitutes their greatest attraction. It is parents living in great simplicity of truth and trust with the Father in heaven that can maintain that childlikeness in the child too.

To this end let us take in the third lesson our Saviour has: "Whoso shall receive one such a little child in my name receiveth me." Let us at their birth receive our children in the name of Jesus, in His Spirit, with His appreciation of their simplicity and humility. Let us receive them in His name, as those whom He loves and blesses and of whom He says, "of such is the kingdom," to be kept and trained for Him and His kingdom alone. Let us receive them in His name, as sent by Jesus to remind us of His own childlike humility and obedience to the Father. Let us receive them day by day in His name, coming as a gift from the Father and the heaven from which He came, to draw us thither too. Let us receive them and cherish them in His name, just as He would receive them, as He did receive them and blessed them. Let us receive them in His name, just as we would receive himself.

Yes, just as we would receive himself. This is not saying too much, for He asks and promises nothing less. "He that receiveth one such little child in my name receiveth me." He that recognizes and loves the humility, the childlikeness, the Christlikeness of the little child and on this account receives and treasures the child, receives Christ himself. This is the promise. With every child something of heaven and of Christ comes into the house. In many cases this is not noticed, not cared for, and all of heaven is pushed aside by the world. Blessed are they who know truly to receive the child in Jesus' name.

Jesus comes with the little one to be that child's and the parents' Saviour. With the child He sets in their midst He takes the parents afresh into His training, teaching them how to be great in the kingdom of heaven. He comes to make their child a blessing to them, so that they may be prepared to be a real blessing in return. He comes to bless parent and child together and make the home what it was meant to be—the picture, the promise, the pathway, to the Father's home in heaven.

Dear parents, let us ask our Lord Jesus most earnestly to open our minds to take in His divine thoughts about the heavenliness of our children, to open our eyes to see Him in them, to bring out hearts into perfect sympathy with himself so that our little ones may day by day be the blessed messengers that lead us to heaven, that bring to us Jesus himself.

* * *

Blessed Lord, open our ears to hear what Thou speakest and our eyes to see as Thou seest. Give us hearts to beat in sympathy with Thine at the sight of every little child; and above all, our Lord, to understand and experience how surely and how blessedly Thou fulfillest Thy promise, "Whoso shall receive one such little child in my name receiveth me."

Lord Jesus, we do ask Thee for a childlike spirit. May the simplicity and restfulness, the love and the loveliness, the trustfulness and truthfulness of the child-nature so dwell in us that in our relationship the heavenly childlikeness of our little ones may not be lost but cherished and maintained through advancing years. Give us to feel very deeply that we cannot truly fulfill our parental calling except as in simplicity and godly sincerity our walk with God be that of little children.

Blessed Lord, we do thank Thee that, however feeble we be and however far short our attainments fall of what we should be, in receiving a child in Thy name we receive Thee. Thou comest thyself to be our teacher and our helper. We pray Thee to strengthen us and all parents in this faith. May we rightly understand that nowhere art Thou nearer or more ready to bless than in the home where the children are received in Thy name, to be saved by Thee, to be trained for Thee. Amen.

THIRTY-FIRST DAY
The Children Come to Jesus

"But Jesus said, Suffer little children, and forbid them
not, to come unto me: for of such is the kingdom of
heaven" (Matt. 19:14).

What deep significance there is in this word, *"Suffer*
little children to come unto me." We suffer, allow, or
permit that which we are not naturally inclined for, which
we would prefer to be otherwise. The mothers had probably heard of the words Jesus had just spoken (see Matt.
18:3-5), and brought their little ones to be blessed of this
wonderful teacher. Jesus saw the disciples rebuking them.
They found it so hard to understand and to follow the
Master; what could the little children have to do with
Him? Jesus hears them and says, Forbid them not; allow
them to come unto me, for of such is the kingdom of
heaven. Among His disciples He loves to have the children;
they are nearest the kingdom, the most fitted for it; the
kingdom needs them as the teachers of the wise and the
great, to show the path through which alone heaven can
be entered.

"*Suffer* little children . . . to come unto me." The word
suffer reminds us how, even still, our wisdom cannot understand that the kingdom and the little ones are especially
fitted for each other. No wonder that with such an attitude
in parents or the Church the youthful grace is quenched,

and the child's religion becomes very much as that of the majority of older people. Let us hear the words of the Master today. Whether you can understand or fully approve, still do not forbid or hinder the children from coming to Jesus; bear with it until you see how He can bless them, until His word, "of such is the kingdom," has entered your heart, and you learn to receive them as He did.

Child-faith consists of that which constitutes the very center of God's revelation—coming to Jesus. In His own well-known words, "Come unto me," our Lord spoke of the blessed rest He would give to all who came to Him to exchange their weary burdens for His loving yoke. This simple gospel is just what a child needs. His faith is ready to believe in the unseen One, so kind and loving. His humility finds no difficulty in confessing sin and the need of help. And nothing appears more simple and natural than that this loving Saviour should be obeyed and followed. As by instinct he reconciles faith and works; he sees at once that trust in Him should beget obedience.

But, above all, the child at once takes in what older people often cannot apprehend—that faith and salvation center in a living Person—Jesus loving and to be loved, Jesus trusted and obeyed, *Jesus himself.* Would that it were so all our life! Coming to Jesus in prayer, in surrender, in love, would be the spontaneous exercise of our faith. Oh, let us not hinder but help our children to come to Jesus!

For this child-faith can be hindered. The words of Jesus suggest the thought. The child is weaker than the older disciple, is under his influence and can be kept back by him. God has given the making of the children into the hands of their elders. And the natural responsiveness of the child, his simple faith and sense of love and duty to Jesus, may be terribly wounded by the example and conduct of those around him. And so Jesus says, "Forbid them not." The word is elsewhere translated, "Hinder them not." The faith of the child is feeble and can so easily be hindered. Christian parents are appointed as guardians to watch and foster its growth. All growth comes from within and depends upon a healthy life. But young and feeble growth needs to be preserved from danger from without and to have provided for it the sustenance it demands.

Parents often have been bitterly disappointed in their children; when they were young they could feel so deeply and speak so beautifully, but they had not lived long before all was lost. It was probably because parents trusted to what was a blessed but still only feeble beginning. They did not watch over the evil influences which the young plant could not yet resist. They allowed the spirit of the world to enter their own religious life or their friends; they allowed company and pleasure and the enjoyment of the world to choke the good seed. Or they failed to supply the needful nourishment. There was not, as the child grew up, the personal speaking of this blessed Jesus, the helping to faith and obedience by the fellowship and example of a warm, living Christianity. The child's faith disappeared because the parents hindered him in coming to Jesus.

How different the result is where this coming to Jesus is fostered and encouraged not only in the little ones but in the growing boy and girl through the years that lead to maturity. We need to be kept from right-hand as well as left-hand errors. On the one side, we must beware of considering a child's religious impressions of little value. Like all beginnings of life and growth, they may be feeble and easily lost; they are still of infinite value as the preparation for that which abideth ever. We must, on the other side, be kept from overestimating or trusting in it. We must remember that the tender plant needs unceasing watching, and that only in the congenial atmosphere of a home holy to the Lord and wholly dedicated to His service can we count on its ripening fruit to eternal life.

We have already suggested what a child's faith needs.

Suffer the child to come to Jesus and remove every hindrance. Believe deeply what Jesus says, "of such is the kingdom," and allow this heavenly element in the child's nature to show itself and to reach out after the Son of God. In your education, may the coming to Jesus to be saved from sin, to have the heart sanctified and satisfied, be your chief end. Beware of coming between the child and Jesus; let the child under your leading have free access to Him. Beware of hindering him by distrust or coolness. Let the warmth of your love to Jesus, your holy example of obedience, your teaching and praying—in a word, your whole living—be a daily help to the child to see Jesus, to live with Him and to long for Him. Jesus Christ is meant to be our everyday friend, our every-hour companion. Let all the wondrous influence you possess in forming your child and fixing his destiny be wielded for this one thing: to satisfy the desire of the Saviour's heart and to make your child wholly His.

These words of Christ were spoken to the disciples who knew Him and confessed Him as the Son of God. They were sound in the faith, Christ's chosen friends. But they understood not His thoughts about the children; this was too high for them because the love of childlikeness is one of the highest things in the kingdom. Many a theologian and preacher and parent is not yet in sympathy with Jesus. Dear parents, you who have taken the Saviour as your only teacher in the revelation of the mysteries of divine love, let Him teach you the unmeasured worth of your little ones. Learn to see in them what He sees. In His light your care of them will become a blessing to yourself and to them.

*　*　*

Blessed Saviour, again do we beseech Thee, open our eyes to see in our little ones what Thou seest; to think of them as Thou dost, as belonging to Thee and the kingdom. Make this so clear to us that it may become impossible to do otherwise than to lead them to Thee. Let

174

Thy claim on them, Thy love to them, be the secret principle that inspires all our education.

And we ask, Lord, for a heavenly wisdom to know how to guide them in coming to Thee and to help them to abide with Thee. Teach us to estimate aright a child's impressions, both in their weakness and in their worth, as the seeds of the eternal life. And may our faith in Thy love to them and in their share in the kingdom be the power by which their young hearts are made strong.

Blessed Lord, Thou art the parents' and the children's Friend. "Come unto me" is Thy one call in every need and for every blessing. We come now, Lord, and ask grace to enable us to bring our children. Grant us Thy Holy Spirit that day by day, year by year, we may possess and train them for Thee alone and for Thy glory. Amen.

THIRTY-SECOND DAY

A Father's Tears

"And straightway the father of the child cried out,
and said with tears, Lord, I believe; help thou mine unbelief" (Mark 9:24).

When Jesus spoke to the disciples about the mothers
who were coming with their little children to Him, He
told them to allow the children to come and forbid them
not. In this story He uses a stronger word. When the
father of the lunatic had told Him that the disciples had
not been able to cast out the evil spirit and Jesus had
reproved their unbelief, He said, *Bring* him unto me."
The expression is a stronger one, setting forth the same
truth. The little ones were quite ready and willing to come
to the loving stranger to be blessed. This poor child, at
times all unconscious or rebellious, had to be brought,
whether he knew it or not. There can be no evil spirit
so strong, no resistance so desperate, but the parent has
the liberty and the power to bring his child to Jesus.
To every disciple, to every father and mother, in every
extremity of sin or need, Christ's voice is heard calling,
"Bring the child unto me."

If we want to understand what it is to bring to Jesus
a child on whom Satan has a hold, we have this most
clearly set forth in the further discourse of this father
with Jesus. When he had told the touching story of how

ever since his childhood the boy had been the prey of this terrible trouble and had pleadingly added, "*If thou canst* do anything, have compassion on us, and help us," Jesus threw the responsibility upon the father, saying, "*If thou canst believe*, all things are possible to him that believeth." The question was not whether Jesus could and would do it but whether the father could believe. If he did, the healing was sure; if he did not, it could not take place.

"If thou canst believe, all things are possible to him that believeth." These well-known words put all the blessings of God's mighty saving love at the disposal of faith. By faith we understand both what God has done and will do. By faith we see Him who is invisible, in the reality of His almighty power and His love towards ourselves. By faith we receive His word into our very heart as a quickening power that works in us the very thought and sentiment that was in His heart when He spoke it. By faith our heart, our nature, our life is opened up to give place to God, so as to let Him be and do in us what He pleases. By faith we become fully conscious of the purpose of His will and of himself as waiting to work it in us. By faith we forsake the visible, ourselves, with our own thoughts and strength; we look to God to do what He has promised and so give Him the glory. Faith is the exercise of a will that yields itself to God's holy will. "All things are possible to him that believeth" because "with God nothing shall be impossible," and faith is union with God.

In speaking these words to the father of the lunatic, Jesus gave to us for all time the secret of successful parental training and prayer. He tells us that it is not only the ministers of His gospel, the watchmen and the workers in fields of special danger or difficulty, but every Christian parent needs to exercise strong faith and who thereby most assuredly secure the salvation of his child. It teaches us that His compassion and power are longing to help us, if we can believe. If not, it is our blame if our children perish.

There are parents who think this is a hard saying. They seek the cause for unconverted and unsaved children in God and not in themselves. How can all the responsibility be thrown on our unbelief? Scripture reveals to us most clearly God's sovereignty; the final decision of the destiny of each man is in His hands. Scripture reveals as clearly man's responsibility and the all-prevailing power of faith. True humility accepts both statements, bowing to the solemn truth Jesus utters here: if the parent can believe the child can be saved.

How this truth ought to affect us, our text tells us. With tears the father cried, "Lord, I believe; help thou mine unbelief." In the agony of the thought that his unbelief may keep the blessing from his child, in the consciousness of the unbelief still in himself, he bursts into tears and casts himself at Jesus' feet to confess that unbelief and ask deliverance from it. It is amid these tears of penitence and confession that the faith is exercised to which the victory is given. The devil is cast out, and the child is saved. Christ's blessed and most heart-searching word had done its work; it had revealed the unbelief but also awakened the faith that brought the blessing.

Christ's word must do the same with every parent, with every father, who pleads for a child's liberation from Satan's power. A father's tears have power. There must be confession and humbling wherever there is to be strong faith. There must be the conviction and confession of the sin of unbelief—that it has been the cause of the blessing being withheld, and that we are verily guilty in being unbelieving. When the disciples asked the Master why they could not cast out this devil, He told them it was because of their unbelief and that this unbelief was caused by their life not being one of prayer and fasting.

Unbelief is not, as many think, a weakness, inexplicable and beyond our power. Unbelief has its reasons: it is the indication of the state of the heart. The worldly man cannot believe. The self-righteous men, the proud man, cannot believe. It is only the pure in heart, the humble, the soul that thirsts for God and forsakes all to follow Christ, that can be strong in faith. And therefore the first step in the path of an overcoming faith is the confession of its sinfulness, and the sins of which it is the index and the symptom.

I have heard parents plead very earnestly with God for the conversion of their grown-up children, secretly fearing that they could not be heard. I saw no sign of confession of parental sin. There are parents whose worldliness, whose lack of living faith, whose self-indulgence and neglect in the education of their children have sown the seeds of which they are now reaping the fruit in the departure of their children from God. And yet they wonder why their children are not more religious. They sometimes pray earnestly for them and try to have the faith, perhaps thinking they have it, that their children will be saved. They may be deceiving themselves. True faith sanctifies. It searches the heart. It confesses the sin of unbelief and all the sins in which that has its root and strength. It casts itself weeping and helpless at the feet of Jesus. There, and there alone, bowing in its weakness, resting on His strength, it obtains the blessing He loves to bestow.

Fathers, you who have sons you would fain bring to Jesus to be saved, come and hear the lessons the Lord would teach you. Let these children first bring you to Jesus in confession, prayer and trust; your faith can then bring them in truth. And in yourself and in them you will experience the all-prevailing power and truth of the word: "If thou canst believe, all things are possible to him that believeth."

* * *

Blessed Son of God, look in mercy upon a parent who now comes to Thee with a child still unconverted and under the power of the evil one. O Lord Jesus, have compassion on us and help us! Let the child be delivered from Satan's power. Oh, make him a child of God!

Lord, I have heard Thy voice, "If thou canst believe," and it has filled my heart with trembling. I have to confess how little my life has been a life of faith, and how my unbelief has hindered the blessing from my child. I have to confess the worldliness and selfishness, the want of entire surrender and obedience to Thee, which made a strong faith impossible. I bow in shame at the thought of all the unbelief that even now comes up in me. Lord, I do believe! Help Thou mine unbelief.

I do believe, Lord, in Thy mighty power. I do believe in thy infinite love. I do believe in Thee as my Saviour, my Friend, my Covenant Redeemer. I do believe, my Lord, that Thou hearest me now for this child. Lord, I believe! Help Thou mine unbelief. I look to Thy word and hold it fast. I yield myself to a life of entire surrender to Thee, to be Thine alone. Blessed Lord Jesus, I do believe! Thou hearest and savest my child. In this faith I praise Thy holy name. Amen.

THIRTY-THIRD DAY
The Sacredness of Motherhood

"He shall be filled with the Holy Ghost, even from his mother's womb" (Luke 1:15).

May God grant us His grace to meditate in holy tenderness and reverence on the truth revealed to us here, a truth of unspeakable worth and power to a believing parent: the mother's womb the work-place of the Holy Spirit. Our Lord taught us that the least in the kingdom of heaven is greater than John the Baptist; if John could be filled with the Holy Spirit from before his birth, how much more, now that Christ is glorified and the Holy Spirit given, can the child of those who have become partakers of the full redemption and the indwelling of the Spirit of Christ.

We find here, at the very opening of the New Testament history, the same truth that came out so strongly in laying the foundations of the covenant with the patriarchs. In preparing and securing servants to do His work, God loves to begin at the very beginning—from before the birth, from the very first conception of life, to take charge and to sanctify the vessel He is to use for His service. The more distinctly we apprehend this part of God's plan with His Church, this root-principle of the economy of redemption, the better shall we understand the holy privilege and duty of parentage. Very specially will mothers be encouraged and strengthened in faith to yield themselves, with all the hopes and joys of motherhood, to be God's chosen vessels for the fulfillment of His purpose and the perfecting of His Church.

Let us look first at what Scripture teaches us of *the mother* in whom the Holy Spirit is thus to work. Of John's parents it is testified: "They were both righteous before God, walking in all the commandments and ordinances of the Lord blameless" (Luke 1:6). The God of nature, who in this world of cause and effect has ordered that like begets like, is also the God of grace. Though omnipotent and ready to work any miracles He pleases, He yet most carefully observes His own laws; and when He wants a holy child, He seeks for holy parents. Throughout Scripture, especially in the New Testament, the blessed indwelling and inworking of the Holy Spirit is promised to the obedient. Man must, in obedience to divine command and under the preparatory moving of the Spirit, build the house; then does the Holy Spirit as the glory and the presence of the Lord take possession and fill it. And so it was of John's parents who walked in all the commandments and ordinances of the Lord blameless, that he would be born who was to be filled with the Holy Ghost from his mother's womb and the forerunner of Him who should baptize with the Holy Ghost. It is of holy parents that God would take a holy child.

The double lesson for every parent, especially for every mother, is of the deepest interest. A righteous and blameless life prepares for and may also count upon the power of the Holy Ghost in the unborn child. Let expectant mothers who would fulfill their holy calling as the ministers of their Lord's purposes study Elizabeth's character: "righteous . . . and walking in all the commandments of the Lord *blameless*." It is to such a life that God chose us, "that we should be holy and *without blame* before him in love." It is to such a life Jesus redeemed us: "He hath reconciled you in his body through death, to present you holy and *unblameable* and unreprovable in

His sight." Every child of God ought to be and can be "*blameless* and harmless, without blemish in the midst of a perverse generation." Especially every mother who would offer her body as the temple of the Holy Ghost should be holy, that in her the vey first beginnings of life may be overshadowed by the Holy Ghost.

Oh, that mothers, and fathers too, understood to what a terrible degree the spirit of the world and the flesh—a life in which blamelessness before God is never expected or sought after, in which sin and selfishness are allowed to have rule—hinder the influence of the Spirit and entail upon the child, more than is needed, the heritage of unholy appetite and passion. A life which in deep humility and the faith of Jesus as our sanctification seeks to walk in obedience and righteousness, blameless before the Lord, will be accepted and honored of Him. Parents, we have a right to ask, and most confidently to expect, the Spirit that is in us to take possession of the life God gives through us. This is the highest and the brightest hope of a holy motherhood: "He shall be filled with the Holy Ghost, even from his mother's womb."

Let us now look at the angel's message about *the child* thus conceived and born: "Thou shalt have joy and gladness; and many shall rejoice at his birth. For he shall be great in the sight of the Lord" (Luke 1:14). Here we find three marks of a child born under the covering of the Holy Spirit. The parents are to "have joy and gladness." Alas! how many a Christian parent has had reason to say in bitter agony, "Would God my child had never been born!" Do you wish to have divinely given and divinely secured joy and gladness in the children that are given you? Oh, let the Holy Spirit take possession of them from before their birth. Yours will be the holy joy of heaven in them as you see the beauty of the Lord upon them.

"And many shall rejoice at his birth." Would you have your child blessed and made a blessing, with many to thank God that they knew him, that he was born? Study the story of John's birth in connection with the story of

Jesus' birth. It was for Jesus' sake, in the power of the
Son of God coming in the flesh, in virtue of his connection
with Jesus, that John was thus filled with the Holy Ghost
from his mother's womb. Plead the coming and the birth
and the redemption of Jesus on behalf of your child; claim
the outpouring of the Spirit upon all flesh and the promise
of the Spirit to you and your children. Your faith will
be strengthened to perfect confidence that your child too
may in his measure be filled with the Spirit and shall
make many to rejoice at his birth.

"And he shall be great in the sight of the Lord." This
sets the crown on the whole. A joy to his parents, a blessing
to his fellowmen, and great in the sight of the Lord is
the Spirit-born child. Among men he may not make a
name, in gifts and talents he may not be great, but
great he will be in the sight of Him who sees not as
man sees. He will be a vessel God can use for His work,
a true way-preparer for the coming of the Lord in His
kingdom.

Mother, God gives you this picture of Elizabeth and
her child of promise with the double lesson: live as she
did, believe and receive what she did. Young mother,
your motherhood is in God's sight a holier and a more
blessed thing than you realize. If you are indeed God's
child, you have in everything been placed under the leading and the rule of His Holy Spirit. Be sure that all the
tender interest and solemn thought, all the quiet trust
and joyful hope which expectant motherhood calls forth
may be sanctified and refined by God's Holy Spirit, and
you be united with your little one under the overshadowing
of His heavenly grace.

*　*　*

Ever blessed God, once more Thou hast shown me
Thy way in preparing a seed to serve Thee. What a deep
interest Thou hast in securing a holy and blameless motherhood! I have seen Thee training a mother for Thy service. Thou dost fill her heart with the thought of the divine

destiny of her child. Thou dost stir her faith to the confident expectation of Thy divine Spirit and blessing on her seed. Thou dost call her in righteousness and blamelessness of life to her holy work. Thou dost in all things teach her that the life she is to bring forth is a holy gift from Thee, to be received and borne in a pure and holy vessel.

O Thou great and glorious God, in deep humility and trembling Thy handmaid bows before Thee, to offer herself to Thy service. O my Father, Thou who dost give the Holy Spirit much more surely than earthly fathers give good gifts to their children, fulfill Thy wondrous promise to Thy child. Let Thy Holy Spirit dwell in me. If it please Thee to make me the mother of a child, oh, let him be filled with the Spirit from the womb. Let me be filled with the Spirit. And let my child be born for this one thing only, that he may be great in Thy sight and a blessing to all around him. Amen.

THIRTY-FOURTH DAY

A Mother's Surrender

"And Mary said, Behold the handmaid of the Lord; be it unto me according to thy word" (Luke 1:38).

We have had occasion to notice the wonderful oneness between mother and child and the extent to which it influences and decides what the child is to be. The life the mother imparts is her own life, in the deepest meaning of the term. When God gave His Son to be born of a woman, this law was not violated; the mother He chose for His Son was doubtless all that grace could make her to be—the fit vessel through whom He should receive His human nature and disposition.

Just as Jesus himself is in everything our example, so we may naturally expect that in His mother God has given us one of His servants who may be an example to other mothers. If the child Jesus be an example to our children, there will be something for mothers to learn from His mother. She to whom the heavenly messenger said, "Hail, thou that art highly favoured, the Lord is with thee: blessed art thou among women"; and to whom also Elizabeth, filled with the Holy Ghost, said, "Blessed art thou among women, and blessed is the fruit of thy womb, . . . and blessed is she that believed," will surely in her words and ways have left an example for every

mother who yields herself like Mary to the Lord, to bear
a child that can be called a son of the Most High. Were
there more mothers like Mary—this we may confidently
say, without forgetting the infinite distance between her
child and ours—there would be more children like the
holy child Jesus.

From the human side, what constitutes the most
marked feature of Mary's motherhood? It is the childlike
simplicity of faith in which she surrenders herself to the
divine purpose: "Behold the handmaid of the Lord; be
it unto me according to thy word." She calls herself the
Lord's slave or bondwoman; she gives her will, herself,
up to Him, to do what pleases Him; in quiet trust and
expectancy she will look to Him to do what He has said.

The same spirit of obedient faith which had once fitted
Abraham to be the father of the promised seed now prepares her to become the mother of Him in whom the
promise is to be fulfilled. Not that there were no difficulties or questionings. We read, "She was troubled at
his saying, and cast in her mind what manner of salu-
tation this should be." When again he had spoken, she
feared not to ask, "How shall this be, seeing I know not
a man?" But when once the angel had spoken to her
of the power of the Most High overshadowing her, she
yielded herself to the divine word. And she became an
example to every mother who would, like her, share the
benediction, "Blessed is she that believed: for there shall
be a performance of those things which were told her
from the Lord." It is the surrender of faith that makes
a blessed motherhood: "Blessed art thou, and blessed
is the fruit of thy womb."

"Behold the handmaid of the Lord." Mary teaches a
mother to yield herself to God for the service of His kingdom, that in her His purpose and glory may be made manifest. It was not by the birth of Mary's son alone that God's
kingdom was to come. Believing parents may look upon
their children as the stones in the great temple of which
Jesus was the cornerstone. Not less than the birth of Isaac
and every child of the chosen race down to Christ is the

birth of each of our children under God's guardianship a link in the golden chain of God's will. Over all the impulses of human love and the instincts of a God-given maternity there hovers a divine purpose, the carrying out of His plan. And nothing will do more to sanctify the life of the wife and mother than when she realizes herself to be the Lord's bondwoman, that from her the chosen seed may be multiplied and from her may be born a generation to serve the Lord. Human love will receive a divine consecration; what otherwise appears to be only natural and earthly is elevated into the heavenlies, into God's will and God's favor; the expectant mother knows herself to be like the angels—one of His servants, doing His commandments, hearkening unto the voice of His word.

"Be it unto me according to thy word." Such is the faith that gives the strength to surrender oneself to God's service. It looks no longer at difficulties or impossibilities; it counts upon God to carry out His purpose and to give the grace and the strength for the work to which He has called us. And it is just this faith that above everything fits for the blessed duties of motherhood, that gives that quiet rest of body and spirit which to mother and babe is health and strength.

What mother is there who, as she first becomes conscious of her new vocation, is not at times with Mary greatly troubled, and does not feel the question come many a time, How can all this be? She finds no rest so sure or sweet as to cast her troubles on her Lord, letting Him do what seemeth to Him good. If the God of nature has created her for a calling, and the God of grace has redeemed her to fulfill that calling in the interests of His kingdom, she assuredly may trust His power and love not to forsake her in her hour of need. "What hour I am afraid I will trust in thee; in God have I put my trust, I will not be afraid"; such words have a thousand times over been the stay of the trembling but trusting handmaid of the Lord.

"Be it unto me according to thy word." To understand

fully the teaching of Mary's example here, there is one trait of her character we must not omit. Twice it is said of her, "Mary kept all these things, and pondered them in her heart." In the holy quiet of meditation and reflection on what God has said, the spirit of trust is cultivated. It is only as God's words are kept and pondered in the heart that they can quicken and deepen a living faith in Him who spoke them.

Every mother who searches Holy Scripture will find many a saying of God with reference to her sacred calling which, if truly received, will fill the heart with confidence and joy. They will teach her to regard everything connected with the birth of the child as a matter of deepest interest to the Father in heaven and of great importance to His kingdom. She will see how all the exceeding great and precious promises may be claimed by her for the little one, before yet it has seen the light. She will see how her receiving the little one in the name of Jesus has the promise of Jesus' presence for herself and for him. She will find that all the ordering and training of the child has been provided for in regulations of divine wisdom and love, and that all the grace needed for carrying out these orders is most surely given to each one who, like Mary, will but be a bondmaid of the Lord and will believe what He has spoken. All of care and fear, of danger and pain in the life of motherhood, all the help and joy and rich reward God has connected with it—all is written in the Book of the Lord; the mother who listens, and waits, and believes will, in view both of what she fears and what she hopes, be able to say, "Behold the handmaid of the Lord; be it unto me according *to thy word*." As she waits her time, let quiet retirement, in which she not only hides herself from the world but opens her whole being to the rays of heaven, let thoughtful, trustful pondering of God's words engage the heart, and she will find how true the word is, "*Blessed* is she that believed."

What a holy and blessed thing the birth of a child becomes in the light of the birth of Jesus! What a holy and blessed task that of the mother becomes in the light of the favor of the Most High God—the means of the fulfillment of His purpose, the promotion of His glory, the experience of His special grace and mercy!

As the mother ponders these things, she will understand something of the deep meaning of that word of Paul, "She shall be saved through the childbearing, if they continue in faith, and love, and sanctification, with sobriety." Just as labor in the sweat of his brow was given to man, to be in his fallen state one of his greatest blessings, so the labor of childbearing was given to the woman that through it and its blessed discipline the salvation of Christ might the more effectually be wrought into her whole character and disposition. It calls and helps to a continuance in that blessed life of faith and trustful dependence, of love and gentleness and motherly kindness, of holiness in the indwelling and sanctification of the Spirit, of sobriety and self-restraint and temperance in which true blessedness is found. It helps, to them who are rightly exercised thereby, to form that perfect womanly character which is one of God's most beautiful gifts on earth. It is in this path of loving acceptance of God's appointment and trustful resting in His promise that the word will come true, a greeting to each expectant mother: Blessed art thou, and blessed is the fruit of thy womb.

* * *

Behold the handmaid of the Lord! Yes, Lord, as Thou hast already looked upon her in Thy mercy and set her apart for the sacred work of bearing and bringing up a seed for Thee, still continue to look upon her and give her all that she needs, to work in her all that is well pleasing in Thy sight. "As the eye of a maid unto the hand of her mistress, so our eyes look unto the Lord our God, until he have mercy upon us." Grant to Thy child the blessed assurance that in this holy calling of motherhood she is indeed Thy handmaiden, called to the fulfillment of Thy purposes, set apart for the service of Thy kingdom. Let this thought teach me to look upon everything connected with the birth of my child as of deepest interest to my Father. Let it encourage me to cast every fear and burden, every care and pain on Him in whose service they come. Let it sanctify all the hope and joy with which Thou dost so wonderfully sweeten pain of childbearing.

And so let it be unto me according to Thy word. In childlike faith, O my Lord, I would take Thy blessed Word, with all its teachings and its promises, as my light and strength. In the time of patient waiting, in the hour of anguish, Thy Word shall be my stay. Let Thy Holy Spirit unfold to Thy handmaiden the treasures Thy Word contains for her as mother that she may know at the right time to receive what Thou hast provided for her. May she be so prepared that the child which has been received according to Thy word may be trained according to that Word and enter into the full enjoyment of all that Thy Word holds out in promise to the seed of Thy people. Behold the handmaid of the Lord! Be it unto me according to Thy word. Amen.

THIRTY-FIFTH DAY
A Mother's Thanksgiving

"And Mary said, My soul doth magnify the Lord, and
my spirit hath rejoiced in God my Saviour. For he hath
regarded the low estate of his handmaiden" (Luke 1:
46-48).

There is perhaps no moment of such exquisite joy,
of deep, unutterable thanksgiving taking the place of pain
and sorrow, as when a mother knows herself to be the
living mother of a living child. Our blessed Lord used
this as the type of that wondrous surprise, that strange
resurrection joy with which His disciples should find Him
whom they mourned as crucified and dead to be the living
One. "A woman when she is in travail hath sorrow, because her hour is come: but as soon as she is delivered
of the child, she remembereth no more the anguish, for
joy that a man is born into the world" (John 16:21).

A mother will find no more fitting expression for her
joy than in thanksgiving to Him to whom she owes so
much. And for the expression of that thanksgiving she
will find in many portions of Holy Scripture the most
suitable language. Often, for instance, the mother has
almost instinctively asked that the words of Psalm 103
be read: "Bless the Lord, O my soul: and all that is
within me, bless his holy name. Bless the Lord, O my
soul, and forget not all his benefits: who forgiveth all

thine iniquities; who healeth all thy diseases; who redeemeth thy life from destruction; who crowneth thee with lovingkindness and tender mercies; who satisfieth thy mouth with good things; so that thy youth is renewed like the eagle's." But as the simple summary of all a mother has to say, no words more beautiful will be found than these of the mother of our Lord: "My soul doth magnify the Lord, and my spirit doth rejoice in God my Saviour. For he hath regarded the low estate of his handmaiden."

In His holy providence the Father has ordered that the first week after the birth of the little one is a time of weakness, a time when nothing is so needed as quiet and rest for the restoration of nature's exhausted powers. The arrangement is one of wondrous grace, giving the mother time to prepare herself again for her new duties. While household duties and ordinary communication are kept at comparative distance, the Lord would keep His child for a little while in the secret place of His holy presence to encourage and instruct her for the solemn responsibilities now again awaiting her. And there is nothing that will be more pleasing to her Lord, more refreshing and strengthening for her own life and a more fitting preparation for blessing to the little one, than that the spirit of thanksgiving should give its bright tone to all her thoughts and hopes. The song of praise, from the lips of the model-mother, should be repeated day by day, from hour to hour: "My soul doth magnify the Lord, and my spirit doth rejoice in God my Saviour. For he hath regarded the low estate of his handmaiden. . . . For he that is mighty hath done to me great things; and holy is his name; and his mercy is on them that fear him from generation to generation."

It is hardly necessary to remind a mother of all there is to stir her to praise. She has but to think of the anxious thoughts and fears that would sometimes come as the solemn hour of her trial rose up before her, and her song is, "I sought the Lord, and he heard me, and delivered me from all my fears." She looks at the precious little treasure that has been given her, with all the love and joy it brings into heart and home; and the words come spontaneously, "What shall I render to the Lord for all his benefits toward me?" As she looks upon the little one in the light of God's purpose and promise, she sees an immortal being, fitted for showing forth God's glory on earth and sharing that glory in heaven, a jewel in Jesus' crown; and her soul bows in trembling wonder at the thought that the charge of keeping and forming such a treasure should be committed to one so feeble. She remembers that through her this child has the promise of the covenant and the earnest of the Spirit; her child is holy because she is one of God's holy ones in Christ.

Mothers, think of all the grace and wisdom and strength provided in Christ to secure to you and your child all that God's love has prepared. Listen to the voice, "My grace is sufficient for thee: my strength is made perfect in weakness," and sing again with Mary, "My soul doth magnify *the Lord*, and my spirit doth rejoice in God *my Saviour* . . . his mercy is on them that fear him, from generation to generation." It is not only God's mercies but God himself in whose love they have their value and their continuance; *it is God himself* in whom Mary, in whom the believer, in whom the grateful mother, is glad and rejoices. True praise uses God's mercies only as the steps of the ladder along which it rises, leaving the mercies behind and rejoicing in God alone.

This spirit of thanksgiving in which we rise up to the God who gave them is of greater worth than can well be expressed. It elevates and sanctifies both the joy, the gift that causes it, and the glad possessor, because it lifts all out of the sphere of nature into the fellowship of the spiritual and the divine. And in this way it is the true preparation for all the work the mother has before her. We saw in Mary's surrender of herself to her God that there were combined in it two elements: the surrender to the work she had to perform ("Behold the handmaid of the Lord") and the trust that counted on God to do for her what He had promised ("Be it unto me according to thy word"). In both of these aspects the thanksgiving and joy of the hour of deliverance, if cultivated and kept up, will be guidance and strength.

"Behold the bondmaid of the Lord." The labor of bearing a child is but the beginning of that labor of love to which God has appointed and set apart the mother. The whole work of rearing and guarding and training the child is now to follow. The spirit of thanksgiving is the best preparation for the altar of consecration. If the mother is indeed to receive grace for the right and successful fulfillment of this new charge, she will need on her part a very distinct consciousness and confession of unfitness, a very definite giving up of herself to be henceforth the Lord's willing, loving slave for this holy work. As she looks at how much there is that has to be parted with and put away, how much that she will have to struggle against and overcome to be the holy mother of a holy child, entirely consecrated to God, the thought may come that the sacrifice and the strain will be too great, that it is impossible to live so strictly, so entirely and peculiarly given up to God's service. We fear to be too different from others; God could bless us and our children even though we are not so very holy.

Oh, that a mother, if such thoughts come, would just pause and think of what God has done! There is the new life given to her and to her precious little one, there is the love and mercy of God and all the promise of more love and mercy to be poured out. Has the thanksgiving been so shallow, has the joy been so selfish and earthly, that there can be any hesitation as to whom these lives shall belong? God forbid! If the thanksgiving has been true, it cannot but lead the mother to say that utterly and entirely she will live for God that she may have grace to train a child who, too, shall utterly and entirely be the Lord's. "The joy of the Lord is your strength"; a mother's joy is the power for a mother's work. The spirit of thanksgiving leads to the altar of consecration where mother and child are laid as living sacrifices to be the Lord's alone.

"Be it unto me according to thy word"; this word of faith and trust gets new meaning after the experience of the first part of its fulfillment. In all the work that waits the mother in the future, the goodness just experienced teaches her to trust. Let her yield herself heartily not to her work but to her God for His work; she may depend upon His teaching and His help and His strength; they are realities. Let her in the joyful spirit of praise read His Word. As she studies what it says of a mother on earth, she should note what it says of the Father in heaven and the abounding grace He has undertaken to supply. Her faith will grow strong that her vow of surrender has been accepted, that its fulfillment is possible and certain, and that the joy of a child born into the world is but the beginning of a joy that shall know no ending. Let thanksgiving lift the heart to God in praise; there faith becomes easy. Let faith lift the heart to God too; there thanksgiving becomes natural, and the life of mother and child may become one unceasing song of faith and love, of surrender and obedience, of thanksgiving and praise.

* * *

Blessed be the Lord, for He hath showed me His marvellous kindness! Bless the Lord, O my soul, and forget not all His benefits! What shall I render to the Lord for all His benefits toward me?

O my Father, in this the time of weakness and gladness of heart, Thy handmaid draws nigh to praise Thy mercy and Thy love. Here am I and this precious child Thou hast given me, the witnesses of Thy power and Thy goodness; may our lives, all our days, devoted to Thee, be the sacrifice of thanksgiving we bring Thee.

Oh, hear the prayer of Thy handmaid! Let my life, now received anew as from Thy hand, indeed become wholly new. In daily communion with my Father, in close following and fellowship with my Lord Jesus, in a very tender yielding to the leading and sanctifying of the Holy Spirit, I desire henceforth to live only and wholly as Thy handmaid.

And with myself, Lord, I offer Thee my precious child. Let the grace I have implored of Thee fit me from the very birth to hold this child as Thy property, a sacred trust from Thee to nurse and train as Thine. This one comes from Thee, O my God, a gift to me; accept my child from me again, a living gift to Thee. Come to Thy handmaid, I pray Thee, in this her time of weakness and thanksgiving; in this time of holy quietness let Thy presence overshadow me and give me the assurance that my prayer is heard, that Thou hast accepted me and my little one to keep as Thine own for evermore. Amen.

THIRTY-SIXTH DAY
Jesus, the Children's Surety

"They brought him to Jerusalem, to present him to the Lord; (as it is written in the law of the Lord, Every male that openeth the womb shall be called holy to the Lord;) and to offer a sacrifice according to that which is said in the law of the Lord" (Luke 2:22-24).

According to the law of God in Israel, a child was circumcised in the home when eight days old. On the fortieth day the mother was to appear in the temple to bring the sacrifice of her purification and to present her child to the Lord. If the child was a firstborn, then the presentation had special reference to the firstborn belonging to the Lord, and the child had to be redeemed. The child Jesus was also to be presented to the Lord, being made under the law and like unto His brethren in all things. This was not only that He might experience everything we pass through but that we might know that every state and condition has been sanctified by His holy presence and merit. By giving us the Spirit which was in Him during those experiences, He will impart to us the blessing and the sanctifying grace that flow from fellowship with Him. This truth has thoughts of wonderful joy and comfort for parents as they bring their little ones to God's home, to present them to the Lord.

Let us study this presentation of the holy child Jesus.

There He is, presented to His Father in heaven by His earthly parents. He is a helpless infant but yet a pleasing sacrifice, a sweet-smelling savor. There, too, He comes as the firstborn among many brethren, the forerunner through whom our little ones too can be acceptable to the Holy One. For now when we present our child to the Lord, He looks down from heaven on the offering and gives to our child the spirit of His holy childhood. He was indeed made like us that we might become like Him; He was made like unto our children that they might be made like Him.

He was not only Mary's firstborn but the Father's firstborn among many brethren. Where the firstfruits are holy the whole family is holy. The presentation of the child Jesus to the Father gives us a right to present ours and makes them acceptable too. Blessed thought! I can place my child beside the holy child and in faith claim that in Him my child is holy and accepted too.

In Israel the presentation of the child was accompanied with a sacrifice to cleanse away the defilement of sin. This we need too. And what a mercy that the mother now can look to the blessed Jesus, the great sin-offering and atonement (Lev. 12:6), for her cleansing from all sin, so that she may be accepted and fitted for being a true mother to this child! And what mercy that the children also share in the efficacy of that great sacrifice even before they know it! From their birth they now are holy to the Lord and may receive that Holy Spirit which is the lawful inheritance of the seed of God's believing people.

The object of this presentation of the children in the temple was especially to acknowledge God's claim upon them and to give them to Him as His property. With what gladness and confidence parents do this when first they have been shown Jesus' presentation in the temple! What does this mean? Has the eternal God not spared His only-begotten Son but given Him up for us and our children? Has He in very deed given His Son, the Lord of glory, to be our and our children's possession, to enter into all their feebleness and misery, to be subjected to a birth needing purification and presentation with sacrifice, and to a death like ours under the curse? And shall we now withhold our children from Him? Let us most gladly present them before Him to be only and wholly His, devoted to His service and glory. Let us place our little one beside this holy child, on His merits, and say, "Father, through Thy holy child Jesus—with Him, in Him, like Him—I present my child to Thee, to be the Lord's only and for ever!"

Be assured that in such a presenting of your child, after the example and in the power and spirit of God's child, there is a rich and sure blessing. Presented to God in Jesus, accepted in Jesus, he may now grow up with and like Jesus. Let your faith lay hold of the holy child-life of Jesus as belonging to your child, as communicable by the power of the Holy Spirit. Let your faith maintain and renew daily the solemn act in which you as parent appeared before the Lord to present your child to Him before you took him back to your home to rear and train. Let your faith rejoice in the divine transaction in which, when you presented your child in the name of Jesus, he *was accepted of the Father as His own*. What we present to God, "according to that which is said in the law of the Lord," that God takes in accordance with His word. And what He takes He keeps. And our faith has only to look to God's taking and keeping to have the joyful assurance that the matter is finally settled between God and us. Let this faith make you strong to train the child for God, in a strength and grace which He will give, to secure His property for himself. Let this faith speak to your child, as he is ready to receive it, of his having been presented with Jesus, like Jesus, in Jesus, to the Father, and of his fellowship in the life and spirit of Him who became the children's Surety.

Let the holy childhood of Jesus overshadow and sanctify the childhood of your little one. Let your children

grow up in His friendship and footsteps. Live in everything
as those who are going to train children to be like Jesus.
If the thought appears too high, ask the Father whether
He does indeed desire your child to be wholly like His
and whether He does expect you to train him so. The
answer will not be withheld. The presentation of Jesus
in the temple will become to you a pledge of the grace
that enables you to train him accordingly.

We all know how, in the economy of grace and in the
work of salvation for man, there are always two powers
in action, the divine and the human. To the former cor-
responds faith that ever looks to God's promise and power;
to the latter, works, without which faith cannot be perfected and which obeys and fulfills the will of God. In
our study of the teachings of God's Word on the parent's
calling, we have found how these two aspects of truth
are presented in turn, and how though at one moment
everything appears to depend upon a parent's faith in
what God does, very soon after a parent's character and
conduct appear to decide all. The two are inseparably
interwoven; the more intently we pursue the one line of
thought, the clearer will the other become. And we shall
see that the deeper our insight into the indispensable necessity of either, the greater will be our felt need of
the other as its complement.

We have here again been meditating on the spiritual
side and apparently speaking less of the practical training of daily life. Let all parents be assured that there
is nothing more intensely practical than an act of real
faith. If our presenting a child to the Lord be the deed
of an intelligent, childlike, heartfelt faith, it will have
its mighty influence on our daily treatment of the child.
If it be renewed from day to day, it will have its effect
on our whole relation to the little one growing up under
our care. As we think of this little one as God's devoted
and accepted property, as we regard ourselves as trustees
to whom he has been committed for keeping and training,
as we realize how God never would expect of our feeble-

ness to take charge aright of an immortal spirit without
providing the grace to do it well, and as we give ourselves
with the child to a life of consecration and holiness, our
faith will be the vital principle ruling all our conduct.
Sanctifying our home life and elevating our education to
what God would have it be, our faith will be the work
of His Spirit, transforming through our life each child,
who, like Jesus, has been presented to Him, into the likeness of the life of Him who is the firstborn among many
brethren.

* * *

Eternal God, who art the Father of our Lord Jesus
Christ and in Him of all that is truly childlike in heaven
and on earth, see us draw nigh to Thee with our little
one to present him to the Lord. We bring him to Thee,
that Thou mayest regard him in Thy great compassion,
cleansing from sin and accepting him as Thine own to
be set apart and sealed as holy to the Lord. We do this
in the assurance of faith and hope, because Thine own
holy child Jesus was once, as the firstborn, presented
in the place and on behalf of all who are brought to Thee.
Blessed God, beside Him and in Him, the children's Surety,
we present our child unto the Lord.

We beseech Thee, enlighten our understanding to apprehend fully all that Thy Son's being made like our children implies and secures. Strengthen our faith to apprehend and accept all the fullness of blessing it has opened
to us. Let the holy childhood of Jesus be the protection
of the childhood of our child. May the fact that he has
been presented to Thee as Jesus was be the beginning
and the power of a likeness that shall take possession
of the whole life. And give grace to Thy servants to be
the worthy parents and guardians and guides of a child
who has been presented to the Lord. For His sake, Oh,
our Father. Amen.

THIRTY-SEVENTH DAY

The Baptism with Water and the Spirit

"John answered, saying, Unto them all, I indeed baptize you with water; but one mightier than I cometh, the latchet of whose shoes I am not worthy to unloose: he shall baptize you with the Holy Ghost and with fire" (Luke 3:16).

Man has a twofold nature: the external and visible; and the internal, unseen, spiritual. Sin brought both equally under the power of the curse. In redemption both are to be made partakers of the glorious liberty of the children of God: "We wait for our adoption, to wit, the redemption of our body." The whole man, body and spirit, is to be saved. All God's dealings with us include both sides of our nature. Through the external He seeks to reach the inner man; the inner is renewed that the blessing may stream out and take possession of the outer man.

It is on this ground that we have the twofold baptism of which our text speaks: the baptism with water and the baptism with the Holy Spirit. John the Baptist teaches us the relationship existing between the two—the insufficiency of the baptism with water in itself and its high value as the pledge and the preparation of what was to come.

First we note the *faith* which the baptism with water warrants and demands as a sign and seal of the baptism of the Spirit. It is a *sign* in which God sets forth the working of regeneration, the cleansing of our nature by the renewal of the Holy Spirit. It is also a *seal*, an assurance that where God has given the water He most certainly gives the Spirit too. When John had come, the coming of Christ was certain too; when John had baptized with water, the baptism with the Spirit was certain too. God gave the one to awaken faith and expectation for the other. So intimate is the connection that our Saviour did not hesitate to speak of being "born of water and the Spirit."

God would teach us that what He has meant to be one and made one in promise, our faith can make one in reality. As in the whole economy of grace the connecting link between God's promise and His fulfillment is our faith, so here too. The promise of God is no empty word, though our unbelief may make it of none effect. In His purpose the water and the Spirit are inseparably united: "What God hath joined together, let no man put asunder." Let not a parent's unbelief rest content without the Spirit. Claim and accept with the most assured confidence the baptism of the Spirit for your child, and in faith believe for it as the divinely secured heritage of thy little one.

Let us now observe the *work* to which the baptism with water calls and pledges us. The whole history of John teaches us that the Spirit could not be received until the way had been prepared for Him. The Baptist knows how little his labors avail until the baptism of the Spirit is given. And yet he labors. He does the double work of preaching repentance of sin and faith in the Lamb of God—a most blessed lesson for the Christian parent.

In some children the workings of the Spirit begin immediately. In others they become manifest at very different stages of later growth. But in all the manifestation of the Spirit needs a parent's education in the lines of John's preaching. The child needs to be taught what sin is and what repentance is. He needs to be led to the giving up of everything that is not according to the will of God.

And he needs to be pointed to Jesus, the Lamb of God, through faith in whom the full influx of the Spirit is to come. Just as in the parent there is to be the harmony of faith and work, so the child no less from its earliest youth has to be trained for a God who asks to be trusted and obeyed. It is by the obedience of faith that parent and child are prepared for the fulfillment of the promise.

Learn one more lesson from John. The secret of the wondrous union between faith and work in him you will find in his deep *humility*. His preaching had been with mighty power. A great revival of religion was taking place. All men were flocking to him; no prophet in Israel had ever preached as he had done. And yet he says, "The latchet of whose shoes I am not worthy to unloose." The more the soul has received of the vision and the fellowship and the power of the Holy One, the deeper the sense of utter nothingness and absolute dependence; but then, also, the deeper the confidence in the truth and power of Him who is seen, the greater the courage for His work. The thought might rise or we might even hear others say that the assured confidence of the Spirit's being given to *our* children may lead to pride or may slacken exertion in their behalf. He who understands what faith is knows the answer. True faith and deep humility are inseparable, because faith is becoming nothing to let God be all. And so true faith and faithful labor are no less inseparable, because faith yields itself to God to use and to work through us. Let it be with the parent as with John; there is nothing makes us so strong to honor God as when we are bound by the threefold cord of strong faith, earnest effort, and deep humility.

Christian parent, have you accepted the promise of the Spirit with the water? Oh, hold that promise fast in a living faith. Praise God unceasingly for His gift to your child, even when you do not yet see its fulfillment. In your daily home life let everything be subordinated to the high destiny for which God has entrusted a child to you: he is to be a vessel filled with His Spirit. Labor earnestly and hopefully with this blessed prospect in view.

As often as these labors show you your impotence or unfaithfulness, look to Him whose servant you are and who has made you the messenger of the Spirit. He will fit you for the work He has given you to do. Jesus has said, "He that believeth in me, out of his innermost being shall flow rivers of living water." Believe in Jesus! Try again, and once again, and ever more again the unexhausted fullness of that word. Live your life by the faith of the Son of God. Through you the Spirit will flow out to your child. And each presentation of a child to God will be the glad reminder of the riches of the inheritance of your child too.

And you ministers of Christ who may read these lines, seek, oh, seek, like John, to testify that He who has sent you to baptize with water has said to you that there is One coming after you who will baptize with the Holy Spirit! Let us pray God to make all His servants indeed ministers of the Spirit. May they have grace to speak and act as men who have realized that the Spirit has been given to follow and to seal the message and the work of faith. And especially may they have grace to lead and train both parents and children into the apprehension of that presence of the Holy Spirit in their home life, through which the family can again take its place as God's first and choicest ordinance for the maintenance and the extension of the kingdom of heaven.

* * *

Lord God, teach me, teach all believing parents, teach Thy Church, to believe that wherever in Thy name the baptism of water is received, Thou waitest to give the baptism of the Spirit too. In the great gift of Thy Son, Thou hast given us Him who baptizeth with the Holy Spirit.

Blessed Lord Jesus, I come to Thee with my children. I bring them to Thee. I claim for them the baptism of the Spirit. In faith I accept and train them to believe in Thee that they may by faith in Thee come into the personal possession of what I have received for them. Yea, before they can yet believe, I offer myself, that through me and the influence of my life Thy blessed Spirit may rest upon them.

Blessed Saviour, give me grace in this faith to train them wisely, according to Thy will, preparing in them the way of the Lord. Amid the consciousness of unworthiness and impotence, may this be my one hope and aim: that my children may daily live under the rule of Thy Holy Spirit. Amen.

THIRTY-EIGHTH DAY

A Faith Home

"There cometh one from the ruler of the synagogue's house, saying to him, Thy daughter is dead; trouble not the Master. But when Jesus heard it, he answered him, saying, Fear not: believe only, and she shall be made whole" (Luke 8:49, 50).

Fear not; only believe! To many thousands that word has been the messenger of comfort and hope. As they struggled under the burden of sin, or sought for help in trial or difficulty, it told them that there was deliverance from fear in believing in Jesus. Faith can banish fear. And yet how many who have found a blessing in this word have forgotten that it is a word that especially belongs to parents. In every other use it is but a loan; it is as parents that we have full right to it. It is Jesus, the Lord of the home, of parents and children, who speaks: Fear not, only believe. The word reminds of the needful double lesson: in our children there is every reason for fear, in Jesus every reason for faith.

When we think of the tendency to evil they inherit from us and the mighty power Satan has in this world, we may well fear. When we see, both in Scripture and in the world around us, how often the bright promise of childhood is blighted and the children of a religious home depart into the ways of evil and of death, we may well fear. When we think of the dangers to which they often are exposed, in the little friends of their childhood, in the schools through which they must pass, in the spirit of the world with which they must come into contact, in the literature and the amusements and the business from which they cannot be kept separate, we may well fear.

And then, when we think of our children, and realize how feeble and unfit and unfaithful we are to take charge of them, the fear grows stronger. Will they indeed secure the blessing prepared for them? We know how the atmosphere we create and breathe through our home is stronger than all precept or external practice. Would God that there were more of earnest, hearty fear of the power of sin and death!

To such the word of Jesus comes: Fear not; only believe. Only believe, for faith is the one condition through which the power and the salvation of God are given. Only believe, for it is by faith that we throw ourselves and our children on Jesus and secure His blessing. Only believe, and let faith look upon God's covenant with us and our seed, seeing how He gives us all the grace we need as parents as well as all the grace our children need. Only believe, because it is faith that is the mighty renewing power in a man's life, teaching him to obey and do all that God has commanded. Only believe—this is the one thing Jesus asks of the parent who truly seeks his child's deliverance from sin and death and fears lest he fail to secure it.

This is now the one lesson we must seek to learn: a parent who has come to Christ with his child has as the first duty faith. Just as with the penitent sinner or the believer seeking more grace, all things are possible to him that believeth. Our domestic, our personal life, must be a life of faith. We must have not only the heart but the home, too, purified by faith. Faith is the one thing God asks for in His children; and if the family constitution indeed be divine and a holy parentage God's first means of grace to the little ones, we cannot be too earnest in reminding each other that parental faith is the only spring of parental duty and parental obedience, parental happiness and parental blessing. *Only believe* must be written on the doorposts of our homes. It must be the animating power of all we are and do for our children. It must indeed be, in the fullest sense of the word, our only care and aim: Jesus said, "Only believe."

It may be well to remember what God's Word says of faith and its actings in that portion so specially devoted to it, Hebrews 11. There we read: faith understands; faith offers a more excellent sacrifice; faith pleases God; faith saves the household; faith obeys when it is called; faith receives strength to bear a child; faith offers up the child; faith blesses the children; faith hides the little one; faith saves the firstborn.

Faith is first the spiritual understanding that receives the revelation of God and His purpose. *It hears His voice*; it listens to His call; it believes His promises. Then it is a divine energy, a living principle of action that carries out God's will and inherits all His blessing. It is especially the parent's grace we see in Noah, Abraham, Sarah, Jacob, Moses' parents, and Moses. In each case it was faith that made it possible, made it simple and easy as parents to be the channels of a divine blessing to their children.

The power to understand God's purpose with our children, to save our household, to obey God's will in all its rule, to offer our children to God, to bless our sons and to save them from the destroyer, all depends upon our faith. The living Christ, in whom is our salvation and our strength, every needed blessing and grace for us and our children—it is He who speaks, "Only believe." It is in the knowledge of what He is—it is in His presence —that such a faith is possible and must prevail.

Has He not redeemed our children as well as ourselves from the power of sin? Has He not come to make the covenant of promise, "thy God and the God of thy house," a brighter and fuller reality than ever it was to Abraham? Has He not secured for us, in the Holy Spirit, a power from on high to fulfill every obligation that rests on us as God's children—this one of keeping our children for Him to whom we belong? Has He not made true all the promises given of old, of God's Spirit upon our offspring, of God's Word not departing from the mouth of our seed's seed forevermore, in that one word on the day of Pentecost, "the promise is to you and to your children"? Can we not count upon Him to give for us and each child just what we need if only we believe?

"Only believe!" Let us take the command literally; faith has never yet been disappointed. Living faith will teach us to see new beauty and worth in our children. Living faith will awaken in us new earnestness and desire in everything to hold and to train them for God alone. Living faith will give its own hopeful and confiding tone to all our communion with God for them and in all our communion with them too. The birth of our children, our love to them, our prayer with and for them, our watching against their sins and reproving them, our teaching and training, their lessons and employments and pleasure—all will be under the inspiring and regulating power of *only believe*.

It hardly need be said that such a faith life in the home is not possible without the faith life in the heart. We cannot be to our children more than we are to God. It is no longer I that live, but Christ that lives in me; I live by the faith of the Son of God. This must be the language of the father, the mother, who would have a home filled with faith. It is not only in moments of special need and prayer or when we are in direct contact with the children that Jesus says, "Only believe." No, day by day, hour by hour, it must be, "I live by the faith of the Son of God."

Christian parent, this life is for you. Learn with each new morning to say: "For this day I accept Jesus for all my duties as believer and as parent." Commit simply, commit fully to Him every duty, every difficulty, every circumstance, every moment, and say confidently, "I know in whom I have believed. It is He who spoke to me as parent the blessed word 'only believe'; and I am persuaded that what I have committed to Him He is able to keep." This is the blessed secret of a faith life and a faith home.

* * *

Blessed Saviour, I thank Thee for this precious word. I have long heard and understood that it is by faith alone the sinner is saved. I have begun to understand and experience that a Christian is to live entirely by faith, and every hour to receive from Thee the life Thou desirest to live in him. Lord, teach me the additional lesson that in the home life faith is just as much the power of blessing and that in all my relationship with my family Thy word still is, "Fear not, only believe." O Jesus, Thou art not only the sinner's but the parent's Friend; in nothing wilt Thou delight so much to reveal Thy saving and sanctifying power as in the family life which Thou hast redeemed to the service of Thy kingdom.

O my Lord, I do pray Thee to teach me and all parents how impossible it is to train our children aright, or be a blessing to them, except as we live the life of faith. Open our eyes to see all that Thou offerest to our faith and how our love to them, our influence on them, our education and our training, may all be inspired and purified and perfected by the faith in the power of Thy finished redemption and Thy abiding presence. Show us how all our own feebleness and our fears, all the waywardness of our children and all the wickedness in the world that tempts them, can be fully met by Thy power and Thy love if we only trust Thee.

O Lord Jesus, do teach us to know Thee as the Saviour of our children from their very birth and in the homes we have to form for them. And let our whole life and communion with them day by day, every day and all the day, be in the faith of the Son of God, who loved us, and gave himself for us. Amen.

THIRTY-NINTH DAY

The Chamber of Death

"And all wept, and bewailed her: but he said, Weep not; she is not dead, but sleepeth" (Luke 8:52).

In God's great school of tribulation there are many classes. In the department where God trains parents, there is one room which all greatly fear to enter. Many, as they are led into it, are seen struggling and murmuring. As its darkness closes in over them, they almost refuse to believe that God is love. Many pass through it with little awareness of the divine comfort or holiness the chastisement was meant to bring; they knew not why they were there and were open to the teaching and the blessing Jesus gives. Others who entered trembling can testify that the chamber of death—for of this we speak— was to them the gate of heaven; it was the death of a little one that first led them truly to know Jesus. As to Jairus with his dead daughter, the child's death was the parent's life.

Let us see how Jesus meets the sorrowing parent in the chamber of death. The first thing He asks is silence and solitude. Jesus comes to the house and finds the crowd making a great tumult. At once He puts out the crowd and goes in alone, with the parents and the three disciples.

One of the things that most effectually hinders the blessing of affliction is too much time spent in fellowship with others, seeking comfort in their sympathy. By clouding the light and the brightness of visible things, the Father draws the soul to himself and to the unseen. "My soul is silent unto God"; "I will hear what God the Lord will speak." He has lessons, often difficult lessons, to teach the parents whose little one has been taken away by death; it is when there is the teachableness that really looks to God himself and waits on Him that the trial becomes fruitful in blessing.

The lessons in the dying chamber of a child are not difficult to state. The parent is led to ask, Have I loved my child in the Lord, or have I looked upon him and treated him as my own possession? Has the spirit of my life and my home been truly an educating of my children for heaven and its holiness? Is there worldliness, selfishness, or sinfulness of which this affliction must remind me? In all I seek for my family, has it indeed been the kingdom first? Affliction can never profit without heart-searching; and heart-searching is impossible except in the holy stillness of soul that is found in separation from man and meeting with God.

Oh, let parents beware, in their time of trial, of the dissipation that comes from too much seeing of friends, from seeking and finding comfort in their company. God wants to see us alone; without this He cannot bless or comfort us. Jesus waits to reveal himself in the power of His great salvation as the surety of the parental covenant too—the Redeemer in whom the parent will find all the grace and blessing promised in the covenant. But He cannot do it except the crowd is put out. He takes His three disciples with Him that all His servants may learn in their ministry that by the bedside of a dying or a dead child Jesus wants to be alone with the parents. Even His ministers are to come in only as they come with Him and point to Him.

He is alone with the parents; now comes the comforting. "Weep not," He says. Jesus does not condemn weeping; He wept himself. Weeping ever touched His heart. And yet He says, "Weep not." "Woman, why weepest thou?" was His very first resurrection word. As the Lamb in the midst of the throne, Jesus leads His redeemed and wipes away all tears.

Jesus says, "Weep not." Weeping is often self-indulgent, a nursing of our grief. It is the fruit of being too absorbed in ourselves, in the object we mourn or in the suffering we endure. Weeping often hinders the voice of God being heard, hinders altogether the blessing the affliction was meant to bring. We are so occupied with what we suffer, and God would have us think of the sin with which we made Him suffer. By taking away a child, God means to take us away from ourselves to make room in the heart for himself. Weeping often only fills us with ourselves. Weeping is often the homage, yea, the adoration, of our own will. God would have us in the affliction learn to bear, and love, and worship His will.

Beloved mourner, hear the voice of Jesus say, "Weep not." He does not say it without a reason. It is not enough that the tumult of the crowd outside is put away and that there is silence in the room; the tumult of thought and feeling must be hushed too; within the soul there must be silence. At the bidding of Jesus the gush of tears must be restrained and the heart must turn to Him. Who is this who thus, with authority, bids us cease our weeping, and what has He to say to justify His injunction?

Jesus leads from the visible to the invisible; where we see only death, He speaks of life. He comes to rouse us to faith, and to it He reveals himself as the living and life-giving one. "Weep not; she is not dead, but sleepeth." With these words Jesus draws near to the lifeless form of each little one over whom a mother's bursting heart is weeping. He reminds her that death has been conquered and that the loved one is not dead, in the terrible meaning which sin gave that word, but truly sleeps, in the deep and blessed sense which that word now has in His mouth.

Your little one is not dead. Judge not by sight. There

is a better life than the life of this earth—the eternal life in which God dwelleth. In that eternal life there is a sleep provided for those who are in Christ Jesus, the blessed waiting-time till He comes to gather all His own. As the life itself and the glory in which it shall be fully manifested is something that has not entered the heart to conceive, so this sleep, too, is something that passes knowledge. We know for certain only that it is a most blessed rest, rest in the bosom of Jesus.

Jesus asks if this is no comfort to know that your little one, whom He took into His covenant before he could know Him, is now resting with Him. He took this one that He might draw you to himself.

Weeping parents, this is God's one purpose and desire, this is God's one great thought of blessing and comfort: in His Son Christ Jesus He has come near to bless and take possession of you. Let this time of affliction not pass without a hitherto unknown experience of what Jesus is as the parents' Friend, Teacher, Comforter, and Sanctifier. You will yet be led to confess how that death has become your greatest gain. The presence and the power and the love of Jesus can more than compensate for the absence and the loss of the child.

* * *

Blessed Lord, in this hour of deep sorrow I come to Thee, my Saviour and the Saviour of my little one. Condescend, I beseech Thee, to come in with me, my Lord, to the chamber of death where Thy weeping child waits for Thee. Oh, come in and be Thou my Comforter and my Teacher. Put out, I pray Thee, the tumult of the crowd, all the sad thoughts and uncontrolled feelings that keep me from hearing Thy voice. Say to the storm, "Be still!" and let Thy presence be the great calm. O my Saviour, speak! I would hear.

Speak, Lord, if it please Thee, of Thy holy will, and Thy right to do with Thine even what pleaseth Thee, and teach me to say, "Thy will be done." Speak, as Thou seest it needful, of any sin and wandering from Thee, of any love of the creature, of any want of love to Thee and delight in Thy fellowship, and make me partaker of Thy holiness. Speak, Lord, and teach me.

Speak, Lord, and comfort Thy child. Reveal thyself to me as the resurrection and the life, the Shepherd who has taken His lamb into His bosom. Reveal thyself as my Shepherd, the one who will see to it that the blessing of the affliction is secured. Come nearer to me with Thy abiding presence. Reveal thyself from henceforth more than ever the house-friend, making thyself at home with us, sanctifying our family life. Come in, Lord Jesus! Come in to me in the chamber of death, and, as Thou hast taken my child to thyself, take me and my beloved home and make us entirely Thine. Amen.

FORTIETH DAY
The Widow's Child

"There was a dead man carried out, the only son of his mother, and she was a widow: . . . And when the Lord saw her, he had compassion on her, and said unto her, Weep not" (Luke 7:12, 13).

Any attempt to set forth the teaching of Scripture on the education of children would certainly be incomplete if it had nothing to say on what always is so sad and difficult, yet often has been a blessed and successful work—a widow's training of her orphan children. There are few sights which attract and claim sympathy, both human and divine. Here is indeed one of the sorest trials that can befall a woman. The husband for whom she left her father's home, on whom she counted and leaned on as her guide and guardian, in whom her life and her love found their joy, to whom she looked as her help and strength in the training of her children—her husband is taken from her, and she is left alone and desolate. The stricken heart seeks in vain for the object of its affection; in temporal prospects perhaps there is nothing to which to cling. The sight of the beloved little ones still left her, instead of being a treasure to which her love now clings, at first only gives new bitterness to the trial. It is not only the heart of man that is touched by this thought; the heart of God too.

Throughout Scripture, from the repeated commands in the law of Moses down to James' testimony that pure religion teaches us to visit "the fatherless and widows" in their affliction, God never forgets the widow. "A father of the fatherless, and a judge of the widows, is God in his holy habitation"; "He relieveth the fatherless and widow"; "Leave thy fatherless children, I will preserve them alive; and let thy widows trust in me" (Ps. 68:5; 146:9; Jer. 49:11). Such words reveal to us the very heart of God.

And now when Jesus came, how could He fail in showing in this too? He was the Father's image; God was in Christ. It is as if the picture of the Master's life would be incomplete without the story of the widow of Nain. In what He said of the widow's mite, we see how His eye watches over a widow's poverty and values, her little (in man's eyes) deed of love. At Nain we see Him as the Comforter of widowed motherhood. Let us go to Nain, the sacred spot where so many a widow has found Jesus her Friend and Lord, to learn what Jesus has to say to a widow weeping over her child. Not only when the tears are those of sorrow over one taken away but those of anxious love or sad distress at the sight of those still left behind, Jesus meets us with His, "Weep not."

Weep not, widowed mother, as you look at your little ones and the heart almost breaks at the thought of their being fatherless. Weep not; come, follow me, as we seek Him who has been anointed "to comfort all that mourn." Weep not as you tremblingly wonder how you are to train and educate them all alone. Let your soul for a little be silent unto Him who came from heaven to say to the widow, "As one whom his mother comforteth, will thy God comfort thee."

Weep not! May the wounded heart not have at least the comfort that the unrestrained flow of its tears does often bring? Let it be enough that Jesus says it. All the other parents whose children Jesus blessed came and asked for help. He speaks to the widow without being asked. Her widowhood is sufficient plea: "When the Lord saw her, he had compassion on her, and said unto her, Weep not." Jesus is looking on you; do not let your tears keep you from looking and listening to Him. Be sure that if it could have been, He would have spared you that cup. Now that it has come, He is looking on you in compassion, waiting to comfort and to bless. In the tenderest love but with the voice of authority Jesus says, "Weep not."

But Jesus was not one who comforts only with words; His words were always followed by deeds. If you will look up and see, He will show you what He will do. To the widowed mother at Nain He gave back the dead son, who had been to her in place of a husband. His believing people know that, though the separation may last a little while, the departed ones who have died in the Lord will be given back to them in glory and forever. Look up to Jesus, the Resurrection and the Life, weeping widow! They who sleep in Jesus will God bring with Him. The resurrection, the meeting again, the being ever with the Lord, are realities—as real, more real, more mighty than the separation and the sorrow. Look up in faith; it is Jesus who speaks. "Weep not."

But oh, the desolation that meantime fills the heart! The sense of utter feebleness and unfitness to fulfill the charge with these boys, these girls, who still live and who do so need a father's wise, firm, loving rule! Dear mother, when Jesus says, "Weep not," He gives what can dry the tears. If Jesus himself were to take the place of the father to these children, would not this make you smile and sing even through the tears? If Jesus would undertake the responsibility of educating those children, of being your adviser and your strength and your assurance of success in your work, would this not be enough to stay those tears? And this is what He comes to do. What promises God gave of old to the widows Jesus comes in human tenderness and in the nearness of the Holy Spirit to fulfill. You may trust your fatherless children to Him;

He will preserve them; He will, in a divine fullness and power of meaning, be the father of the fatherless.

It may be that a widowed mother reads these words but they have little meaning. Though a Christian, she has yet to learn the full meaning of living by faith, to count the unseen things of faith surer and clearer than the things of sight; the promise appears all vague and distant. She hardly dares hope for the reality of Jesus doing this for her. She does not feel as if she is good or holy or believing enough, that her children should receive such a wonderfully special and divine guidance.

My sister, if you would learn what Jesus would have of you, that you may with confidence depend upon your children being preserved and blessed by Him, and your tears pass away in the sunlight of His love and care, come and listen. Of a widow He asks but one thing: "Let thy widows *trust in me.*" *Trust me!* This was what He claimed from the widow of Nain; this is what He asks of you. *Trust Jesus!* This is the message I bring you this day in your weeping, anxious widowhood. *Trust Jesus!* Trust Him for yourself.

Let each thought of your departed one lead you to say, "I have Jesus with me—I will trust Him." Let the consciousness of sin and shortcoming, of unfitness for your mother's work, wake the prayer, "Jesus! I will trust Thee to make me what I should be." Trust Him with your children, with their temporal and their eternal interests.

The life of trust needs a life of undivided, simple, childlike surrender. Be wholly His and He will prove himself wholly yours. Tarry in prayer and supplication, in the silent, restful committal of every care and fear to Him. Really trust Him; in every prayer make this the chief thing: "I have now entrusted my need to Him; I trust Him with it; I am confident He is mighty and faithful to keep that which I have committed unto Him." Trust Him wholly; they who wholly trust Him, find Him wholly true.

And if ever the double trial of the widow of Nain should be yours and you have to mourn the loss not only of a husband but of an only son, oh, remember that there Jesus still is the Comforter of the widow doubly desolate! This will be the time in which you will find Him become doubly precious; you will have grace to say, "My flesh and my heart fail; but God, but Jesus, is the strength of my heart and my portion for ever."

* * *

Blessed Lord Jesus, how shall I praise Thee for that thoughtful love which would not give us the record of Thy life without the story of the widow of Nain? Blessed be Thy name for the revelation of the special place the widow has in Thy heart, the tenderness of that compassion which drew nigh to her before she ever knew that she might look to Thee!

Lord Jesus, for every widowed mother we now pray to Thee. Teach each one to come to Thee with her fatherless children. We bless Thee that there are thousands of widowed mothers who have proved how wonderfully Thou canst bless the feeble and how richly Thou hast blessed their children.

Teach the widow, we pray Thee, to put her trust in God. Thou art able and Thou art willing to do what man dare not expect, what man counts impossible, if we honor Thee by trusting Thy love. O Saviour, help the feeble faith of every widow. Let her desolation and her sorrow and her feebleness compel her now wholly to cast herself with her children on Thee, to depend upon Thee alone. Draw thyself nigh, O Thou compassionate one, and reveal thyself. Speak into the depths of the sorrowing, anxious heart Thy word of comfort: Weep not!"

Oh, let Thy widowed child hear Thee speaking, see Thee come to take charge and provide and care for the education of her children. Teach her that her one work is to trust Thee, in separation from the world, in holy devotedness to Thee, trust Thee for a more than human guidance, a divine guidance and blessing on her children. Let her continue in prayer and supplication in daily communion with Thee the unseen one, the portion of her children. Let her then fully know how truly Thou art the widow's Friend, the Saviour and the Friend of her children. Amen.

FORTY-FIRST DAY

The Sick Child

"There was a certain nobleman, whose son was sick at Capernaum . . . he went unto [Jesus], and besought him that he would come down and heal his son: for he was at the point of death" (John 4:46, 47).

In the wonderful training of the parent through the child, God uses a child's sickness as one of His special means of blessing. And in the parent's training of the child, the sick-room often has been the place when the parent first fully found his way to the child's heart, to guide him to Jesus and the distinct confession of faith in Him. The beautiful story of the nobleman of Capernaum teaches us how sickness is to be met, to be healed, to be blessed.

How is sickness to be met? God's great gift to sinful men is Jesus; in His Son He meets our every need. And the one great thing God asks of us is a spirit of faith— the trustful surrender to Jesus, allowing Him to be to us all that the Father would have Him be. And because He has been given to us, not only as individuals, but as parents, to accept on behalf of our children, the one thing that God asks of the parent is faith—trust in Jesus.

As faith in God was the one thing by which the saints of old pleased God, so faith in His Son is the one supreme grace by which the Christian parent can please

God and obtain His blessings on his children. And all God's leadings and dealings have this one object and purpose, to make us strong in faith, giving glory to God.

When God allows sickness to come upon the child of one of His believing people, perhaps still young or an infant, and the parents' hearts are agonized by the sight of his pain or the fear of losing him, the question comes with terrible force, Why does God permit all this suffering? The answer Scripture gives is this: for the trial and so for the purifying and the strengthening of faith. God's one purpose with parent and child is to work and increase faith in them. By faith they become capable of receiving the revelation of God's glory and showing it forth again; by faith God can dwell in them and work through them. God's one desire is that they should more fully believe in His Son; and our one desire should be to meet the sickness by faith in Jesus.

The one great lesson the story of the nobleman teaches us is the growth and increase of faith in the dealing with Christ. His faith begins as a general faith in what he has heard of Christ's compassion and power; this brings him into contact with Christ. He believes in Jesus as a healer. It becomes a distinct faith in the promise he received of healing: "the man believed the word that Jesus had spoken unto him." He believes in Jesus as the healer of his child.

The faith in Jesus the healer is perfected to faith in Him as Saviour and Lord: "himself believed, and his whole house." At first the focus of the nobleman was on his sick son; as he met Jesus and talked with Him, his focus moved to Christ himself. His general faith became specific for the salvation of his whole household.

How is the sickness to be healed? The answer to the second question of our story is very simple: by the power of Jesus. In Matthew Christ's healing work is presented as the natural result of His atoning work (Isa. 53; Matt. 8). He took upon himself our human nature, and, having redeemed it, lifted it into the glory of the eternal life in heaven.

When on earth, He delighted in healing the sick, something His loving heart could do even when He could not save their souls. In His Word He left the assurance that the prayer of faith would save the sick, because the prayer of a righteous man availeth much. He has a thousand times over led His children by His Spirit to apply the promise of His doing whatsoever we will in asking and receiving healing for a sick child. His great desire in sickness is to educate us into that simple, child-like faith, which though it cannot give account of its assurance to reason yet through the Holy Spirit has the assurance that its petition is granted, that it has what it asks. Let us claim the life of the beloved sick one for God's glory in him and in us as parents. The word of Jesus can come to us as real as to the nobleman: "thy son liveth."

How is sickness to become a blessing? The Lord Jesus used it as a means of drawing to himself; when it had done this He took it away that the healing might bind to himself. When the sickness had done its work, the healing perfected what had been begun. The sickness had brought the nobleman to Jesus in hope and expectancy; the healing left him a confirmed believer along with his household.

There is a very prevalent opinion that sickness is better than health for true piety. In the life of Christ and in His work we see no token of this. Health obtained directly from Jesus in the prayer of faith, health received consciously as a gift of redeeming love, is one of the most wonderful spiritual blessings—a bearing in the body the mark of the hand of Jesus. Let each parent whom our Lord leads into this school of sickness realize this fully, that health, asked and received in faith, may be a token of even more intimate contact with Jesus than the blessing of the sickbed ever has been. As this is understood, we shall feel courage to make known our desire for health in which there is power for God's glory. The new revelation of the power and the love of Jesus may make us and our household believers as never before—full of

226

faith and devotion to Him who has blessed us.

Parents, our sick children are God's messengers to lead us to Jesus and to faith in Him. The sickness has a message and a blessing. It calls us to search the heart and life and home: Have we held our children wholly for God, trained them as holy to the Lord? It comes to make the heart tender and humble and to draw it out to Jesus. Oh, let us beware lest in all the care and sorrow the sickness occasions, in all the means by which we seek deliverance, in all the fear of losing our child, we miss God's purpose. He wants to bring us, subdued and quiet, in faith and hope to Jesus. Let us pray to God very earnestly that we may not miss the blessing of the sickness.

And, much more, let us accept the greater blessing of the healing. The exercise of faith honors God more than anything. Availing ourselves of our privilege, trusting Jesus' word and power, learning to know Him as indeed our helper, experiencing His healing power in distinct answer to our faith—it is this that binds to Christ. We learn to know Him as the Living One. We have the token of the acceptance of our surrender and our trust. Our home has become the scene for the display of His kingly power. It has sealed afresh the parental covenant. We and our home become the Lord's as never before.

* * *

Blessed Redeemer, we have learned that sickness has but this one purpose—to draw us to thyself. When Thou wast on earth, the sickness of a child was one of the cords with which the Father drew men to Thee. And still He takes parents into the sickroom of their little ones that there they may learn to seek and find Thee, to wait for and to receive the revelation of Thy power and love.

Lord Jesus, teach us, we pray Thee, in all the time of our children's sickness to learn the blessed lesson of coming to Thee and trusting Thee. We may be most sure that Thou art watching over us to teach, to comfort, to sanctify, and to heal. Teach us especially that Thou art still the same as when on earth, mighty to bid the sickness depart and to free from the power of death. To spare the life of a child for Thy service, to gladden and sanctify a parent's heart by Thy grace for the Father's glory, Thou art still ready to hear the prayer of faith and raise up the child. Oh, grant us this faith that we may honor Thee and not hinder Thee from proving with what compassion Thou hearest a parent's cry.

And grant, Lord, when Thou graciously hast heard and given back a child to the parent's faith, that the blessed fruit may be the parents with their whole house believing in Thee as never before. May all see that Jesus is now Lord and Master, the beloved Friend of the home. As the sickness leads to seek Thee, may the healing bind to Thee and Thy blessed service. Amen.

FORTY-SECOND DAY

Feed My Lambs

"Jesus saith to Simon Peter, Simon, son of Jonas, lovest thou me more than these? He saith unto him, Yea, Lord; thou knowest that I love thee. He saith unto him, Feed my lambs" (John 21:15).

Peter was a fisherman. After the first miraculous draught of fishes, the Lord had said, "Follow me, and I will make you fishers of men." Peter's work on earth was the symbol of his heavenly calling. After the second miraculous draught of fishes, in the days preceding the ascension, our Lord no longer calls Peter a fisherman but a shepherd. There is deep significance in the change. One great point of difference between the fisherman and the shepherd is that while the former catches what he has neither reared nor fed, seeking only what is full grown and casting away all the little fish out of his net back into the sea, the shepherd directs his special attention to the young and the weak; on his care for the lambs all his hope depends.

The type of the fisherman gave no place for the Master to give special charge concerning the children of His Church. The shepherd's calling at once suggested the words, "Feed my lambs," and sets forth the deep importance and the blessed reward of giving first place to the little ones of the flock. Peter and Christ's ministers were not to feed only the sheep; the prosperity of the Church would especially depend upon their feeding the lambs. What was said to them is very applicable to parents as under-shepherds, who each have their little flock of lambs to keep and rear for the Master. Christ's commission to His Church through Peter shows the place the little ones have in His heart and teaches us to think of the weakness, the value, the need, and the hope of our children.

"*Feed my lambs*," Jesus says, reminding us of the great care necessary for our children. I was once leaving a sheep farm in company with its master towards evening. There were threatening clouds; just as we left he hurried back to call his son and cry out, "Take great care of the lambs! There is a storm coming." The Lord is just about to ascend the throne; one of His last words is, Care for the lambs. The sheep is a weak and helpless animal; how much more the little lamb! It cannot care for itself.

The Master would have every minister and every parent realize how utterly dependent the child is on the care of those to whom he is entrusted. He cannot choose the company under whose influence he comes. He knows not yet to choose between good and evil. He knows nothing of the importance of little words or deeds, of forming habits, of sowing good or bad seed, of yielding to the world or God. All depends upon his surroundings; and parents especially have the children in their power. What a solemn responsibility to lead and nourish them carefully, to feed them not with the husks of this world's thoughts and pleasures but with the milk for babes which our Father has provided, then to lead them on in the green pastures!

"*Feed my lambs*"; the words remind us of the high value of the little ones. In the lambs the shepherd sees the possibilities of the future; as the lambs, so the coming flock. The Church of the next generation, the servants with whom, in but a few years' time, Jesus will do His work of converting and saving and blessing men, are the children of today. Alas! how little we have understood the admonition to feed the lambs. He says more; He says,

"Feed *my* lambs," for of such is the kingdom. Not only for what they are to become but for their childlike simplicity and heavenliness, He loves them and counts them of great worth. For the lesson they continually have to teach grownups, for all the influence they exert in making their parents and elders gentle and humble and trustful, for all the blessings they bring to those who receive them in the name of Jesus, they are to Him of unspeakable worth, the most beautiful part of His flock. Let us try to catch His spirit as He cries, "Feed *my* lambs."

Oh, let us learn to look upon our children in the light in which Jesus looks upon them! Let us pray for the Holy Spirit to make the familiar words *Jesus' lambs* a deep spiritual reality to us until our hearts tremble at the thought. Our little ones are His lambs; we are daily to feed them as such that they may grow up as the sheep of His pasture.

"*Feed My lambs*"; the children's great need is here set before us. Food is the condition for growth. Food is something received from without, to be assimilated and taken up into our very life. The body has its food from the visible world. The mind is nourished by the thoughts that enter it. If the spirit feeds, through the mind, on thoughts from the Word of God, it will grow. The little ones cannot seek pasture for themselves; Christ looks to parents to bring to them day by day not a chapter of the Bible just read over and in most cases beyond their comprehension but some of the thoughts of divine wisdom and love, without which the soul cannot possibly grow. The mother studies daily how to let the child have something to eat and what he is to eat; she ought no less carefully to feed each lamb entrusted to her care. The one desire and aim must be to rear him for the Lord. The consecration of the child to the Lord must be the chief thing in life.

"*Feed my lambs*"; the words tell the provision Christ has made for His weaker ones. To whom were the words spoken? To one of whom the question had been asked,

"Lovest thou me?" and who had answered, "Yea, Lord, thou knowest that I love thee." Only one who is inspired by love to Jesus can truly take charge of the lambs. This is the examination of fitness for the duty of parent and shepherd of the lambs, "Lovest thou me?" This is the provision Jesus has made for the lambs; true love to Jesus can do the work.

Let every parent who longs to know how he can obtain the needed qualification for his work give in his name for this examination. Let Jesus search your heart—once, twice, a third time—until the remembrance of past unfaithfulness brings tears and the answer comes, "Lord, thou knowest all things, thou knowest that I do love thee." Alas! the blight of so many a Christian home is the lack of the conscious, fervent, and confessed love of Jesus. Nothing influences a child like love; the warmth of a holy love to Jesus will make itself felt. There may be a great deal of religion, of teaching, of praying; it is only love that will conquer.

Love to Jesus will lead to obey Him very carefully, to walk with Him very closely, to trust Him very heartily. Love to Jesus will make the desire to please Him very strong and the charge He gives us to keep very precious. Love to Jesus will make our testimony of Him very personal. The food with which we feed the lambs will have the warmth of a divine love about it. Jesus wants parents who love Him, who love Him with their whole heart and strength; this is the provision He has thought out for His little lambs.

The religion of Jesus is a religion of love. Of the Father it is said, "God is love." Jesus himself is the gift of a love that passeth knowledge. His own life and work is one of love—love stronger than death. When the Holy Spirit comes to us, He sheds abroad in our hearts the love of God. Our whole relation to the divine is to be one of love. And our relation as parents and children was meant to be one of love. It was to restore this that Jesus came. And He does it by calling parents to love himself and then, receiving the little ones in His name, for His sake, and in the fervor of His love, to take charge of them. The love of earth He purifies and elevates by the love of heaven. And the home is consecrated by the light of Jesus' love resting on the children, and the power of His love dwelling in the parents, and the whole of education being made a work of love for Him.

Christian parents, see and accept your blessed calling; you are the shepherds of the divine love to tend and feed the lambs. In His Church the Chief Shepherd has many shepherds to care for the flock, but none who can so care for the lambs as the parents. "He maketh him families like a flock." It is to parental love, inspired and sanctified by redeeming love, that Jesus looks for the building up of His Church. Let us pray very earnestly that our eyes will be opened to see things as Jesus sees them, to realize by the Holy Spirit what He feels for our little ones, what He expects of us and is ready to do for us in giving us wisdom and strength. "Feed my lambs"; when this word is made the law of a parent's duty, what gentleness and love will it inspire, what heavenly hope, what faithful, watchful care, and what an unceasing life of faith in the love and grace and blessing of Jesus on our home! Let us hear the voice saying to us, "Lovest thou me? Feed my lambs."

* * *

Blessed Saviour, Thou art the good Shepherd of whom my soul hath said, "The Lord is *my* shepherd, I shall not want." I bless Thee for the tender love that did not forget the little ones but didst so carefully commit them to the charge of Thy servant Peter at his installation to the office of shepherd. I bless Thee for the holy privilege Thou hast bestowed on me of being a parent, and also bearing Thy commission, "Feed my lambs." I bless Thee with my whole heart for the honor and blessedness of being, in my little sphere, what Thou art in Thine—a gentle, loving shepherd. O my Lord, may my daily experience of the way in which Thy shepherd-love does its work on me be a daily lesson to teach me how to feed my little flock of lambs.

Blessed Master, I beseech Thee open my eyes to look upon my children as Thou dost, to regard them always and only in the light of Thy claim upon them. Open my eyes to see what a holy life of fellowship with Thee, of separation from the world and its spirit, of watchfulness and trust, is needed to do my duty to Thee and Thy lambs. Take away every thought of reluctance and fear of difficulty and burden, and let me see how a simple, childlike life with Thee is the best, the only true training for doing a parent's work aright.

And to this end, my Lord, fill me with Thy love. Let love to Thee, a bright, obedient love, be the atmosphere of the home in which my children grow up. O Thou who art Thyself the Lamb of God and dost allow my children to bear the same name, to be God's lambs, oh, let Thy holy love in my heart be the inspiring power of all my communion with Thee and with them. And let me so prove how wonderfully Thou art my Shepherd and how blessedly I am their shepherd.

For Thy name's sake. Amen.

FORTY-THIRD DAY
The Holy Spirit in the Family

"For the promise is unto you, and to your children"
(Acts 2:39).

We have not forgotten the frequent use in the Old Testament of the words, "thou *and* thy house," "thee *and* thy seed," "you *and* your children," "me *and* my house." These were expressions of the blessed bond that made the whole family one in God's sight and partners in God's covenants and blessing. God be praised! The expression is found in the New Testament too: "you, and to your children." Nowhere could it have found a place of deeper significance than here in Acts. On the day of Pentecost the Church of Christ, which had just been born by His resurrection from the dead, receives its baptism with the Holy Spirit; the word is heard, "For the promise is unto you, *and* to your chidren." All the blessings of the new dispensation, the ministration of the Spirit, are at once secured to our children.

The promise is of the Spirit of the glorified Jesus in all His fullness, the baptism of fire and of power. When we are baptized in the name of the Father, of the Son, and of the Holy Ghost, we confess our faith in the Holy Trinity. The Holy Spirit, not only as one with the Father and the Son but as being the third person, brings the full and perfect revelation of the divine glory.

All that in the Old Covenant had been promised by God, all that had been manifested and brought near to us of divine grace in Jesus, the Holy Spirit is now to make our very own. Through Him all the promises of God are fulfilled, all grace and salvation in Christ becomes a personal possession and experience. God's Word calls our children the children of promise; it is especially of this promise of the Holy Spirit that they are the heirs. The secret of a godly education is to bring them up in the faith and for the fulfillment of this promise. *In the faith of the promise* we must learn to look upon the aid and the presence of the Spirit in our daily training as absolutely necessary and indispensable but also as most positively secured to us. In all our praying for them and living with them, we must learn to count upon and expect the direct working of the Holy Spirit. So we shall educate them *for the fulfillment of the promise*, that their lives more than our own may, from their youth up, be in the power of the Spirit, holy to the Lord.

To *you* the promise is and to your children. The very thought of training children every day in dependence upon the Holy Spirit's presence and with the expectation of His filling the children appears to some too strange and high; it is impracticable. The reason for this thinking is simply that they have not yet learned to understand and enjoy the abiding of the Spirit as essential to a true Christian life. The promise of the Spirit is to *you*; as parents realize in their own personal experience that it is only the continual leading of the Spirit which enables them to live as God intends that they will have the capacity for believing, in its full meaning, the promise of the Spirit for their children. Only then can they become the ministers of the Spirit to their families.

Oh, that the Church of Christ understood the place and the power which the Spirit of God is meant to have in every Christian, in every Christian home! All the complaints about the neglect or the failure of religious education have their root in this: the Holy Ghost is not expected, is not accepted as the only sufficient strength of the believer for all his God asks of him. As *you* parents receive the promise and live and walk in the Spirit, will you receive it for your children too?

As in nature, so in grace, you *and* your children have been linked together for good or for evil. Physically, intellectually, morally, they are partakers of your life. Spiritually it may be so too. The gift of the Spirit and His gracious workings, to you and to them, does not consist of two distinct separate acts; no, but in and through you He would come to them. Your life, your daily influence, is the channel through which His quickening and sanctifying grace would reach them.

If you are resting content with the thought that you are saved, without seeking to be truly filled with the Spirit—if your life is still more carnal than spiritual, with more of the spirit of the world than of God—do not think it strange if your children grow up unconverted. You are hindering the Holy Spirit. You are breathing day by day into your children the spirit of the world. You are, though it may be unconsciously, most effectually using all your influence to train them into man's religion, in harmony with the spirit of the world, instead of God's religion, in the power of the Holy Spirit sent down from heaven. In spite of your influence, through the faith of others the blessing may reach them, but you have no reason to expect it except as you yield yourselves to be the channel for its conveyance. If nothing else has yet roused us, would that we would see that for our children's sake nothing less is needed than for us to be filled with the Holy Ghost.

To you is *the promise*, and to your children. *The promise!* Too many look upon a promise of God as a mere word or thought—something that is without power until they from their side do what is needed to make it effectual. They do not know that the word of God has in it a living, mighty energy, a divine seed-life, and that if they will but hide and keep it in their hearts, it will beget the faith through which the blessed fulfillment comes. I come this day to every parent who reads this with a wonderful message. *The promise*, the promise of the Holy Spirit in His fullness and His power, is to you and to your children. A promise means that God in His infinite power has bound himself to do what He has said, and that He will most certainly do it for us as soon as we claim it in faith. And the promise here means that the Holy Spirit, with His quickening, sanctifying, and gladdening grace, is ours, waiting to come and to be in our home, in our family life, all that we need to make it holy and happy. And however far our home life may be from God's ideal, and however impossible it appear to us that in our circumstances and with our difficulties we shall ever succeed in making it very different, if we will but claim and hold fast the promise in the prayer of faith, God himself will fulfill it. A promise needs two things: the receiver must believe and claim it; the giver must fulfill it and make it true. Let our posture be that of simple, trustful faith in God for ourselves and our children, counting on the promise: God is faithful, who will also do it.

Dear parents, let us open our hearts to take in the promise of God as a divine quickening power; it will itself beget in us the very state of mind which God requires before the fulfillment comes. Let us look upon ourselves as the divinely appointed ministers of the Holy Spirit, to prepare and train our children under His influence from their youth up, and let us yield ourselves wholly to His guidance and working. To train a child aright means training him to be a temple of the Holy Spirit, living ourselves in the power of the Spirit. Let no sense of shortcoming or feebleness discourage us; to you is the promise, and to your children. Let us place our lives as parents under the leading of the Holy Spirit. That will mean placing our whole life under His leading, because we can be to our children only what we really are to God. Let the spirit of praise and thanks unceasingly fill us, because God has bestowed the wondrous grace upon us to make our family life the sphere for the special working of His

238

Spirit. Let our unceasing prayer and our confident expectation be that, by the power of the Holy Spirit from heaven, our home on earth shall be coming continually nearer to the home in heaven, of which it is meant to be the image and the preparation.

* * *

O Thou thrice-holy God, how shall we bless Thee for the promise that our home is to be Thy home, the abode of Thy Holy Spirit, and that in the happy life of love between parents and children the Spirit of Thy divine love is to be the link that binds us together? Glory to Thy name, O my God, for the promise of the Holy Spirit to us *and* to our children!

O God, we come to set wide open the doors of our beloved home to Thee, and to place it with our whole family life at the disposal and under the rule of Thy Holy Spirit. We beseech Thee, let Him take possession. As parents we desire to claim the fulfillment of the promise. May our love to our children and our desires for them, our daily relationship with them and our influence on them, all be under the continual overshadowing of Thy Holy Spirit. May our whole life, the invisible atmosphere that surrounds us and that fills our home, be that which Thy Holy Spirit breathes, holiness to the Lord.

We claim the promise for our children. We desire, in simple, childlike faith, to count upon it as a settled thing between Thee and us that they are the heirs of the promise of the Spirit. Give us grace, O Father, as often as we see in them signs of sin that make us sad, tendencies and dispositions that make us fear, influences around them that bring danger; oh, give us grace to plead the promise in the assurance of faith! O our Father, we would live ourselves, we would guide our home life, we would train each child day by day under the leading of the Holy Spirit. May the holy reverence, the deep, quiet joy, the tender watchfulness, the death to self and the flesh, the life of faith in Jesus, which mark His presence, ever be ours. Amen.

FORTY-FOURTH DAY
Parental Self-culture

"Thou therefore which teachest another, teachest thou not thyself?" (Rom. 2:21).

Nothing is more inconsistent and vain than the attempt to teach others without teaching ourselves. Only what the teacher has really mastered and thoroughly made his own can he successfully communicate to others. In the higher sphere of the life-truth which a parent has to impart, it holds far more good; it is the lesson I first teach myself that I can really teach my child. One of the first laws in the science of home education is that it depends far more on example than precept; what parents are avails more than what they say. There is not one of the great lessons for the child which the parent must not first himself learn. Let us look at some of them.

The great aim of education is to give the child, when grown up to manhood, the perfect mastery and the ready use of all the wondrous powers with which God has endowed him. To this end *a wise self-control* is one of the first virtues. As a state cannot prosper if there be no wise, intelligent ruler to make its laws and provide for its needs as they arise, there cannot be happiness in the little empire within man's bosom unless everything be subject to a ruling power. The child cannot be trained too early to form habits of quiet thoughtfulness in speech and act, giving time and opportunity for mind and will to hold their rule.

This training comes far more through example than precept. It is the atmosphere of a well-regulated home, the influence of the self-control which parents exhibit, which unconsciously set their mark on the child. When parents give way to impulse and temper, perhaps at the very time when professing to reprove or restrain the child's temper, the effect of the good advice they mean to give is more than neutralized by the evil influence of the spirit displayed. It is the spirit that influences. The child may never look up and say this, but God's Word on his behalf says, "Thou that teacheth another, dost not thou teach thyself?"

If parents honestly watch themselves, they will often discover the causes or the helps to their children's failings in themselves. Such discovery ought to lead to very earnest confession before God, to a very hearty surrender to the teaching of Jesus and the Holy Spirit. We can depend upon the divine renewal to fit us for true self-control; and what we so by grace teach ourselves will in due time influence our children also.

But the self-control must know its object and the path to reach that object. The child finds both in the word we have already repeated often—*obedience*. He must control himself to be able to render obedience to his parent that he may be trained to his liberty and his glory, obedience to God. Here again the parent's obedience will be contagious; it will inspire the child. If the parent's position be one of privilege and liberty and command, the child may feel that the burden of obedience is all put upon him, the weaker one.

"Johnny," said a father once to a child, who was hesitating about obeying his father's will, "whose will must you do, your own or Dad's?" "Dad's will," was the reluctant answer. And on it followed at once the question, "But whose will must Dad do, then?" The father was able at once to answer, "God's will," and to explain how he considered such obedience to a wiser and a better will than his own his greatest privilege. He could at once take his place by the side of his child as also having to give up his own will. The parent who in all things seeks to do the will of his God and can in his prayers, in his children's presence, appeal to his God too, will find in the witness of such a life a mighty power to inculcate obedience in the child. When, on the contrary, the seeking of our own will marks our relationship with our children, we need not wonder if our education is a failure. Let us turn at once and hearken to the voice, You who teaches another, do you not teach yourself?

Especially does this hold true of that great commandment which is the fulfilling of the law. Family life has been ordained of God as the sphere where love can be cultivated. In nothing is our self-control to be more proved than in loving others, in restraining everything that is selfish or unloving. In the daily life of our children with each other and their companions, we have in miniature the temptations to which later life will expose them. For the exercise of the virtues of gentleness and forbearance, of forgiveness and generosity, of helpfulness and beneficence, continued opportunity will be found. Principles must not only be inculcated but the trouble taken to lead the child to do the right thing easily and lovingly.

Many would like to help the poor, for instance, but do not undertake this project because of not knowing how to set about it. It is one of the highest parts of a right Christian education to make benevolence the chief object of life and to awaken the desire to live to make those around us better and happier. But we feel at once how all this can only be attained as the parents teach themselves and, for their own sakes as well as their children's, cultivate the virtues they teach.

In the daily life of the family the parents must seek to show that love is the law of their life. It must be understood that unkind words, harsh judgments, and unloving reports form no part of their conversation. In the relation-

242

ship with each other, with children, with employees, with
friends and the world around, love, God's love, must be
sought after and manifested. In sympathy with the needy
and wretched, in thoughtful study of everything by which
those who have none to care for them can be helped or
comforted, in the actual loving self-denial exercised for
the sake of the poor or the suffering, the example of Christ
and His love must be reduced to practice in daily life.
Thus alone can education to a life of love be truly successful.

"Thou therefore which teachest another, teachest thou
not thyself?" With what searching light these words ask
whether as parents we are doing the first and most needful
thing for being successful teachers of our children: teaching ourselves. Yes, parents, teach yourselves. If we are
to train our children wisely, we must go through a new
course of training ourselves. We have to put ourselves
to school again, and to be teachers and scholars in one.
Of the two scholars whose education has to go on simul-
taneously, the parent and child, the parent will often find
that the child makes more progress. The lessons which
the attempt to train a child teaches parents are often
of greater importance and difficulty than those the child
has to learn. It is especially well if the first lesson is
learned—the need of self-teaching, the need of teachableness, the need of continual daily learning.

Let the parent who begins to see this realize what
it means to become a scholar. All schooling requires time
and trouble, patience and payment. Teaching that costs
nothing is of little value. No one can become even fairly
competent to train a child for eternity without making
sacrifices. Take time to study God's Word and what it
says of a parent's duties. Study man's moral nature, with
its wonderful capacities, as the sacred trust committed
to your care. Teach yourself to cultivate that nature to
its highest fitness for God's service; it will be the best
preparation for teaching your children aright. And if you
feel a great need for the help of some friend to stimulate
and to guide, let Jesus be that teacher. He came and

taught himself, that He might know to teach us; He learned obedience that He might show us the way. He came to show us the Father; He will so reveal the Father's love and grace, the fatherly tenderness of our God, that we shall be full of joyful assurance that He will not refuse to teach and enable us to be true fathers and mothers to our children. And we shall understand that to be ourselves teachable, obedient, loving children of the heavenly Father is the surest way of having our children teachable, obedient, and loving too.

* * *

Gracious God, I come again to seek the grace I need for filling rightly my place as a parent. I ask of Thee to imprint deep on my heart the solemn thought that I can effectually teach my children only what I really teach myself, and that I can expect only the truth that influences my own life really to influence theirs.

O my God, I think with shame of how much I reprove in them that is only the reflection of what they have seen in me. I confess how much there has been wanting of that spirit of childlike love and self-denial, of joyful obedience to Thee and thoughtful self-sacrifice for others, which would have been to them the highest education. O my God, forgive me what is past, and give me grace in everything to teach myself what I want to teach my children.

Make me feel deeply that it is as I live as an obedient child with my Father in heaven that I can teach my children and expect them to be obedient to me. Lord, may childlike simplicity and obedience be the atmosphere my home breathes, the bond that makes parents and children one. As I think of my own slowness in learning, may I be very patient and gentle with my children, and yet full of hope that the lessons I impart to them will have their effect.

Jesus, Master, teach Thou me, that with Thy teaching I may teach my loved ones. Amen.

FORTY-FIFTH DAY

Baptized into Christ

"How shall we, that are dead to sin, live any longer therein? Know ye not that so many of us as were baptized into Jesus Christ were baptized into his death? Therefore we are buried with him by baptism into death; that like as Christ was raised up from the dead by the glory of the Father, even so we also should walk in newness of life" (Rom. 6:3, 4).

"Ye are complete in him . . . , buried with him in baptism, wherein also ye are risen with him through the faith of the operation of God, who hath raised him from the dead" (Col. 2:10-12).

In writing both to the Romans and the Colossians, Paul pleads with believers to live a life of separation from sin and the world—a life of holiness and liberty—and uses their baptism into Christ as his great argument. He unfolds the spiritual meaning of baptism, a union with Christ both in His death and His life, and shows how this is both the obligation and the possibility of a walk like Christ's in newness of life. Baptism is the symbol of the deep spiritual mystery of our perfect oneness with Christ; as it is understood and believed, it is the pledge of an abiding union and the ever-growing likeness to Him.

The parent needs continually to remember what God meant baptism to be. Without this he cannot educate the child into the possession of what God intends for him.

Without this he cannot live himself, in the power of his baptism, that life which alone can lead the child to the blessing God has in store for him. Let us try and understand what, in the full light of the Holy Spirit's teaching, baptism really is.

The great lesson we are taught is that in baptism the death and resurrection of Jesus Christ are set forth. Scripture teaches us how the old world, in the time of Noah, had been destroyed and renewed again by a fearful baptism of water. The old nature, mankind in its sinfulness, had perished under the water. From the water a new and cleansed world had emerged; Noah the believer had been brought forth, as begotten again from the dead. Scripture teaches us how at the birth of Israel God's firstborn son among the nations, that fearful baptism had not been wanting. Under Pharaoh's rule the Egyptians and the Israelites had been mixed up, very much one. In the Red Sea, Pharaoh, the old man, had perished; out of the waters that were death to Egypt, Israel came forth as God's firstborn, to sing the song of redemption.

The Holy Ghost teaches us (1 Pet. 3:20 and 1 Cor. 10:2) to regard the waters both of the flood and the Red Sea as types of baptism and its spiritual meaning. As the Jew, at John's command, went in under the water, he not only thought of the water in its cleansing power. His life was so tainted by sin that nothing but the giving up, the death of, the old life, and the reception of a new life could really cleanse him. Going in under the water meant the drowning, the death of the old nature, the putting off of sin in confession and repentance; the coming up out of it, the profession and the hope of a new life.

John's baptism of water was but a preparation; Jesus Christ alone could give the true baptism, the true deliverance from the old nature. But even He could not do this until He himself had undergone His own baptism into death. In Him the two elements, the old and the new, which in the flood and the Red Sea were represented by two separate parties—in Him they were united. The power of sin He bore in His own flesh—"Our old man was crucified with him." He descended into the great deep, where He had to cry, "All thy waves and thy billows are gone over me" (Ps. 42:7). It was this prospect that made Him say, "I have a baptism to be baptized with, and how am I straitened till it is accomplished." And again, "Can ye indeed drink of the cup that I shall drink of, and be baptized with the baptism that I am baptized with?" This was Christ's baptism, a terrible reality—a baptism into death.

But this was only the one half. There was also "the coming up out of the water," the entrance on a new life redeemed from destruction. That new life, typified in Noah and Israel, symbolized in John's baptism, now became a reality. Jesus was raised from the dead in the power of a new victorious life that can die no more. "We were buried with him, through baptism into death; that like as Christ was raised, we also might walk in newness of life." "Ye were buried with him in baptism, wherein ye were also raised, through faith in the working of God who raised him."

Baptism is, in the power of the Holy Spirit, our participation with Jesus Christ in the deepest and most mysterious experiences of His life; as our faith ever looks to, rests on, claims, and yields itself to the working of God who raised Him, we experience the power of His death and His life working in us; our life becomes conformable to His, that life of His which died and lives forevermore. Reckoning and knowing ourselves to be indeed dead unto sin and alive unto God in Christ, we have the power to walk in newness of life, we are made free from sin and live as the servants of God and of righteousness. As often as the flesh suggests that we must sin or tells us, with the Colossians, to seek our strength in carnal help and ordinances, God's Word reminds us of our strength: We have been baptized into Christ, into His death and into His life.

Yes, believing parent, your life is the means of grace,

the medium appointed and consecrated by God, through which the life of the risen One is to become the life of your child. It is through your life—not your teachings, or prayers, or beliefs, for these are but parts of yourself—but through your life, representing the sum of all you are, and of the influences you exercise upon your child, that God would have him inherit the blessings.

What an urgent call for the parent to live truly the life of a baptized one, as one who has been made one plant with Christ in the likeness of His death and resurrection. Let no believing parent say or think that this truth, that this life, is too high for him. If he be a true believer, this Christ who died but lives again, is his life, his blessedness. He cannot taste the true blessedness of the life of faith, he cannot praise or honor God aright, he cannot abide fully in Christ, unless he accepts Him fully in all He is and gives.

Live to this end as people who have been baptized into the death of Christ, with the flesh crucified, yourselves crucified to the world, made free from sin, bearing daily the cross and the dying of the Lord Jesus. Live as those who in baptism have been raised again by the faith in the working of God who raised Jesus. Let your faith claim all the power of His resurrection life; all that God wrought in Him, He will work in you (Eph. 1:20, 2:6; 1 Pet. 1:21). Let the whole of your education be in this faith in the working of God to make true to your child all He promised in raising Jesus from the dead. Live as one baptized into the death and life of Christ.

Lead your child to Jesus, to whom he alone belongs. Lead him to the cross, to take it up and bear it in the love of Jesus. Help him, as sin and self come up, as the flesh and the world tempt, to practice the blessed self-denial which Jesus links with the cross. Guide him in that path of bright and loving obedience, where truest happiness is found. Speak to him of Jesus, the risen One, as a living friend, as the power of his new life. Long before he can understand the theology of it, let the im-

pressibility of his young heart have been won for Jesus
and a life like His, devoted to His service.

* * *

O my God, with my whole heart I thank Thee for all
the blessing and power that is secured to me by my having
been baptized into Christ and into His death. And that
Thou hast set me apart as parent so to live as one baptized
into Christ's death, that first my life, and later on my
teaching too, may lead my child to know this blessed
life in Christ.

O my Father, I humbly ask Thee to deliver me from
all ignorance and unbelief concerning this wonderful baptism into Christ's death and my fellowship in it. Enlighten
my understanding, strengthen my will, and help my faith
in Thy mighty working, that my own life may be in the
full power and fellowship of the death and the resurrection
of Jesus. As crucified to the world, as dead to sin in
my Lord Jesus, I yield myself to walk in newness of life
with Him.

I ask Thy grace, O my God, that a baptism into the
death of Christ, as it has been pledged in the water, may
now come true to my child through the Holy Spirit in
full power. May this be my one aim in education: to have
the power of the cross, as it crucifies to the world, and
lifts up unto God, revealed in those Thou hast given me.
And may the life of Christ be manifest in me and my
home to the glory of Thy holy name. Amen.

FORTY-SIXTH DAY

The Heritage of Holiness

" . . . else were your children unclean; but now are they holy" (1 Cor. 7:14).

Let us bless God for this precious statement. There is not a deeper or more distinctly divine word in Scripture than holy; in this statement the whole treasure of holiness, with all that revelation teaches us concerning it, is made the heritage of our children. God's holiness and our children are meant for each other; as parents we are the God-ordained links for bringing them into perfect union. If we would do this, we must *understand* and *apply* this precious truth.

The revelation of God's holiness was a very gradual one, because it was the opening up of the mystery of the Holy Trinity. There was first holiness as seen in God, its source and fountain; then in Christ, the Holy One of God, our sanctification; then in the Holy Spirit, as the Spirit of holiness in the Church. By gradual steps we can rise from the lower to the higher use of the word and enter into the fullness of divine meaning which the word has as used of our children.

Holy. The word expresses a relation. Whatever was separated unto God and made His property was called holy. "The Lord will show who are *his* and who is *holy*: the man whom the Lord shall choose, he is holy." Apart from the moral character, even an inanimate object which had been given to God and taken by Him to be His own, was holy. And so the first and simplest thought our faith must take in and fill with spiritual meaning is this: our children belong to God. The very fact of their being born of believing parents make them His in a very special sense. Just as in olden times the children of the slave were the property of the master as much as the slave himself, so the Lord's redeemed, who love to call themselves His bondservants, have no desire to look upon their children in any other light than themselves—wholly and absolutely His. "Now are [your children] holy."

Holy. The word suggests a destiny. It is of great importance, as we study the word holy in Scripture, to notice how everything that is called holy had a use and purpose; every holy day and thing, place and person, had its service to fulfill. Let the Christian parent beware of looking upon holiness as a mere means to an end, simply as the way to get safely to heaven. Oh, it is infinitely more! Let him realize that his child is God's property, to be used in this world as God directs, to be trained with the one purpose of doing God's will and showing forth His glory. The more clearly this is apprehended and made the distinct object of the work of prayer and education, the more speedily shall we be led to grasp its higher meaning and gain the path to the blessing it offers.

Holy. The word is the pledge of a divine life-power. Though we find that God himself uses the word holy sometimes of external relation or privilege and at others of real spiritual blessing, we must remember that the former always had the latter in view as its aim. Let us beware of emptying the word holy of its divine truth and power. If God calls our children holy because of the covenant in which He has taken them up, it is because they are born from a believing parent who is holy in Christ, and therefore they are holy too. The child of true believers, having soul and body under the rule and indwelling of the Holy Spirit, inherits from his parents not only the sinful disposition, but habits and tendencies and attitudes which the child of the heathen or the infidel does not share. These are the true seed-germs of holiness, the working of the Holy Spirit from the mother's womb. Even where it cannot be seen and is but very feeble, there is a secret heritage of the seed of holiness implanted in the child of the believer. And with this there is given, in the word holy, the promise of the divine life and power to make reality and personal possession what is the child's in covenant and in birth to holy parentage. There is secured to him the Holy Spirit in whom the holiness of God has reached its full manifestation.

In promising the Holy Spirit to His disciples, our Lord said He would be a river of living water flowing from them to others. The believer has a power to influence those with whom he comes in contact; his faith is to save his household, since the child born of him inherits a blessing in the very life he receives from one who is sanctified by the indwelling of the Holy Spirit. In the mother's womb the child can receive the Holy Spirit. Oh, let us be sure of it, when God gives our child the name of holy, there is the beginning and the pledge of a divine power, even the work of His own Holy Spirit. Let nothing less than this be what our heart reads in God's words: Your children are holy.

Holy. The word describes a character. God's holiness is His infinite moral perfection—that He hates and destroys the evil, that He loves and works the good. Holiness is the divine energy of which perfect righteousness and infinite love are the revelation. It is correspondence with himself that God seeks and that He gives. "Be ye holy; I am holy; I make holy." In calling your children holy, God invites you to have them partakers of *His* holiness; without this, holiness is but a name and a shadow. It is the work of the Christian parent to train his children in dispositions and habits, ways of thinking and feeling and acting, that will be in harmony with the fact that they are holy in Christ and belong to the Holy Spirit. "Holy in all manner of conversation" is what your children are to be—separated from the world, its spirit and its service; consecrated to God, His Spirit, and His will.

It is as we begin to understand that our children are holy that we shall apply it rightly. We shall find it a word of great power in our dealings with both God and our children. With God it will be the strength of our prayer and faith. We shall feel liberty to claim that we be not sent away with a mere possibility, a promise without fulfillment, a covenant right without a personal experience. No. We may be sure that when our children are called holy, all that is implied in the word *holy* is meant for them.

As we study the wonderful word in the story of Israel, in the character of God, in the person of Jesus, in the work of the Spirit of holiness, we shall find the assurance that it is all for them. As we plead for the conversion of our children, we shall say with holy boldness, Hast not Thou said they are holy? As we plead still more earnestly that they may not only be saved but truly and fully sanctified, vessels meet for the Master's use, we shall most confidently cry, O Thou who hast laid the name of holy on them, it cannot be Thy will it should mean anything less than all Thy power and love can give. As in its light we confess how little we have realized the holiness of our children, the blessed heritage of holiness they have in us as believing parents, we shall yield ourselves more than ever to train them as holy to the Lord.

And so the word will exercise its mighty influence in our dealings with our children. We shall think of our home and family as His home, the dwelling-place of His holiness. We shall learn to look upon sin in our children, upon the spirit of the world or conformity to it, as at utter variance with a child which the Holy God has set apart for holiness. We shall write "holiness to the Lord" upon our doorposts. We shall realize that the first need of a parent whose children God calls holy is to be very holy; that personal holiness is the indispensable condition for educating a holy child. "Your children holy" will lead us to look to our own position, "Ye are holy in Christ Jesus," and to our own example and conduct as the channel through which the knowledge and the love and the power of holiness are to come to them. And as we hear the words spoken of Jesus used by God himself of each child as it is born, "that holy thing which is born of thee," "thy holy child," we shall realize that nothing but a life in the holiness of God, a life entirely under the leading of the Spirit of holiness, can fit us for watching over and training the children God has given us.

* * *

O my God, my meditations on this word of the Holy Spirit have made me feel deeply the need of His divine light to teach me what it means to Thee. Lord, show me, I pray Thee, the thoughts and the purposes of Thy heart when Thou sayest to Thy believing people whom Thou hast sanctified in Christ, "Your children are holy." Show me, my God, how in this word there is secured to my child all that treasure of sanctification which is prepared in Christ, and which the Spirit of sanctification makes our personal possession.

O blessed God, Thou art the Thrice Holy. The glory which the seraphim praise and worship without ceasing is the glory of Thy holiness; in it all Thy attributes have their perfection and their beauty. Thou hast revealed thyself as the Holy One who makes holy, Thy Son as Thy Holy One, Thy Spirit as the spirit of holiness. Thou callest Thy people Thy holy ones, and even of their little ones thou sayest, "Your children are holy."

O my God, Thy words are never like men's words, empty thoughts; they are full of meaning, of life, and of power. Oh, make these words of Thine quick and powerful in our hearts that we may understand and rejoice in and hold fast the infinite blessing they bring us. And grant, Lord, that as we love and train, as we pray and believe for our children, it may all be with this one object as our motive and aim, that we and they may be holy to the Lord, realizing and showing forth the glory of His holiness. Amen.

FORTY-SEVENTH DAY

The Reign of Love

"Ye fathers, provoke not your children to wrath" (Eph. 6:4).

"Fathers, provoke not your children to anger, lest they be discouraged" (Col. 3:21).

"Charity suffereth long, and is kind; . . . seeketh not her own, is not easily provoked" (1 Cor. 13:4, 5).

"Teach the young women . . . to love their children" (Tit. 2:4).

The apostle had noticed in the houses he visited how sadly education often suffers from a want of love. He speaks especially to fathers on two occasions, warning them to provoke not their children to wrath. His words suggest three thoughts: a child is often very provoking, a father often allows himself to be provoked, the result often being that he again provokes the child to wrath. Instead of being the help and the strength of his child in seeking what is good, he discourages and hinders him. Paul's warning opens up to us the whole subject of giving reproof or punishment in the right spirit, of the need for patience and wisdom and self-control, of the secret of a parent's rule being a reign of love.

Let us mark first that fathers are here especially addressed. They are expected to take a part in the management of the children. There are many fathers who neglect this and seek to throw the work entirely on the mother. When returning home from the day's labor, they do not feel inclined to trouble themselves; the children are regarded more as a burden and a weariness than as a charge entrusted by the Lord to be met in the spirit of love and gladness.

God has joined to the meekness and gentleness of the mother the firmness and strength of the father; it is as each takes his share in the work, becoming the helper of the other, that the divine blessing may be expected. On this account it is of such great importance that in addition to the daily united devotions at the family altar, there should be set times when father and mother join in reading and conversation and prayer on the training of their children. One half-hour a week set apart for this purpose, if it were for only one year, would bring a rich reward. It would be a training school for parents and draw attention to many an important lesson which is otherwise not noticed in the presence of work. It would give the opportunity for the mother to call for and receive the father's aid and guidance. It would bring the blessing on conjugal and parental love, of which Peter speaks: "Ye husbands, dwell with your wives according to knowledge, giving honor unto the woman, as unto the weaker vessel, as being also joint heirs of the grace of life; to the end that your prayers be not hindered." Let every father accept his calling to take his part in the training of the children.

"Ye fathers, provoke not your children unto wrath." Ordinarily the child has first provoked the father. A child is sometimes wayward, often thoughtless, always feeble and ignorant, so that even what was well meant may be the cause of annoyance. It is when the nature of the child, especially the weakness and sinfulness, is carefully and lovingly taken into account that the parent will be able patiently to bear with him and rightly to train him. It is the privilege and honor of the parent to have this immortal spirit, with all the failings and with all the trials of patience it involves, entrusted to his charge, with the view of his being the artificer through whom God is to make of him something of beauty and of glory for himself. Let parents take into account the weakness and the willfulness of their children; let them not be surprised or taken unawares by what may be trying to temper and to patience; they will see the need for preparing themselves for their holy work by faith in Him who fits us for every work He gives us to do.

"Ye fathers, provoke not your children to wrath." There is much in some children that is provoking; there is much in some fathers that is easily provoked. Beware above everything of giving way to such provocation; it has been the ruin of many a child. To educate a child is impossible without self-control. "Ye have need of patience"; "Let patience have its perfect work."

The whole life of the Christian is meant by the Father in heaven under the guidance of the Holy Spirit to be one of watchfulness and self-recollection. In home life these graces are specially indispensable. The sudden outbreaks of temper in children, the little vexations arising from their disobedience or neglect or mistakes, their little quarrels and naughtinesses all are so many occasions on which a father needs the love that is not easily provoked. God meant the rule of the family to be like His own, a reign of law inspired by love.

"Ye fathers, provoke not your children to wrath." However provoking the child may have been, however much inclined the father may be to feel provoked, he must see to it that he does not provoke the child to wrath. One provocation calls forth another—an angry father, giving way to his failing of being provoked easily, makes an angry child.

There is innate in each human bosom a sense of the dignity of government and the duty of submission to authority. The calm, quiet assertion of authority helps greatly to bring the offender to the acknowledgement of the justice of his punishment. When the parent, instead of trusting to this, gives way to anger and passion in the sharp reproof or hasty punishment, the child's passion is roused too and he is angry and vexed. Passion ordinarily rouses passion. The parent is the teacher and example of the child, appointed of God to meet and conquer outbreaks of his passion by the gentle firmness of love. How sad when the very opposite is the case: a father's hasty anger inflames a child's passion, and he becomes his provocation to wrath!

"Lest they be discouraged." In the struggle between good and evil that goes on in the child, there is nothing needed more than encouragement to believe the victory of the good is within his reach, that goodness is possible and pleasant. To inspire a child with a holy confidence in what he can accomplish is one of the blessed secrets of success in training. In training a horse the utmost care is taken never to overtax it or give a load that might lead to failure; at each difficult place you see its master all alert with voice and hand to inspire it with confidence; it must not know that it cannot succeed. A child should never be allowed to feel that his immaturity is not taken into account, that his little reasonings are not regarded, that he has not received the pity or the help or the justice he expects. This will take a love which children all too little receive and a thoughtfulness which parents all too little bestow.

"Ye fathers, provoke not your children to wrath." The education of a child needs above everything self-training. This was one of the objects for which God created the family relation and one of its chief blessings. Without his knowing it, your child is God's schoolmaster to bring you ever nearer to Christ. Not only the child's tenderness and lovingness call forth the love of your heart—his waywardness and willfulness call for it still more as they put it to the test and school it in forbearance and gentleness. Study to have every token of your displeasure, every reproof and every punishment, so marked by love that through it all the child may really be encouraged into goodness.

But it is not by reproof and punishment, however gently

and wisely administered, that parents will keep their children from getting provoked or discouraged. This is but the negative side; the positive is of more importance. Prevention is better than cure. Cultivate ever in yourself and the child that state of feeling which takes away the opportunity of his coming into collision with you. Endeavor by your own tranquillity, gentleness, and kindliness to promote the same feelings in the child. Count upon the wonderful ascendency and influence over children that sympathy gives in both its aspects. Throw yourself in sympathy into their interests, entering into their state of mind and feeling. Expect them—for their nature is as keenly susceptible to sympathy for others as from others—to enter into your spirit and temper and instinctively to yield themselves to its influence. And as you seek to maintain the rule of love—not the mere love of natural instinct but of love as a principle of action, earnestly sought in prayer from above and carefully cultivated in all your family life—you will find that the children will catch its spirit and become your helpers in making your home the reflection of the life of love in which the heavenly Father guides and trains His children.

*　*　*

Gracious God and Father, the longer we listen to the teaching of Thy Word on our duty as parents, the more deeply we feel the need of a divine grace for doing that work right. I come to Thee with the humble confession of my sin. How often sin in the child has been met by sin in the parent, calling forth in the child new sin, and discouraging him in the battle with it. And Thou meanest the parent to be to the child the model of a holy, patient love, uniting and helping his feebleness and by his example encouraging him into the assurance that he, too, can conquer.

O God, we beseech Thee to open our eyes that we may know our holy calling. Give us a deep conviction that nothing but Thine own Spirit, dwelling in us day by

day, can fit us for training sinful beings in a life of holiness; that nothing but the most entire surrender to walk
with Thee, to be in everything guided and possessed by
Thy Spirit, can prepare us for the work of parents.

O God, we pray Thee especially for a baptism of love,
of Thine own love. May a holy wisdom and patience in
meeting each outbreak of evil be given us. May the power
of a love that enables us to bear and yet to conquer as
well as to inspire our child with confidence in us and
the victory of good fill our lives. O God, we would train
our children after Thy mind, to be a pleasure to Thee;
be Thou our help. Amen.

FORTY-EIGHTH DAY

The Nurture of the Lord

"Ye fathers, provoke not your children to wrath: but bring them up in the nuture and admonition of the Lord" (Eph. 6:4).

We know the great importance between instruction and education, between teaching and training. The former is the communication of knowledge, secular or religious; the latter is the development of the faculties, both intellectual and moral, to help the child really to do and be what the teaching has set before him. The two words the apostle uses correspond exactly to our expressions and might be translated "nurture them in the training and teaching of the Lord."

Let us note first the spirit which must pervade the upbringing of our children: Nurture them in the discipline and admonition *of the Lord.* Our children are the Lord's; their whole education must be animated by this thought. We train them for Him, according to His will and in His spirit. It is the Lord's own training of which we are to be His ministers to them.

Jesus Christ—the Son of God, our Lord and Master, with His personal presence, His love and rule in heart and home—must be our aim; we must educate our children "unto the Lord." That they may know and love Him, that they may be fitted to obey His will and to serve

Him, must be the goal of our education. And it can be this only as we very earnestly study His will and the rules He has laid down in His Word for parental duty, as we wait for His Spirit to guide and to sanctify us for our work. Our whole nurture is to be the nurture of the Lord.

The two parts God has joined together may not for a moment be separated. The child's emotional nature, with all its sensitiveness and impressibility, is first developed. For the due regulation of this, the Creator has endowed it with two great powers—*willing* and *knowing*. Training seeks to influence the will, the power which really makes a man; teaching supplies the knowing by which the willing is to be guided and strengthened. The nurture of the Lord is to bring up the child that he may be a vessel meet for the Master's use, with every faculty of spirit, soul, and body prepared for doing His will. The training and teaching must work in harmony for securing this blessed object. All instruction and admonition has the forming of the will, of character as a completely fashioned will, as its purpose.

The word education is so often used of what is merely instruction that I would like to use the word discipline to give the idea the apostle intended. The foundation of a useful and happy life will be found in the habit of order and self-control, the ready submission to law and obedience to duty. When not impulse or circumstance, not our likes or dislikes, but the steady purpose and power of knowing and doing right rule the life, one of the chief objects of education has been attained. Discipline uses the means and exercises the power needed for securing this result. The discipline of the Lord has reference not only to what may be considered more directly religious but to the child's whole being, spirit, soul, and body.

Whatever contributes to the healthy development of the powers God has bestowed on us is included in the nurture of the Lord. There are what may be called physical virtues, at the foundation of which is order. "Order is heaven's first law" throughout the immeasurable spaces of the universe, and in the minutest atoms that the mind can conceive there reigns a divine order. Everything owns submission to law. How little is availed that a child or a man is converted if the power of self-control, the power of at once doing what is seen to be the right in its time and place, has not been cultivated. Conversion will not give this; the parent has to prepare the home in which the Spirit of God is to dwell and to find its servants.

The habit of order cultivated in a little child in external things can pass on into his intellectual training and become a mighty power in his moral and spiritual life. And it leads to that other foundation—virtue, decision of character, firmness of purpose, strength of will. In submitting to order in the external, the child learns that for everything there is an ought and a must, and that his welfare will be found in entering at once and heartily into that ought and what it requires. Let every parent seek, in nurturing a child for the Lord, to discipline into a fixed habit the innate sense of the rightness of order and decision. They will become ruling principles, in the wake of which other natural virtues will easily find their place.

Then come what may be called the legal virtues—those distinctly commanded in God's law, such as obedience, truthfulness, justice, and love. Parents cannot too often or too earnestly remind themselves of the power of single acts often repeated to become habits, and the power of habits to aid in giving ascendency to the principles that underlie the acts. Our moral no less than our bodily powers are strengthened by exercise. Conscience may in early life be so disciplined by the divine blessing to become habitually tender and ready to act. The innate sense of right and wrong, the feeling of guilt and shame following on sin, the authority of God's Word—all these the discipline of a wise training appeals to in nurturing for the Lord.

And then there are the virtues that belong more distinctly to the New Testament and the great redemption it reveals—faith in and love for Jesus, the indwelling and leading of the Holy Spirit, the self-denial and holiness and humility of a Christlike life. All this is not to be a matter of only the promise of the Spirit, working all unconsciously in the children; they are to be trained into it. To be temples of God through the Holy Spirit, to bear the image and be fit for the service of the Lord Jesus, must, from the outset, be the aim of the divine nurture in which we seek to bring up our children.

For such training to be successful, it is absolutely necessary that there be authority; the nurture must be in the discipline of the Lord. To this end it is not enough that the parent as the superior assert the right God has given him; the authority derived from God must become a personal possession by the influence the parent acquires over the child. The parent must prove himself worthy of his place; his ascendency will depend upon the weight of his moral character. To acquire such influence must be a matter of study and effort and prayer.

All who wish to govern children not by force but by influence, not against their will but by means of it, not in virtue of a position in which they have been placed but in the power of a life that proves them worthy of that position and that secures an instinctive acknowledgment of their authority, must make not only their own duty but especially the nature and the needs of childhood their careful study. Only then can the education of our children become, instead of being a series of experiments and failures that teach us wisdom when it is too late to benefit by them, the wise and well-ordered commanding of our household that they may keep the way of the Lord.

True authority has its root and strength in a life in which we exhibit ourselves what we ask of our children. A life of childlike trust in the Father's love, of submission to His authority and surrender to His training will make itself felt through the home. It will awaken our sympathy for a child's needs and failings. It will awaken their sympathy with our teachableness of spirit and our quiet restfulness in the divine rule. And the nurture of our children

will be to ourselves and to them truly the Lord's nurture—
God's nurturing us by means of them that He may nurture
them by means of us.

* * *

Blessed God and Father, who hast appointed us Thy
servants to bring up our child in a training and teaching
which is to be Thine own, we come again with the prayer
for wisdom and grace to perform our task aright. We
ask of Thee to show us the difficulty and the sacredness
of our task, to show us, too, the nearness and sufficiency
of Thy help. We want especially to realize that it is as
we yield ourselves to Thy training and teaching, walking
with Thee as loving, obedient children, that we shall have
power to nurture them aright.

We ask for grace to combine the admonition that points
out the way with the discipline that trains to walk in
it. We would form our children's character to that order
and self-restraint, to that submission to law and authority,
in which is the secret of happiness. We would give their
body and mind such a healthy development that they may
be formed the fit and ready instruments of a spirit under
the leading of Thy Holy Spirit. Blessed Father, we look
to Thee for the grace we need to do this work.

We will trust Thee to show each of us wherein we
are in special danger of coming short. We will trust in
Thee to accept our childlike desire to obey Thee and,
notwithstanding our failings, to bless our home. We claim
the merit and the presence of Jesus our Lord. We claim
the power of a full salvation for us and our children.
Amen.

FORTY-NINTH DAY
Home Rule

"A bishop then must be . . . one that *ruleth well* his own house, having *his children in subjection* with all gravity; (for if a man know not how to rule his own house, how shall he take care of the church of God?) . . . Let the deacons be the husbands of one wife, *ruling their children* and their own house well" (1 Tim. 3:2, 4, 5, 12).

It is most thought-provoking that among the qualifications for office bearers in the primitive church—bishop, elder or deacon—in each case the state of their household should have been taken into account and failure there should have been considered sufficient to bar them from the office for which personally they otherwise might have appeared fit. It reminds us once again of the closeness of the link between parents and children and the organic unity of the home as a whole. From the household you can infallibly judge what the parents are; the parents make it. Here is the outgrowth and the expression of their life, the mirror in which often with startling faithfulness their hidden failings are revealed.

Some may be inclined to doubt the truth of this statement. They have so often heard, they know, of pious parents whose children have turned out ill. Is all the blame to be laid on the parents? We have no power to change evil nature; grace alone can do it. Is it not going too far to put the blame for unbelieving or unruly children on the parents and count such a father unfit for holding office in the church or household of God because his own household is not what it should be? And yet just this is what the Holy Spirit does. He teaches Paul to connect unbelieving and unruly children with the failure of the home rule and unfitness for church rule. He thus stirs us to search out what causes the training of children by parents, who otherwise appear fit to be leaders in the church, to be robbed of power and promised blessing. We are to seek for causes of failure in the home rule.

The first answer may be suggested to us by the words of Paul, as he argues from failure at home to failure in the church. We may go a step backward and argue from failure in the family to failure in the person; *the wrong in the home reveals something wrong in its head.* We have more than once seen that the secret of home rule is self-rule, first being ourselves what we want our children to be. The wonderful power of the will with which man has been endowed was meant to make him in the first place his own master.

And yet how many Christian parents there are to whom real self-control in daily life is quite foreign! It is not the thought of God's will nor the rule of their own will that guides and decides their conduct, but in conversation and action, in likes and dislikes, they are led away by the feelings of the moment. Because they trust that they are God's children and that Christ's blood pardons their sins, that their prayers will be heard, they hope for the salvation of their children. And yet their education is setting up the most effectual barrier against God's grace. Pleasing themselves, allowing their inclination or temper to be the rule of language and conduct, they give the most effectual contradiction to their profession of being the servants of God's will.

Would that all Christian parents might learn the lesson that a quiet self-recollection and self-control, that a calm stillness of soul that seeks to be guided by God's Spirit, is one of the first conditions of success in our own spiritual life and so in the sacred influence we wish to exert on our children. "In quietness and confidence shall be your strength"; nowhere will the unconscious but strong influence of this restfulness be felt so soon as in family life.

But there may be other causes. A Christian parent may not be wanting in self-control and yet fail. The reason will very possibly be found in *neglect of the duty of ruling.* With some this may come from an entire ignorance of the solemn place a parent occupies. They have never thought seriously of the extent to which the souls and wills and characters of the children are in their hands. They have never taken any trouble to think carefully of the work entrusted to them. They may pray earnestly at times that their children may be saved; they know not that it is of more importance to pray daily that they themselves may be fitted to guide their children aright.

With others the neglect of the duty rests on wrong principles thoughtlessly adopted. They admire a strong will; in the waywardness or self-assertion of a child's will they often see nothing but cause of amusement or admiration. They wish to see their child grow up a strong, bold character, able to do and dare; they would not for anything weaken his will. They know not that a wayward will is a curse; and that a will that masters itself by obedience is the truly strong will. No wonder that the children later on will be disobedient or unruly.

And then with others the neglect of the duty comes from simple weakness and sloth. They admit that it is their duty. But it is so hard; it takes so much time and thought. It is so trying to their love to punish or to thwart the child and, under cover of the name of tenderheartedness, the authority with which they have been entrusted of God is neglected and abused. Let parents take time and thought to realize: to rule a child is as distinctly God's command as to love and care for him. The interests of parent and child demand it; the time and labor spent in cultivating this grace will be richly rewarded.

But still there are parents in whom neither of the causes of failure mentioned hold good. They do rule themselves and they do seek to rule their children, and yet they have failed. The cause must be sought deeper: the lack of the divine blessing must be found in the *lack of true faith and consecration*. There are some children easily ruled; there are others of nervous temperament or wayward disposition who appear to defy control. "The things that are impossible with men are possible with God." Education is a work in which the parents are meant to be God's servants, His fellow-workers; but to work with God means to walk closely with Him. It is to the soul that is wholly given up to Him and seeks undividedly to do His will that the power of faith will be given to hold fast the covenant, living in the assurance that God himself will do the work.

Let there be simple, childlike heart-searching to see if there has not been in our aims for our children desire for worldly honor or position; the spirit of the world is the most secret but most certain hindrance to true faith. Let the surrender of ourselves and our children—not only to God's mercy, to save, but to God's will, to rule and use—be complete and unreserved. We shall find God to be our ally, our covenant-helper in training the children, and with Him on our side we must prevail. To have had power with Him in prayer is the sure guarantee of victory with the child.

Parents, the work entrusted to us is holier than we know. The precious instrument, so delicate, so wonderfully made, though marred by sin already and so exposed to its power, is of such inconceivable worth. To take charge of an immortal soul, to train a will for God and eternity, surely we will shrink from it. But we cannot. If we are parents, the duty is laid upon us. But, thank God, sufficient grace is prepared and promised too.

If we do but give up our home and our life to God for Him to come in and rule, He will himself take possession and by the gentle influence of His Holy Spirit bow their will to himself. And the discipline which our ruling of the children brings will be the best preparation for our ruling in God's house—the ruling of which Jesus speaks: "He that is chief among you, let him be servant of all."

If, for the sake of serving God in our homes, we deny ourselves to acquire real influence and power to rule our children, He will count us worthy of influence and power with our fellowmen and in His Church. Faithfulness in the home rule will give power to take care of the Church of God—will be, as it was with Abraham, the secret of admission to the counsel of Him who rules the world, to the power that prevails with God and men.

* * *

Adorable Lord God, we worship Thee as the Ruler of the universe. Righteousness and judgment are the foundation of Thy throne. Thou art gracious and full of compassion; slow to anger, and of great mercy. Thy kingdom ruleth over all; and Thy rule is everywhere the fountain of all blessing and good.

O Lord, it hath pleased Thee to ordain that in each home on earth Thy heavenly rule should have its reflection. Thou hast given to parents power and authority over their children to rule in Thy name. Thou hast promised to give them all needful wisdom and strength for maintaining that authority and ruling their children well.

We have to confess with shame how often this holy trust of ruling in Thy name has been neglected and abused. We beseech Thee to forgive us. We beseech Thee to deliver us from all that hinders that rule. We desire to take it up as a life-work in Thy strength. May a holy self-rule fit us for a happy home rule. We desire to make the work Thou givest us a study and a pleasure, to fit ourselves carefully for doing it well. Be Thou our teacher and our help.

Lord Jesus, we do indeed yield our homes and our

children, our lives and all our powers, to be wholly Thine. Thou art able to keep that which we commit to Thee. Keep our homes as Thy sacred dwelling-place where we and our children serve Thee in righteousness and love, in peace and in great joy. Amen.

FIFTIETH DAY
Children and Scripture

"When I call to remembrance the unfeigned faith that is in thee, which dwelt first in thy grandmother Lois, and thy mother Eunice" (2 Tim. 1:5).

"But continue thou in the things which thou hast learned and hast been assured of; knowing of whom thou hast learned them; and that from a child thou hast known the holy scriptures, which are able to make thee wise unto salvation through faith which is in Christ Jesus" (2 Tim. 3:14, 15).

If we connect these two passages, we find in them the true relation in which children and Scripture ought to stand to each other. Between the unfeigned faith of the mother and grandmother and the faith of Timothy, Scripture had been the connecting link. Scripture needs the believing parent as its messenger. The believing parent needs Scripture as the vehicle for the communication of his faith. A parent's faith teaching the word of faith may count upon the child's faith as the fruit of his labors.

God has so ordered that it is mostly through the Holy Spirit dwelling in His saints that the word is brought to sinners in the power of the Spirit. It is one Spirit dwelling in the word and in the child of God; in the combined action of the two the word is made a blessing to others.

One of the highest honors God has for the believing parent is that He has made him the minister of His holy Word to his children. It is the unfeigned faith of father or mother, a faith which lives on and according to the word, and speaks of it in the power of personal testimony and experience, that will be used of God to awaken a child's faith. In real living faith there is something contagious; the life of the Spirit breathes in it and makes its words a blessing. This truth suggests some very precious lessons a parent should seek to learn.

Teach your child to *believe* the Word of God. Of old God sought above everything to train His saints to be men of faith. There is nothing more pleasing to Him than faith. Faith is the soul's surrender to God, to hear what He says, to take what He gives, to receive what He works, be entirely at His disposal. Faith in God begins with faith in His Word, and there is no habit a parent can cultivate in a child of deeper importance than that of a trustful acceptance of all that God has said.

In an age of doubt and questioning, teach your child to accept what he cannot understand, even what appears mysterious and contrary to reason, because God who is wise and great has said it. Teach him to believe in His love, in the gift of His Son and in the life through Him as realities which come true to us as our faith simply trusts the Word and is assured of what it says. Teach him day by day to look upon every promise, every truth in the Word, as the food for faith, meant to make our faith and through it our life stronger. Parents, a child is naturally trustful; guide his young trust to that Word which never fails. The child wants to trust; the Word wants to be trusted; let your unfeigned faith bring them into contact.

To the end teach your child to *know* the Word of God. Faith depends upon knowledge. Timothy had *known* the sacred writings as able to make him wise unto salvation. If the grace of God is to save us, it must teach us. It is a wisdom from above; we must love God with the mind as well as the heart. Let the parent seek to give the child a clear and intelligent apprehension of the great truths of salvation God has revealed. He will not entrust this work to school or church; it is astonishing how vague the knowledge thus obtained often is.

Let family worship be so ordered as to be really helpful in the knowledge of God's Word. Try always to make it clear at what stage in the history of the kingdom and in the progress of revelation it was that the word you read was given. Take trouble to lodge in the mind not only the truths and the history of the Bible but especially to store in the memory some of God's own words. Be not content with the child's learning and saying his text at fixed times; it is often forgotten as soon as said. But seek to have some of these words, by frequent repetition, so rooted in the mind that nothing can efface them. Teach the child to know the book itself too—to be at home in it, to feel at ease in it. To be taught by unfeigned faith thus to know the sacred writings is an inestimable blessing.

Teach your child to *love* God's Word. This is more difficult than teaching to believe and to know it. Often the assent of faith and an interest in the knowledge of Scripture has very little of real love to it. To teach this is no easy task. Its first requisite is, of course, that we love it ourselves. "Oh, how love I thy law," is an expression of piety which many an earnest believer will be afraid to utter. Love and joy ever go together; what I love I rejoice to possess. Reverence and respect for God's Word, the earnest study of it, and the desire to be guided by it—these are good, but they do not necessarily breathe that bright spirit of delight which says to God, "Oh, how I love thy law!"

And yet it is love to which a child's heart is especially susceptible. Childhood is the age of feeling and impression; the child can be won before he can give a reason of his hope. And a parent's holy, tender love to the Word of God will be the surest means of inspiring the child's love. Let this be a distinct matter of desire and prayer and of careful study too: so to guide the child in his familiarity with the Bible that he may not only not dislike it, not only like it for its stories and its study, but truly and heartily love it as the Father's Word. This will indeed be the token of divine grace and the preparation for all blessing.

And then teach your child to *obey* the Word of God. God connects all believing, knowing, loving, with *doing*; obedience is God's test of uprightness and reality. Teach the child to make what the Father has said the standard of conduct. Let him see and hear that you do so. In our ordinary Christianity, children are educated into the belief that God's commandments are grievous. The idea of obedience to Him, wholehearted and unceasing, being simply happiness is never thought of. And yet this is the only religion that really will be mighty to plant itself in the hearts of our children.

The Bible must not be as a law continually holding us in check, keeping us from what we would like, and demanding what is difficult. No! With our children we must take up an entirely different position. As the Father's redeemed ones the children of His covenant and kingdom, we must say, with the only-begotten Son, "I delight to do thy will, O God; yea, thy law is within my heart." It is His covenant promise to work this in us and our children. If in Christ Jesus we enter into the blessed life of the liberty of God's children, our children will learn from us how impossible it is to us to read the Father's Word and not do it. Our study of it with them will have this as its one purpose: we want to know and do the will of God.

The custom of family worship is to be found in almost every Christian family. Every day a portion of God's holy Word is read there. But, alas, in that reading there is often little power or blessing. Many an earnest Christian parent looks more to his private reading for profit and nourishment. And yet the daily gathering of the family around the Word of God might become a season of real spiritual refreshment and nourishment! If only the same care we take to have a properly prepared meal placed on the breakfast table and each child served with just what he needs were taken to see that the children really receive and enjoy the feeding with the divine Word!

Let parents make a real effort to have their family worship so ordered, to lead the children into the holy place, to be presented before the Lord, to be fed with the bread each one requires, and to receive the Father's blessing for the day. Let them prepare for reading of the Word with the family. Let the reading be of God's Word, in His presence, and waiting on His Spirit.

Beware of the hurry which gives just time enough for the hasty reading of a chapter. Family worship becomes a dead and deadening form, hardening children into a habit of careless dealing with the Word and with God himself. A few moments devoted to a quiet, loving calling of attention to what God says and to making the personal application, encouraging the children to take and keep the Word, may be the beginning of great blessing.

Parents, God's Word is your child's heritage from the Father in heaven. And you are commissioned to lead him into the knowledge and the love and the possession of its treasures. Make it a matter of earnest prayer that you may wisely and rightly do it. Let that Word dwell richly in you in all wisdom. In giving His promises, Jesus said that if we abide in His word, His words will abide in us.

Let your life be one of unfeigned faith, that lives and delights in doing God's word. Such faith will pass on into your children. The quiet confidence that comes from God's Word is a power that makes itself felt with our children. And if you often feel that you know not how to bring the Word aright to them, or see in them things that hinder its reception, be still of good cheer—you have God to do the work, to make the Word effectual. Pray and believe for the Holy Spirit's working; He will make the word, which you speak and live in unfeigned faith, the seed of faith to your children too.

* * *

Gracious God, we ask Thee to give us a very deep sense of the blessedness of this part of our work as parents, to bring Thy holy Word to them. May the privilege Timothy had be that of our children—from earliest youth to have the unfeigned faith of a loving parent as the interpreter of holy Scripture. May a deep, full, and very joyous faith in Thy blessed Word be the power in which all our Scripture teaching comes to them. Help us to see clearly how their hearts are claimed by Thee, to be filled with Thy words, that these may be in them the seeds of all holy thoughts and dispositions.

We ask of Thee the grace of wisdom and faith and patient faithfulness to bring Thy Word day by day to our children. May our family worship every day be a holy season of communion with Thee, the unseen one, in which we lead our children into Thy presence to hear Thy voice speak and to receive Thy teaching. O our God, we yield ourselves to the supremacy and the power of Thy holy Word; let it so abide in us that our life may be the shining forth of its holy light. Let us be so full of faith and love and obedience to the Word that our dear children learn from their youth to love and believe and obey it too.

Father, forgive us that this has been too little so. Wilt Thou not by Thy mighty power make it so now? Amen.

FIFTY-FIRST DAY
Believing Children

"Ordain elders . . . if any be blameless, the husband of one wife, having *children that believe, not unruly*" (Tit. 1:5, 6).

God expects that the children of believers should be believers too. There is nothing so honoring or pleasing to God as believing Him; nothing so opens the way for His blessing and love to flow in and take possession of us than that we believe Him. And the very object and purpose of God in the institution of the parental covenant is that believing parents should educate believing children. They are the children of the promise; God and His grace are theirs in promise. A promise has no value but as it is believed; parents who truly believe will understand that it is their privilege and their duty to train "children that believe."

On the day of Pentecost with the outpouring of the Holy Spirit, Peter announced that the foundation principle of God's covenant with Abraham was to remain unchanged and children were still to be regarded as the heirs of the promise. As ordained by God in Paradise, the household was still to be the channel for the transmission of the blessing of the Spirit. Faith was not to be an individual thing but to embrace the household, and then from the parent out to pervade it.

It is in harmony with this that we so often find in the Acts—that book of the Acts of the Holy Ghost—mention made of the household. "Cornelius feared God with all his house." "Lydia was baptized, and her household." To the jailor of Philippi Paul said, "Believe, and thou shalt be saved, and thy house," and "he was baptized, and all his, immediately," and "he rejoiced greatly with all his house, having believed in God." "Crispus, the ruler of the synagogue at Corinth, believed in the Lord with all his house."

In the epistles of Paul we find that he four times uses the expression, "the church in thy house"; he does not say the church assembling in thy house, but the church which is in thy house, referring evidently to the circle of believers constituting the family. Though in these cases no express mention is made of children, the principle of the organic unity of the family, on which the idea of a household rests, assures us that the children were comprehended in it too. And it is so clear to Paul that believing parents ought to have believing children that when such is not the case he regards it as a matter of blame, as a sure index that there has been something wrong on the part of the parents, that their own faith and life has not been what it should be. They are at once debarred from holding any place of honor or influence in the Church of Christ. When the father, as the ruler of the church in the home, has not trained children that believe, he is unfit for taking care of the house of God. Children that believe are to be looked for from parents whose life is truly that of faith. Let us try to once again take home the lesson God would teach us.

Even children can be believers. Trustfulness, the power of simply believing what is told, of resting on what love has promised, is one of the most beautiful traits of true childlikeness. It is this wonderful power of a child's heart, of which the parent avails himself every day and which often fills him with such gladness, that must be guided heavenward and led to cling to God and

His Word, to Jesus and His love. There is nothing more natural to children than to believe; it is through a parent's faith that the Holy Spirit loves to take possession of the child's faith and makes it the living link to a living Saviour. As the child grows, the faith may grow—a deep and hidden root of life that even amid temporary coldness or declension still holds onto the blessed Saviour.

God expects our children to grow up believers. We ought to expect it too. The very nature of faith in God ever seeks to think as He thinks, to count upon Him for what with man and nature is impossible, to make His promise and His power the measure of its hope. Let us take time to realize that God's wonderful promise to our children is meant so to take possession of us that it shall fill us with the sense of His holy power waiting to fulfill it and draw us to live in His presence and in the presence of our children as the channels of that power and that blessing. The confidence that our children will grow up true believers—something much higher than the confidence that they will eventually be saved—will exercise its influence on us and on them. On us as a daily call to a life of pure holiness and consecration; on our children in the creation of an atmosphere of faith around them in which they breathe and live. In our homes God expects that there shall be children that believe.

The proof that our children are believers will be their conduct. Paul writes, "elders . . . having children that believe, *not unruly*." Faith is ever perfected by works; like every other function of life, it can grow and become strong only by action. A life of faith is always a life of obedience. And a child's faith must prove itself in a child's obedience—that is, obedience to the parents. Children that are allowed to be unruly and disobedient and self-willed will speedily lose their childlike faith. What is said of men—that having thrust from them a good conscience they have made shipwreck of the faith—holds good of children too.

Faith is surrender. I yield myself entirely to the

influence of the news I hear, of the promise I receive, of the person I trust. Faith in Jesus is entire surrender to Him, by Him to be ruled and influenced and mastered. Faith in Jesus is the surrender to Him and His will. Faith in Jesus to be saved by Him, is the surrender for Him to let Him save us in the way He has opened up— the way of trusting, loving, holy obedience. Let parents seek to lead the little one's simple faith in Jesus to this surrender. Let them claim the child's obedience to themselves as obedience to Jesus. Let them educate the child to obey conscience in Jesus' name; their home will be the happy proof that believing children are not unruly.

If ours are not children that believe, let us seek the cause in none but ourselves. God's promise is sure, and His provision is perfect. It may be that the spirit of the world so prevails in heart and home that while the Sunday talks teach the children faith in Jesus, the week-day life trains them to faith in the world, to a surrender to its spirit and rule. Or it may be that while we are earnestly engaged in religion and religious work there is but little of true spirituality, of the joy and the love and the power of holiness which alone make religion a reality. Religion has been an occupation like any other; and the holy presence of Jesus has not been felt by our children. Or even when there has been a striving after this, there may have been failure in our not devoting ourselves to the holy task of training children; we have entrusted the work to others, and neglected the self-denial and the study needed to fit ourselves for the work of ruling them well and of guiding them in the ways of the Lord. Let us seek very honestly and very earnestly to discover the reason for failure, to solve the sad enigma: we are believers, we have a faithful God, and yet we have not what He claims, "children that believe, not unruly."

God calls us to heart-searching and confession and return. And even if we have children that believe but who have not the power and devotion as we could wish, let us turn to God with humbling and a new surrender.

Our home life needs the power of a true consecration. The warm light of a Saviour's love and the joy of His near presence shining from us—it is this our homes need as the secret of a successful education.

Each new step in the path of entire separation to God and of larger faith in His abiding and keeping presence must make itself felt in the family. If there are circumstances and influences that appear to make it impossible, let us remember what faith can do: it can bring Almighty God and His power into the scene. It may not obtain at once what it asks. But it can live the life God wants His child to live, it can keep the soul in peace and rest; it can in secret exert its slow but sure influence.

It is the faith of an entire surrender that our homes need; this faith will transform them into what God would have, the nurseries of believing, obedient children. Both with God and with our children, let us ponder and remember this well: there is no power so mighty as that of a quiet, restful faith, that knows that God has given what we have asked, that He has taken charge of what we have entrusted to Him, and that in His own hidden, silent ways He is already working out what He has undertaken. Parents who are believers, who believe with their whole heart and strength and life, will have "children that believe, not unruly."

* * *

Blessed Lord God, the God of the families of Israel, we thank Thee for each message that reminds us of what Thou wouldst have our children be, as the proof of the reality of our faith in Thy Word and our life in Thy love. We pray Thee, blessed Lord, to print it deep in our hearts that in every believing home Thou dost expect and dost seek for believing children. Lord, as trees of Thy planting, the fruit from them Thou seekest we yield to Thee.

When Thou dost not find this fruit we beseech Thee to reveal to us the cause. Whether it be unbelief or worldliness, the want of ruling well or the want of living well, reveal, we pray Thee, the sin that it may be confessed and cast out. Reveal especially if it is chiefly the want of our undivided consecration to Thy will, with its consequent want of a full assurance and experience of Thy presence, that is the secret cause of all our failure.

Blessed Lord Jesus, it was Thy presence, the tidings of Thy being so near and so loving and so mighty to bless, that drew many parents to trust Thee when Thou wast on earth. O our Lord, it is Thy presence with us which will strengthen our faith and give us children that believe. We do set our homes open to Thee. Come in and reign. Be our joy and gladness every day. We have yielded ourselves to live each moment under Thy rule; we have believed in Thine acceptance of our sacrifice to keep us abiding in Thee; oh, give us the wisdom and sweetness, the faith and the power to be a blessing to our home. Oh, give us children that believe, children whom in the power of faith Thou canst use for Thy glory. Amen.

FIFTY-SECOND DAY

The Children Which God Has Given

"Behold, I and the children which God hath given me" (Heb. 2:13).

These words were originally used by the prophet Isaiah: "Behold, I and the children whom the Lord hath given me are for signs and for wonders in Israel." The prophet and his family were to be God's witnesses to certain great truths which God wanted His people not to forget. In the Epistle to the Hebrews, these words of the Holy Spirit are put into the mouth of Christ; He was confessing His relation to those whom He is not ashamed to call His brethren. They are words of the believing parent who presents himself with his children before the Lord in the consciousness of that wonderful unity of the Spirit in which the family is one before God.

As we draw our meditations to a close, these words invite us to gather up all that the Word has taught us of the purpose and the promise of our God, of the work of love committed to us and the abounding hope in which we may look to the fulfillment of what God has led us to expect.

"Behold, I and the children which God hath given me." Let this be the language of a deep and living faith as we think of the wonderful ground of our unity. I am one with my children in virtue of God's eternal purpose, when

He created man and instituted the family. He meant the parent to beget children in his own likeness, to impart his own life and spirit to them, to have one life with them. When sin entered, the promise and the covenant were given to restore the blessing that had been lost; again, the parent was in faith to receive for the child and communicate to him the grace God had bestowed. In virtue of that promise I am one with my children, and my children are one with me, in the enjoyment of the love and the life that comes in Jesus.

In that faith I present myself before the Father with that same "Behold!" with which Jesus called the Father to look upon Him and His, and I say too, "Father! behold, I and the children whom thou hast given me." *Thou* hast given them me, with a divine giving, to be inseparably and eternally one with me. God hath given them me, in the power of the complete redemption of His Son with the sure and full promise of His Holy Spirit for them as for me. God hath given them me to keep and train for Him and then present before Him as mine and His too.

In this faith I want day by day to look upon my little God-given flock, to believe that they are one with me in the possession of all the promises and blessings of the covenant, of all that the love of my God can give. When for a time it may appear as if they are not growing up as one with me in Christ, my faith will still say, "Behold, I and the children thou hast given me." And even when the thought of past sin and neglect in my training makes me fear lest my guilt is the cause of their being unconverted, I will still say, looking to the blood sprinkled on the doorposts of my home: "Behold, I and the children whom Thou hast given me. We are one; we must be one through Thy grace; we shall be one to all eternity."

In Jesus Christ nothing availeth but faith working by love. "Behold, I and the children which God hath given me"—when spoken in loving faith, the words become the inspiration of love for the work God has committed to it. The bond between a parent and child is a double one—there is the unity of life and of love. What apparently has become two lives, love voluntarily and joyfully links together and makes to be one. This love in nature cares for and rears and nurtures the child. It is this love that God takes possession of and sanctifies for His service. It is this love that becomes the strength for the difficult and yet delightful work the parent has to do.

Love is always self-surrender and self-sacrifice. It gives itself away to the beloved object; it seeks to enter into it and become one with it. True, full love has no rest apart from perfect union with the beloved; all it has must be shared together. And God calls His redeemed ones who are parents to love their children, to identify themselves with them, to seek and claim their salvation as much as their own. And as the Spirit of Christ takes possession of the heart, the parent accepts the call. In the unity of a love that cannot think of itself without the children, that is ready to sacrifice everything to make them partakers of its own blessedness, the parent learns to say with a new meaning, "Behold, I and the children whom God hath given me."

I and the children! I, the author of their life, the framer of their character, the keeper of their souls, the trustee of their eternal destiny. I, first blessed that I may bless them, first taught how my Jesus loved me and gave himself for me, that I may know how to love and how to give myself for them. I, having experienced how patient and gentle and tender He is with my ignorance and slowness and willfulness, now set apart not to think of my ease or comfort but in the meekness and gentleness and long-suffering of Christ to watch over and to bear with their weakness. I, made one with these children, that in the power of love I may be willing to study what they need and the way I may best influence them; to train myself for the work of ruling well, and training them to self-rule. I, walking in the obedience and the liberty of a loving child of God, guiding them in the happy

art of an obedience to authority that is always free—
freedom that is always submissive to law.

Yes, I *and* the children! The consciousness grows upon
me that, in the unity of love, what I am the children
may and will be. And the more tenderly my love to them
is stirred up, the more I feel the need to be wholly and
only the Lord's, entirely given up to the love that loves
and makes itself one with me. This will fill me with a
love from which selfishness shall be banished, giving itself
in a divine strength to live for the children that God has
given me.

When faith and love thus have spoken, hope will have
courage to take up the song, and in full assurance to
say, "Behold, I and the children which God hath given
me!" We are inseparably and eternally one. Hope is the
child of faith and love. Faith is its strength for waiting
and watching, love its strength for willing and working
Hope ever looks forward. It sees even in this life,
when things are dark, the unseen God coming through
the clouds to fulfill His word. It sings the song of victory
when others see nought but defeat. Amid all the struggles
through which it may see a loved child passing, amid
all trials of faith and patience, hope speaks: "In his word
do I hope: I will hope continually, and will praise thee
yet more and more." Through its own buoyant tone it
inspires with hopefulness the children when discouraged
in the fight with evil; it seeks to be the morning star
of the home. It looks forward to each one of the circle
being not only a saved one but a sanctified one, fit for
the Master's service here on earth.

And as often as it looks for the blessed hope, the
appearing of our Lord Jesus, and the glory that is to
follow, hope rejoices in the full assurance of an unbroken
family circle in heaven. It even now trembles with joy
as it thinks of the privilege that waits it when the Son
has presented himself with His brethren in His "Behold,
I and the children whom God hath given me," of also
coming forward to fall down and worship and say likewise,

"Father, behold! here am I too, and the children which Thou hast given me." May God teach us to rejoice in this hope! "Now the God of hope fill your hearts with joy and peace in believing, that ye may abound in hope in the power of the Holy Ghost."

"Behold, I and the children which God hath given me." Beloved fellow-believers, whom God has honored to be parents, shall we not seek to have the spirit of these words breathe through our whole home life? It is God who has given us the children; it is He who regards them as one with us in His covenant and blessing and teaches us to regard them so too. His love calls and fits for a life of self-sacrifice and unselfishness; His grace will accept and give success to our efforts to be one, perfectly one with our children in the power of faith and love and hope. In God's sight and promise we are one; in our life and love and labor let us be one with them too; we shall be one through the glory of eternity.

* * *

Our gracious Father, we do thank Thee for all the blessed teaching of Thy Holy Word concerning our children. We thank Thee that it has set them before us in Thine own light, as created by Thee, though ruined by sin, redeemed in Christ, and now entrusted to us to keep and care for, while the Holy Spirit renews them to Thine eternal life and glory. We thank Thee that Thou thyself hast come as our teacher to fit us for teaching them. We pray Thee for Thy blessing on each word of Thine, that we may indeed become such parents as Thou wouldest have us be.

O Lord, we pray Thee to establish in our thoughts and hearts and lives all the wonderful truths that gather round the home life. We would count Thy covenants and its promises as exceeding precious to us. Our faith would see the names Thou givest to our children, children of the covenant, of the promise, of the kingdom, as written on their foreheads. We would treasure all the promises of Thy Spirit and Thy blessing as their sacred heritage. We would read of all Thy dealings with Thy saints in the birth of their children and their upbringing for Thy service as the revelation of Thy will with ours. We do accept all Thy warnings and all Thy instructions concerning children as the law of our home. O Lord, open our eyes that we may ever have before us the picture of a believing home as Thou willest—as Thou willest to make it for us.

Above all, blessed Lord Jesus, let Thy presence and Thy love and Thy joy, filling the parents' heart, be the power to fulfill the Father's will and to win our children's love. It is in Thee all the promises are Yea and Amen; come thyself and accept our consecration to be wholly Thine; come thyself and let our home be the abode where Thou lovest to tarry. Then shall it be blessed indeed, and each of us say with never-ceasing gladness of hope, "Behold, I and the child God hath given me."

Even so, Lord Jesus. Amen.